COMMENTED RECAST VAT DIRECTIVE

APRIL 2014

A PRAGMATIC VIEW ON EUROPEAN
VALUE ADDED TAX

Comments, References and Notes

by

António Calisto Pato / Marlon Marques

Copyright © 2014 TaxEye

The text in this book is of unofficial nature. The authors, publisher and any other person involved in preparing, publishing or selling this book are not responsible for the results of any actions taken on the basis of the information contained in it nor for any errors or omissions contained therein.

TABLE OF CONTENTS

TABLE OF CONTENTS 3
VISIT US 7
INTRODUCTION TO THIS BOOK 8
TITLE I - SUBJECT MATTER AND SCOPE 9
TITLE II - TERRITORIAL SCOPE 20
TITLE III - TAXABLE PERSONS 26
TITLE IV - TAXABLE TRANSACTIONS 34
    Chapter 1 Supply of Goods 34
    Chapter 2 Intra-Community Acquisition of Goods 39
    Chapter 3 Supply of Services 41
    Chapter 4 Importation of Goods 43
TITLE V - PLACE OF TAXABLE TRANSACTIONS 58
    Chapter 1 Place of Supply of Goods 58
        Section 1: Supply of Goods without Transport 58
        Section 2: Supply of Goods with Transport 58
        Section 3: Supply of goods on board ships, aircraft or trains 61
        Section 4: Supplies of gas through a natural gas system, of electricity and of heat or cooling energy through heating and cooling networks 63
    Chapter 2 Place of an Intra-Community Acquisition of Goods 64
    Chapter 3 Place of Supply of Services 66
        Section 1: Definitions 66
        Section 2: General rules 66
        Section 3: Particular provisions 67
            Subsection 1: Supply of services by intermediaries 67
            Subsection 2: Supply of services connected with immovable property 67
            Subsection 3: Supply of transport 68
            Subsection 4: Supply of cultural, artistic, sporting, scientific, educational, entertainment and similar services, ancillary transport services and valuations of and work on movable property 69
            Subsection 5: Supply of restaurant and catering services 70
            Subsection 6: Hiring of means of transport 70
            Subsection 7: Supply of restaurant and catering services for consumption on board ships, aircraft or trains 71
            Subsection 8: Supply of electronic services to non-taxable persons 71
            Subsection 9: Supply of services to non-taxable persons outside the Community 72
            Subsection 10: Prevention of double taxation or non-taxation 73
    Chapter 4 Place of Importation of Goods 74
TITLE VI - CHARGEABLE EVENT AND CHARGEABILITY OF VAT 103
    Chapter 1 General Provisions 103
    Chapter 2 Supply of Goods or Services 103
    Chapter 3 Intra-Community Acquisition of Goods 106
    Chapter 4 Importation of Goods 106
TITLE VII - TAXABLE AMOUNT 109
    Chapter 1 Definition 109
    Chapter 2 Supply of Goods or Services 109
    Chapter 3 Intra-Community Acquisition of Goods 114

Chapter 4 Importation of Goods 114
Chapter 5 Miscellaneous Provisions 116
TITLE VIII - RATES 122
    Chapter 1 Application of Rates 122
    Chapter 2 Structure and level of Rates 123
        Section 1: Standard Rate 123
        Section 2: Reduced Rates 123
        Section 3: Particular Provisions 125
    Chapter 3 126
    Chapter 4 Special Provisions applying until the Adoption of Definitive Arrangements 126
    Chapter 5 Temporary Provisions 130
TITLE IX - EXEMPTIONS 134
    Chapter 1 General Provisions 134
    Chapter 2 Exemptions for Certain Activities in the Public Interest 134
    Chapter 3 Exemptions for other Activities 139
    Chapter 4 Exemptions for Intra-Community Transactions 142
        Section 1: Exemptions related to the Supply of Goods 142
        Section 2 Exemptions for Intra-Community Acquisitions of Goods 144
        Section 3 Exemptions for Certain Transport Services 145
    Chapter 5: Exemptions on Importation 146
    Chapter 6 Exemptions on Exportation 150
    Chapter 7 Exemptions Related to International Transport 153
    Chapter 8 Exemptions Relating to Certain Transactions treated as Exports 155
    Chapter 9 Exemptions for the Supply of Services by Intermediaries 157
    Chapter 10 Exemptions for Transactions relating to International Trade 157
        Section 1: Customs warehouses, warehouses other than customs warehouses and similar arrangements 157
        Section 2: Transactions exempted with a view to export and in the framework of trade between the Member States 162
        Section 3: Provisions common to Sections 1 and 2 163
TITLE X DEDUCTIONS 173
    Chapter 1 Origin and Scope of Right of Deduction 173
    Chapter 2 Proportional Deduction 177
    Chapter 3 Restrictions on the Right of Deduction 181
    Chapter 4 Rules Governing Exercise of the Right of Deduction 182
    Chapter 5 Adjustment of Deductions 185
TITLE XI - OBLIGATIONS OF TAXABLE PERSONS AND CERTAIN NON-TAXABLE PERSONS 189
    Chapter 1 Obligation to Pay 189
        Section 1 Persons liable for payment of VAT to the tax authorities 189
        Section 2: Payment arrangements 199
    Chapter 2 Identification 208
    Chapter 3 Invoicing 210
        Section 1: Definition 210
        Section 2: Concept of invoice 211
        Section 3: Issue of invoices 211
        Section 4: Content of invoices 220
        Section 5: Paper invoices and electronic invoices 225
        Section 6: Simplification measures 232
    Chapter 4 Accounting 235
        Section 1: Definition 235

Section 2: General obligations 235
Section 3: Specific obligations relating to the storage of all invoices 236
Section 4: Right of access to invoices stored by electronic means in another Member State 239
Chapter 5 Returns 240
Chapter 6 Recapitulative Statements 245
Chapter 7 Miscellaneous Provisions 251
Chapter 8 Obligations Relating to Certain Importations and Exportations 252
    Section 1: Importation 252
    Section 2: Exportation 254
TITLE XII - SPECIAL SCHEMES 255
Chapter 1 Special Scheme for Small Enterprises 255
    Section 1: Simplified procedures for charging and collection 255
    Section 2: Exemptions or graduated relief 255
    Section 3: Reporting and review 260
Chapter 2 Common Flat-Rate Scheme for Farmers 260
Chapter 3 Special Scheme for Travel Agents 267
Chapter 4 Special Arrangements for Second-Hand Goods, Works of Art, Collectors' Items and Antiques 269
    Section 1: Definitions 269
    Section 2: Special arrangements for taxable dealers 270
        Subsection 1: Margin scheme 270
        Subsection 2: Transitional arrangements for second-hand means of transport 276
    Section 3: Special arrangements for sales by public auction 278
    Section 4: Measures to prevent distortion of competition and tax evasion 282
Chapter 5 Special Scheme for Investment Gold 283
    Section 1: General provisions 283
    Section 2: Exemption from VAT 284
    Section 3: Taxation option 284
    Section 4: Transactions on a regulated gold bullion market 285
    Section 5: Special rights and obligations for traders in investment gold 286
Chapter 6 Special Scheme for Non-Established Taxable Persons supplying Electronic Services to Non-Taxable Persons 287
    Section 1: General provisions 287
    Section 2: Special scheme for electronically supplied services 288
TITLE XIII DEROGATIONS 296
Chapter 1 Derogations Applying Until the Adoption of Definitive Arrangements 296
    Section 1: Derogations for States which were members of the Community on 1 January 1978 296
    Section 2: Derogations for States which acceded to the Community after 1 January 1978 297
    Section 3: Provisions common to Sections 1 and 2 304
Chapter 2 Derogations Subject to Authorization 306
    Section 1: Simplification measures and measures to prevent tax evasion or avoidance 306
    Section 2: International Agreements 307
TITLE XIV - MISCELLANEOUS 309
Chapter 1 Implementing Measures 309
Chapter 2 VAT Committee 309
Chapter 3 Conversion Rates 309
Chapter 4 Other Taxes, Duties and Charges 310

TITLE XV - FINAL PROVISIONS 311
    Chapter 1 Transitional Arrangements for the Taxation of Trade between Member States...311
    Chapter 2 Transitional Measures applicable in the Context of Accession to the European Union 313
    Chapter 3 Transposition and Entry Into Force..318
ANNEX I..320
ANNEX II...321
ANNEX III..322
ANNEX IV..324
ANNEX V 325
ANNEX VI..326
ANNEX VII...327
ANNEX VIII 328
ANNEX IX..329
ANNEX X 330
ANNEX XI..332
ANNEX XII...334
VAT E-CONSULTANT APP 363

VISIT US

at

WWW.EASYGOTAX.COM

And test our **VAT e-Consultant**

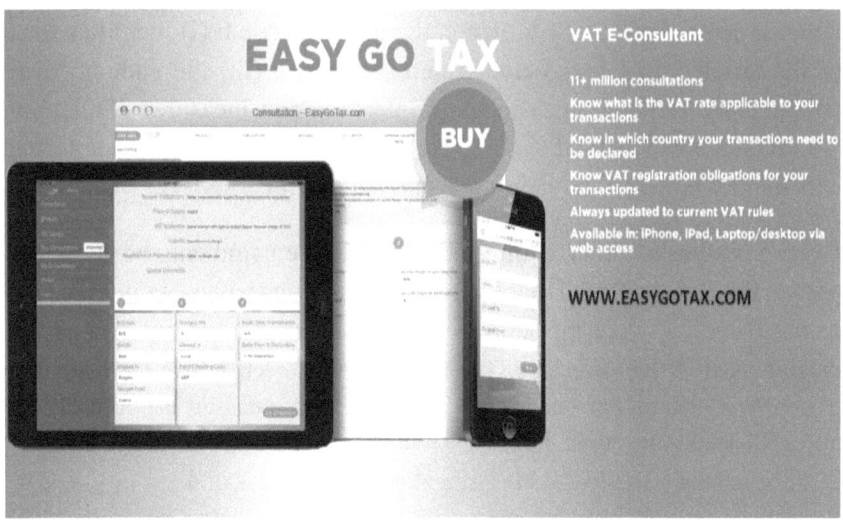

Introduction to this book

The authors of this book are international tax lawyers who have worked both on the service-providing side with law firms and Big4 and in in-House with US and Mexican Multinationals and have been based out of different jurisdictions (Switzerland, Luxembourg, Netherlands, Italy, Portugal, Brazil).

This book is primarily a compilation of the Recast VAT Directive, updated up to April 2014 to which the authors added: (i) identifications of the articles, in [ ]; (ii) cross references in [ ], (iii) the authors' own commentary (iv) reference to the implementation measures regulation, (v) reference to the VAT Committee meetings and (vi) reference to the explanatory notes on invoicing rules issued by DG TAXUD.

Every text that is either within [ ] or within the comments boxes is not part of the Recast VAT Directive. All bolds or underlines within the text of the Directive were introduced by the authors and are not part as the original text of the directive. The Recast VAT Directive here reproduced is of unofficial nature. For binding interpretation, please consult the original text as published in the Official Journal, which you can find at http://europa.eu/legislation_summaries/taxation/l31057_en.htm.

RECAST VAT DIRECTIVE

Title I - Subject Matter and Scope

Article 1 [Definition & Object]

1. This Directive establishes the **common system of value added tax** (VAT).

2. The principle of the common system of VAT entails the application to goods and services of a **general tax** on **consumption** exactly **proportional to the price** of the goods and services, however many transactions take place in the production and distribution process before the stage at which the tax is charged.

On each transaction, VAT, **calculated** on the price of the goods or services **at the rate applicable** to such goods or services, shall be **chargeable after deduction** of the amount of **VAT borne** directly by the various cost components.

The common system of VAT shall be applied up to and including the retail trade stage.

Article 2 [Transactions Subject to VAT]

1. The following transactions shall be **subject to VAT**:

    (a) the **supply of goods** for consideration within the territory of a Member State by a taxable person acting as such;

    (b) the **intra-Community acquisition of goods** for consideration within the territory of a Member State by:

    (i) a taxable person acting as such, or a non-taxable legal person, where the vendor is a taxable person acting as such who is not eligible for the exemption for small enterprises provided for in Articles 282 to 292 [*Special scheme for small enterprises*] and who is not covered by Articles 33 [*distant sales*] or 36 [*place of supply for goods installed or assembled by or on behalf of supplier*];

    (ii)   in the case of new means of transport, a taxable person, or a non-taxable legal person, whose other acquisitions are not subject to VAT pursuant to Article 3(1) [*supply during section of passenger transport*], or any other non-taxable person;

    (iii)   in the case of products subject to excise duty, where the excise duty on the intra-Community acquisition is chargeable, pursuant to Directive 92/12/EEC [Directive on the *general arrangements for products subject to excise duty and on the holding, movement and monitoring of such products*], within the territory of the Member State, a taxable person, or a non-taxable legal person, whose other acquisitions are not subject to VAT pursuant to Article 3(1) [*supply during section of passenger transport*];

(c) the **supply of services** for consideration within the territory of a Member State by a taxable person acting as such;

(d) the **importation** of goods.

2. [*Means of Transport*]

    (a) For the purposes of point of paragraph 1(b) [*intra-Community transactions*], the following shall be regarded as **"means of transport"**, where they are intended for the transport of persons or goods:

        (i)   motorized **land vehicles** the capacity of which exceeds 48 cubic centimeters or the power of which exceeds 7.2 kilowatts;

- (ii) **vessels** exceeding 7.5 meters in length, with the exception of vessels used for navigation on the high seas and carrying passengers for reward, and of vessels used for the purposes of commercial, industrial or fishing activities, or for rescue or assistance at sea, or for inshore fishing;

- (iii) **aircraft** the take-off weight of which exceeds 1,550 kilograms, with the exception of aircraft used by airlines operating for reward chiefly on international routes.

(b) These means of transport shall be regarded as "**new**" in the cases:

- (i) of motorized **land vehicles**, where the supply takes place within six months of the date of first entry into service or where the vehicle has travelled for no more than 6,000 kilometers;

- (ii) of **vessels**, where the supply takes place within three months of the date of first entry into service or where the vessel has sailed for no more than 100 hours;

- (iii) of **aircraft**, where the supply takes place within three months of the date of first entry into service or where the aircraft has flown for no more than 40 hours.

(c) Member States shall lay down the conditions under which the facts referred to in point (b) [*definition of new means of transport*] may be regarded as established.

3. "**Products subject to excise duty**" shall mean energy products, alcohol and alcoholic beverages and manufactured tobacco, as defined by current Community legislation, but not gas supplied through a natural gas system situated within the territory of the Community or any network connected to such a system.

Article 3 [intra-Community acquisitions NOT subject to VAT]

1. By way of derogation from Article 2(1)(b)(i)[intra-Community acquisitions], the following transactions shall **not be subject** to VAT:

   (a) the intra-Community acquisition of goods by a taxable person or a non-taxable legal person, **where** the **supply of such goods** within the territory of the Member State of acquisition **would be exempt** pursuant to Articles 148 and 151 [exemptions related to International Transport and Certain Transactions treated as Exports];

   (b) the intra-Community acquisition of goods, other than those referred to in point (a) and Article 4 [other intra-Community acquisitions not subject to VAT], and other than new means of transport or products subject to excise duty, by a taxable person for the purposes of his **agricultural, forestry or fisheries business** subject to the common flat-rate scheme for farmers, **or** by a taxable person who carries out only supplies of goods or services in respect of which **VAT is not deductible**, **or** by a **non-taxable legal person**.

2. Point (b) of paragraph 1 shall apply only if the following conditions are met:

   (a) during the **current calendar year**, the total **value** of intra-Community acquisitions of goods **does not exceed** a threshold which the Member States shall determine but which may not be less than **EUR10,000** or the equivalent in national currency;

   (b) during the **previous calendar year**, the total value of intra-Community acquisitions of goods **did not exceed** the threshold provided for in point (a).

The threshold which serves as the reference shall consist of the total value, exclusive of VAT due or paid in the Member State in which dispatch or transport of the goods began, of the intra-

Community acquisitions of goods as referred to under point (b) of paragraph 1.

3. Member States shall grant taxable persons and non-taxable legal persons eligible under point (b) of paragraph 1 the **right to opt** for the general scheme provided for in Article 2(1)(b)(i) [*intra-Community acquisitions*].

Member States shall lay down the detailed rules for the exercise of the **option** referred to in the first subparagraph, which shall in any event cover a period of **two calendar years**.

Article 4 [Other intra-Community acquisitions not subject to VAT]

In addition to the transactions referred to in Article 3, the following transactions **shall not be subject to VAT**:

(a) the intra-Community acquisition of **second-hand goods, works of art, collectors' items** or **antiques**, as defined in points (1) to (4) of Article 311(1) [*definitions of second hand goods, works of art, collectors' items and antiques*], where the vendor is a taxable dealer acting as such and VAT has been applied to the goods in the Member State in which their dispatch or transport began, in accordance with the **margin scheme** provided for in Articles 312 to 325 [*margin scheme for taxable dealers of second-hand goods, works of art, collectors' items and antiques*];

(b) the intra-Community acquisition of **second-hand means of transport**, as defined in Article 327(3) [*definition of second-hand means of transport*], where the vendor is a taxable dealer acting as such and VAT has been applied to the means of transport in the Member State in which their dispatch or transport began, in accordance with the transitional arrangements for second-hand means of transport;

(c) the intra-Community acquisition of second-hand goods, works of art, collectors' items or antiques, as defined in points (1) to (4) of Article 311(1) [*definitions of second hand goods,*

WWW.EASYGOTAX.COM

works of art, collectors' items and antiques], where the vendor is an organizer of sales by **public auction**, acting as such, and VAT has been applied to the goods in the Member State in which their dispatch or transport began, in accordance with the special arrangements for sales by public auction.

Comments to Title I RVD: Subject Matter and Scope

A - Comments

A1. What is VAT?

Before tackling any topic, it is of the outmost important to have it clearly defined.

VAT is, obviously, a tax, i.e. a compulsory and unilateral levy imposed upon someone (individual or corporation) by a state or equivalent and enforceable by law.

Everyone deals with VAT on a daily basis. Whenever you go to a supermarket within the European Union, when checking out and paying, you will be paying not only the price of the product you're buying, you will also be paying for VAT which is added to the final price of the product. Despite the fact that the final consumer in this example will be supporting the payment of the tax, he is not per se the taxpayer (if you understand tax payer as the entity that needs to pay the tax to the Exchequer). In such an example, the Supermarket or its suppliers will be the taxpayers (as will be further explained in the following sections).

If we take a step further, from a technical perspective, VAT is defined as an indirect tax, payable on the consumption of goods and services, general in nature, neutral and exactly proportional to the price of the goods and services on which it is computed.

The next paragraphs will take you through each of these characteristics.

A1.1 - Indirect tax

VAT is qualified as an indirect tax, as it is shifted towards the consumer instead of being directly supported by the taxpayer (as this is the case with direct taxes such as personal income tax or corporate income tax). The tax burden is supported by the final consumer while he is not the taxable person, i.e. the person responsible for collecting and paying the taxes to the tax authorities.

Contrary to what happens in direct taxes (such as personal or corporate income tax) where the taxable person is not only responsible for paying the taxes, but it is also the one that economically supports the tax burden, in VAT, the States "delegate" the tax collection function to the taxable persons (in charge of paying the VAT to the exchequer) however the taxable persons do not actually support the tax burden as they shift the cost of the tax to the final customer (by adding the tax cost to the price of goods or services). Thus the final consumer supports economically the VAT, even though he is not the taxable person (and very often will not even realize that he is supporting it, from where the attraction State authorities have for this type of tax as it bears less of a psychological effect as compared to direct taxes that directly reduce our earnings by taxing income).

Take an example (assuming a country Alpha where sale of apples is subject to 6% VAT) where Supermarket "X" sells, among other products, apples.

Mr. "B" buys €10 of said apples for consumption.

The sale from Supermarket "X" to Mr. "B" is subject to VAT and supermarket "X" is the taxable person, thus the person liable for charging the VAT in this transaction. Therefore Supermarket "X" needs to charge Mr. "B" the price of the apples (€10) adding the VAT applicable to the transaction (€0.6).

What happens then is the following:

Supermarket "X" will invoice a total price of €10,60 and will declare an output VAT of €0.60 in its VAT return; Supermarket "X" will deliver this amount to the tax authorities (for the purpose of this example let's assume that this is the only transaction occurring in the taxable period at stake).

Mr. "B", in this example, is the one that economically supports the tax as he paid the €0.6, while Supermarket "X" only serves as an "intermediary" or if you prefer an "agent" collecting the VAT on behalf of the tax authorities.

A1.2 - General

VAT is also a general tax in the sense that it aims to tax all expenditures incurred for the consumption of goods or services to take place, at all stages of the production, distribution and overall supply chain and not only the final sale to the customer.

Let's take another example the following set of transactions assuming again 6% VAT on the sale of fruit as well as on the provision of cutting & packaging services:

Example set of business transactions

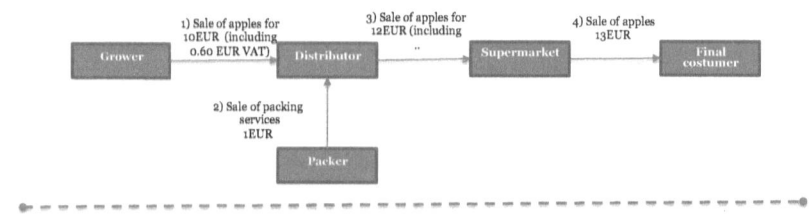

Summary of resulting VAT treatment

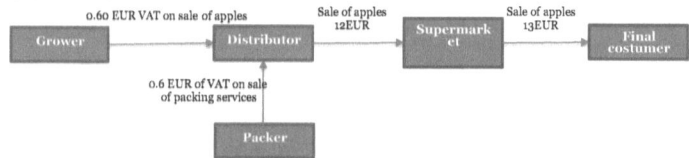

1. Grower "A" sells apples to Distributer "B" for €10;
2. Distributer "B" buys the apples, transports them to Packer "C" where apples are cut and packed for €1;
3. Distributer "B" transports and sells the "packed apple pieces" to Supermarket "D" for €12;
4. Supermarket "D" sells the apple pieces to final customer Mr. "E" for €13;

On the first transaction, Grower "A", as taxable person, will collect €0.60 of VAT and submit that amount to the Treasury; this act of collecting VAT from your customer is called a VAT output. On the other hand, Distributer "B" incurs a VAT input, i.e. it pays VAT on the acquisition of a good/service.

On the second transaction, Packer "C" collects €0.06 VAT (VAT output of €0.06) and submits that amount to the exchequer;

On the third transaction Distributor "B" collects €0.72 VAT (output VAT). As it has incurred in an input VAT of €0.66 (paid on the acquisition of the apples and to the packer) he can deduct (offset) one amount against the other and only needs to pays the difference to the Treasury i.e. €0.06;

On the fourth transaction, Supermarket "D" collets €0.78 output VAT. As it has previously incurred an input of €0.72 now it only needs to submits the difference to the treasury i.e. €0.06;

The outcome is that the Treasury receives a total of €0.78 which is fully supported by the final customer and taxes all the stages of the production, distribution and supply chain for this product (value added in the cutting and packaging process is also included).

All expenditure, which is incurred in order for the apples to reach the final consumer is taxed, thus the tax being general as per opposition to taxes that are specific (for example an excise duty or customs duties that tax solely the product and not all related expenditures; or a duty that would imply the levy of €1 per kg of apples sold to the customer).

A1.3 - Neutral

As it can be seen by the previous example, VAT is (aimed at being) neutral, i.e. it is collected fractionally at each stage of the production or distribution chain but the deduction mechanism ensures that within the territory of a member state similar goods and services bear the same tax burden, whatever the length or type of the production and distribution chain.

Experience shows, however, that such neutrality, though simple in theory, is not always achieved in practice namely in cases where the taxpayer is not well organized or due to poor lawmaking or poor transposition of the directive into domestic law, or simply by poor application of VAT rules by Tax Administrations and Courts.

Fact is that VAT more often than desired may become a cost to tax payers and drive the way the tax payer organizes its supply chain organization.

A1.4 - On consumption

Take again example 2. Despite being collected at each step of the chain, VAT ends up being fully supported by the final consumer.

What happens then, if the goods go through all a production and distribution chain and fail to reach final consumer? Let's take example 2 and imagine that Transaction 4 never took place due, for example, a fire in the warehouse. Supermarket "C" never obtains a VAT output (as the apples are not sold) and the apples are never sold to a final costumer. In this case the company may have a VAT credit against the Tax Authorities and may be entitled to receive a refund for the VAT input it incurred. The logic behind it is that as the goods never end up being consumed, there should be no VAT charged.

A1.5 - Proportional to the price of the goods and services

On each transaction VAT is calculated on the price of the goods or services at the rate applicable to such goods or services. Thus, assuming a rate in a given country of 21% for supply of computers, a domestic sale of a computer that costs €100 will imply charging VAT in an amount of €21 while same transaction for a computer that costs €1000 will imply charging €210.

B – Implementation measures (see Regulation 282/2011)

Article 2

The following shall not result in intra-Community acquisitions within the meaning of point (b) of Article 2(1) of Directive 2006/112/EC:

(a) the transfer of a new means of transport by a non-taxable person upon change of residence provided that the exemption provided for in point (a) of Article 138(2) of Directive 2006/112/EC [*the supply of new means of transport, dispatched or transported to the customer at a destination outside their respective territory but within the Community, by or on behalf of the vendor or the customer, for taxable persons, or non-taxable legal persons, whose intra-Community acquisitions of goods are not subject to VAT pursuant to Article 3(1), or for any other non-taxable person*] could not apply at the time of supply;

(b) the return of a new means of transport by a non-taxable person to the Member State from which it was initially supplied to him under the exemption provided for in point (a) of Article 138(2) of Directive 2006/112/EC [*the supply of new means of transport, dispatched or transported to the customer at a destination outside their respective territory but within the Community, by or on behalf of the vendor or the customer, for taxable persons, or non-taxable legal persons, whose intra-Community acquisitions of goods are not subject to VAT pursuant to Article 3(1), or for any other non-taxable person*].

Guidance notes on art. 2: This article deals with the exemption in respect of the acquisition or return of a new means of transport on transfer of residence.

Article 3

Without prejudice to point (b) of the first paragraph of Article 59a of Directive 2006/112/EC [*which states that in order to prevent double taxation, non-taxation or distortion of competition, Member States may, with regard to certain services, consider the place of supply of any or all of those services, if situated within their territory, as being situated outside the Community if the effective use and enjoyment of the services takes place outside the Community*] the supply of the following services is not subject to VAT if the supplier demonstrates that the place of supply determined in accordance with Subsections 3 and 4 of Section 4 of Chapter V of this Regulation [*Location of Customer regarding place of supply of services*] is outside the Community:

(a) from 1 January 2013, the service referred to in the first subparagraph of Article 56(2) Directive 2006/112/EC [*Short term hiring of means of transport*];

(b) from 1 January 2015, the services listed in Article 58 Directive 2006/112/EC [*Supply of electronic services no non-taxable persons*];

(c) the services listed in Article 59 of Directive 2006/112/EC [*Supply of services to non-taxable persons outside the EU*].

Guidance notes on art.3: Without prejudice to the use and enjoyment provisions (Article 59a of the VAT Directive1), the supply of the following services is not subject to VAT if the supplier demonstrates that the place of supply is outside the Community:

•services listed in Article 59 of the VAT Directive supplied to non-taxable persons outside the Community;

- short-term hiring-out of a means of transport as listed in Article 56 (from 1 January 2013);
- services listed in Article 58 of the VAT Directive supplied to non-taxable persons (from 1 January 2015).

Article 4

A taxable person who is entitled to non-taxation of his intra- Community acquisitions of goods, in accordance with Article 3 of Directive 2006/112/EC [*intra-Community acquisitions NOT subject to VAT*], shall remain so where, pursuant to Article 214(1)(d) or (e) of that Directive [*rules regulating VAT identification number*], a VAT identification number has been attributed to that taxable person for the services received for which he is liable to pay VAT or for the services supplied by him within the territory of another Member State for which VAT is payable solely by the recipient.

However, if that taxable person communicates this VAT identification number to a supplier in respect of an intra-Community acquisition of goods, he shall be deemed to have exercised the option provided for in Article 3(3) of that Directive [*right to opt for the general scheme*].

Guidance Notes on art.4: This article relates to certain circumstances where a person is entitled to non-taxation of intra-Community acquisition of goods.

C – Guidelines VAT Committee
Meeting 17, 18, 19, 20, 22, 23, 25, 26, 34, 45, 54, 94, 96

Title II - Territorial Scope

Article 5 [Definitions]

1. For the purposes of applying this Directive, the following definitions shall apply:

   (a) "**Community**" and "**territory of the Community**" mean the territories of the Member States as defined in point (2);

   (b) "**Member State**" and "**territory of a Member State**" mean the territory of each Member State of the Community to which the Treaty establishing the European Community is applicable, in accordance with Article 299 of that Treaty[see comments to Title II], with the exception of any territory referred to in Article 6 of this Directive;

   (c) "**third territories**" means those territories referred to in Article 6;

   (d) "**third country**" means any State or territory to which the Treaty is not applicable.

Article 6 [Territories out of Scope]

1. This Directive **shall not apply** to the following territories forming part of the customs territory of the Community:

   (a) Mount Athos;

   (b) the Canary Islands;

   (c) the French territories referred to in Article 349 and Article 355(1) of the Treaty on the Functioning of the European Union[see comments to Title II];

   (d) the Åland Islands;

(e) the Channel Islands.

2. This Directive **shall not apply to the following territories** not forming part of the customs territory of the Community:

   (a) the Island of Heligoland;

   (b) the territory of Büsingen;

   (c) Ceuta;

   (d) Melilla;

   (e) Livigno;

   (f) Campione d'Italia;

   (g) the Italian waters of Lake Lugano.

Article 7

1. In view of the conventions and treaties concluded with France, the United Kingdom and Cyprus respectively, the Principality of **Monaco**, the Isle of **Man** and the United Kingdom Sovereign Base Areas of **Akrotiri** and **Dhekelia** shall not be regarded, for the purposes of the application of this Directive, as third countries.

2. Member States shall take the measures necessary to ensure that transactions originating in or intended for the Principality of **Monaco** are treated as transactions originating in or intended for **France**, that transactions originating in or intended for the Isle of **Man** are treated as transactions originating in or intended for the **United Kingdom**, and that transactions originating in or intended for the United Kingdom Sovereign Base Areas of **Akrotiri** and **Dhekelia** are treated as transactions originating in or intended for **Cyprus**.

Article 8

If the Commission considers that the provisions laid down in Articles 6 and 7 are no longer justified, particularly in terms of fair competition or own resources, it shall present appropriate proposals to the Council.

Comments to Title II RVD: Territorial Scope

A – Comments

See Comment to Title IV, pgs. 39 and following.

B – Guidelines VAT Committee
Meeting 10, 14, 15

C – Others
Treaty establishing the European Community

Article 299

1. This Treaty shall apply to the Kingdom of Belgium, the Czech Republic, the Kingdom of Denmark, the Federal Republic of Germany, the Republic of Estonia, the Hellenic Republic, the Kingdom of Spain, the French Republic, Ireland, the Italian Republic, the Republic of Cyprus, the Republic of Latvia, the Republic of Lithuania, the Grand Duchy of Luxembourg, the Republic of Hungary, the Republic of Malta, the Kingdom of the Netherlands, the Republic of Austria, the Republic of Poland, the Portuguese Republic, the Republic of Slovenia, the Slovak Republic, the Republic of Finland, the Kingdom of Sweden and the United Kingdom of Great Britain and Northern Ireland.

2. The provisions of this Treaty shall apply to the French overseas departments, the Azores, Madeira and the Canary Islands.
However, taking account of the structural social and economic situation of the French overseas departments, the Azores, Madeira and the Canary Islands, which is compounded by their remote-ness, insularity, small size, difficult topography and climate, economic dependence on a few products, the permanence and combination of which severely restrain their development, the Council, acting by a qualified majority on a proposal from the Commission and after consulting the European Parliament, shall adopt specific measures aimed, in particular, at laying down the conditions of application of the present Treaty to those regions, including common policies.
 The Council shall, when adopting the relevant measures referred to in the second subparagraph, take into account areas such as customs and trade policies, fiscal policy, free zones, agriculture and fisheries policies, conditions for supply of raw materials and essential consumer goods, State aids and conditions of access to structural funds and to horizontal Community programs.
 The Council shall adopt the measures referred to in the second subparagraph taking into account the special characteristics and constraints of the outermost regions without undermining the integrity and the coherence of the Community legal order, including the internal market and common policies.

3. The special arrangements for association set out in Part Four of this Treaty shall apply to the overseas countries and territories listed in Annex II to this Treaty.
This Treaty shall not apply to those overseas countries and territories having special relations with the United Kingdom of Great Britain and Northern Ireland, which are not included in the aforementioned list.

4. The provisions of this Treaty shall apply to the European territories for whose external relations a Member State is responsible.

5. The provisions of this Treaty shall apply to the Åland Islands in accordance with the provisions set out in Protocol 2 to the Act concerning the conditions of accession of the Republic of Austria, the Republic of Finland and the Kingdom of Sweden.

6. Notwithstanding the preceding paragraphs:

(a) this Treaty shall not apply to the Faeroe Islands;
(b) this Treaty shall not apply to the United Kingdom Sovereign Base Areas of Akrotiri and Dhekelia in Cyprus except to the extent necessary to ensure the implementation of the arrangements set out in the Protocol on the Sovereign Base Areas of the United Kingdom of Great Britain and Northern Ireland in Cyprus annexed to the Act concerning the conditions of accession of the Czech Republic, the Republic of Estonia, the Republic of Cyprus, the Republic of Latvia, the Republic of Lithuania, the Republic of Hungary, the Republic of Malta, the Republic of Poland, the Republic of Slovenia and the Slovak Republic to the European Union and in accordance with the terms of that Protocol;
(c) this Treaty shall apply to the Channel Islands and the Isle of Man only to the extent necessary to ensure the implementation of the arrangements for those islands set out in the Treaty concerning the accession of new Member States to the European Economic Community and to the European Atomic Energy Community signed on 22 January 1972.

Treaty on the Functioning of the European Union

Article 349

Taking account of the structural social and economic situation of Guadeloupe, French Guiana, Martinique, Réunion, Saint-Barthélemy, Saint-Martin, the Azores, Madeira and the Canary Islands, which is compounded by their remoteness, insularity, small size, difficult topography and climate, economic dependence on a few products, the permanence and combination of which severely restrain their development, the Council, on a proposal from the Commission and after consulting the European Parliament, shall adopt specific measures aimed, in particular, at laying down the conditions of application of the Treaties to those regions, including common policies. Where the specific measures in question are adopted by the Council in accordance with a special legislative procedure, it shall also act on a proposal from the Commission and after consulting the European Parliament.

The measures referred to in the first paragraph concern in particular areas such as customs and trade policies, fiscal policy, free zones, agriculture and fisheries policies, conditions for supply of raw materials and essential consumer goods, State aids and conditions of access to structural funds and to horizontal Union programs.

The Council shall adopt the measures referred to in the first paragraph taking into account the special characteristics and constraints of the outermost regions without undermining the integrity and the coherence of the Union legal order, including the internal market and common policies.

Article 355

In addition to the provisions of Article 52 of the Treaty on European Union relating to the territorial scope of the Treaties, the following provisions shall apply:

1. The provisions of the Treaties shall apply to Guadeloupe, French Guiana, Martinique, Réunion, Saint-Barthélemy, Saint-Martin, the Azores, Madeira and the Canary Islands in accordance with Article 349.

2. The special arrangements for association set out in Part Four shall apply to the overseas countries and territories listed in Annex II.
The Treaties shall not apply to those overseas countries and territories having special relations with the United Kingdom of Great Britain and Northern Ireland, which are not included in the aforementioned list.

3. The provisions of the Treaties shall apply to the European territories for whose external relations a Member State is responsible.

4. The provisions of the Treaties shall apply to the Åland Islands in accordance with the provisions set out in Protocol 2 to the Act concerning the conditions of accession of the Republic of Austria, the Republic of Finland and the Kingdom of Sweden.

5. Notwithstanding Article 52 of the Treaty on European Union and paragraphs 1 to 4 of this Article:
(a) the Treaties shall not apply to the Faeroe Islands;
(b) the Treaties shall not apply to the United Kingdom Sovereign Base Areas of Akrotiri and Dhekelia in Cyprus except to the extent necessary to ensure the implementation of the arrangements set out in the Protocol on the Sovereign Base Areas of the United Kingdom of Great Britain and Northern Ireland in Cyprus annexed to the Act concerning the conditions of accession of the Czech Republic, the Republic of Estonia, the Republic of Cyprus, the Republic of Latvia, the Republic of Lithuania, the Republic of Hungary, the Republic of Malta, the Republic of Poland, the Republic of Slovenia and the Slovak Republic to the European Union and in accordance with the terms of that Protocol;
(c) the Treaties shall apply to the Channel Islands and the Isle of Man only to the extent necessary to ensure the implementation of the arrangements for those islands set out in the Treaty concerning the accession of new Member States to the European Economic Community and to the European Atomic Energy Community signed on 22 January 1972.

6. The European Council may, on the initiative of the Member State concerned, adopt a decision amending the status, with regard to the Union, of a Danish, French or Netherlands country or territory referred to in paragraphs 1 and 2. The European Council shall act unanimously after consulting the Commission.

Title III - Taxable Persons

Article 9 [Definition of Taxable Person and Economic Activity]

1. **"Taxable person"** shall mean any **person** who, **independently**, carries out **in any place** any **economic activity**, **whatever** the **purpose or results** of that activity.

Any activity of producers, traders or persons supplying services, including mining and agricultural activities and activities of the professions, shall be regarded as **"economic activity"**. The exploitation of tangible or intangible property for the purposes of obtaining income therefrom on a continuing basis shall in particular be regarded as an economic activity.

2. In addition to the persons referred to in paragraph 1, any person who, on an **occasional basis**, supplies a new means of transport, which is dispatched or transported to the customer by the vendor or the customer, or on behalf of the vendor or the customer, to a destination outside the territory of a Member State but within the territory of the Community, shall be regarded as a taxable person.

Article 10 [Independently]

The condition in Article 9(1) that the economic activity be conducted **"independently"** **shall exclude employed** and other persons from VAT in so far as they are **bound to an employer** by a contract of employment or by any other legal ties creating the relationship of employer and employee as regards working conditions, remuneration and the employer's liability.

Article 11 [VAT group]

After consulting the advisory committee on value added tax (hereafter, the "VAT Committee"), each Member State may regard as a single taxable person any persons established in the territory of that Member State who, while legally independent, are closely bound to one another by financial, economic and organizational links. [VAT group and IGP (article 132(f) are two different VAT concepts]

A Member State exercising the option provided for in the first paragraph, may adopt any measures needed to prevent tax evasion or avoidance through the use of this provision.

Article 12 [Occasional building transactions]

1. Member States may regard as a taxable person anyone who carries out, on an **occasional basis**, a transaction relating to the activities referred to in the second subparagraph of Article 9(1) and **in particular** one of the following transactions:

    (a) the **supply**, before first occupation, of a **building** or **parts** of a building and of the **land** on which the building stands;

    (b) the supply of **building land**.

For the purposes of paragraph 1(a), "**building**" shall mean any structure fixed to or in the ground.

2. Member States may lay down the detailed rules for applying the criterion referred to in paragraph 1 (a) to conversions of buildings and may determine what is meant by "the land on which a building stands".

Member States may apply criteria other than that of first occupation, such as the period elapsing between the date of completion of the building and the date of first supply, or the period elapsing between the date of first occupation and the date of subsequent supply, provided that those periods do not exceed five years and two years respectively.

3. For the purposes of paragraph 1(b), "**building land**" shall mean any unimproved or improved land defined as such by the Member States.

Article 13 [Not Taxable Persons]

1. **States**, **regional** and **local government authorities** and other **bodies governed by public law** shall **not be regarded as taxable persons** in respect of the activities or transactions in which they **engage as public authorities**, even where they collect dues, fees, contributions or payments in connection with those activities or transactions.

   However, when they engage in such activities or transactions, they shall be **regarded as taxable persons** in respect of those activities or transactions where their treatment as non-taxable persons would **lead to significant distortions of competition.**

   In any event, bodies governed by public law shall be **regarded as taxable persons** in respect of the activities listed in Annex I[*see comments to Title III*], **provided that** those activities are not carried out on such a small scale as to be negligible.

2. Member States may regard activities, exempt under Articles 132, 135, 136 and 371, Articles 374 to 377, Article 378(2), Article 379(2) or Articles 380 to 390c, engaged in by bodies governed by public law as activities in which those bodies engage as public authorities.

Comments to Title III RVD: Taxable Persons

A - Comments

A1. General considerations

Generally, the transactions that fall within the VAT scope are the supply of goods and services for consideration within the territory of a Member State carried out by a taxable person acting as such. Thus: i) supply of goods and services; ii) for consideration; iii) within the territory of a Member State; iv) carried out by a taxable person acting as such.

The main question here is determining what is a taxable person acting as such. How can you identify whether one or several of the parties to a transaction are regarded as a taxable person(s) from a VAT perspective.

As seen in our list of core elements that need to be analyzed in a transaction to identify the applicable VAT (if any), the identification of the parties of the transaction as Taxable Persons (or not) should be the first step to be taken.

Indeed, only transactions carried out by a Taxable person fall within the scope of VAT. If neither party to a transaction is characterized as a Taxable Person, then the transaction falls outside the scope of VAT and the analysis stops there, as nothing is required from a VAT standpoint (e.g., the entity does not have to register for VAT, nor issue invoices, nor, charge any VAT in the transaction or in case only the acquirer is a non Taxable Person VAT may be charged but it is not recoverable, etc).

On the opposite, in case the conclusion of the analysis of element a. is that either one or more parties to the transaction are taxable person(s), the supply may fall within the VAT scope (the remaining elements need to be analyzed) and it can trigger different VAT compliance obligations (e.g. VAT registration and issuance of invoices, charging of VAT, recoverability or deduction, etc).

A2. Qualifying as taxable persons

A2.1 - Taxable Person

To qualify as a taxable person certain conditions have to be met. Taxable person is:

- Any person who,
- Independently and
- On a Regular basis,
- Carries out any Economic activity,
- Whatever the Purpose or Results of that activity.

A2.2 - Any person who...

Any person means exactly that: any person. The concept is broad enough to include anyone with or without legal personality and must be interpreted in the largest possible sense. This includes Individuals, Companies, Partnerships and any other legal entity independently of its form.

Important to know: this notion makes no restrictions in terms of nationality, establishment or country of incorporation (please note that Establishment can however influence liability, as will be seen in a subsequent chapter). Meaning that, for instance, a foreign individual or entity performing taxable transactions in an EU Member State is considered as much a taxable person as an individual or entity of with the nationality or established that member state.

One other point that is imperative to keep in mind is that Public authorities (States, regional and local government authorities and other bodies governed by public law) shall not be regarded as taxable persons regarding the activities or transactions in which they engage as public authorities, even in the cases where they collect duties, fees, contributions or payments in connection with those activities or transactions.

Two exceptions to this rule:

i - If it is considered that their treatment as nontaxable persons would lead to significant distortions of competition, they shall be regarded as taxable persons concerning those activities or transactions.

ii – In all cases, in respect to the activities listed below, provided that those activities are not carried out on such a small scale as to be negligible:

- Telecommunications services;
- Supply of water, gas, electricity and thermal energy;
- Transport of goods;
- Port and airport services;
- Passenger transport;
- Supply of new goods manufactured for sale;
- Transactions related to agricultural products, carried out by agricultural intervention agencies pursuant to Regulations on the common organization of the market in those products;
- Organization of trade fairs and exhibitions;
- Warehousing;
- Activities of commercial publicity bodies;
- Activities of travel agents;
- Running of staff shops, cooperatives and industrial canteens and similar institutions;
- Activities carried out by radio and television bodies unless the activities, other than those of commercial nature, are carried out by public radio and television bodies.

A2.3 - ...Independently and...

To be considered a Taxable Person, the person needs to be carrying on its economical activity independently.

This excludes of the qualification as Taxable Person any person who is conducting the economic activity which VAT liability is under analysis bound to an employer by a contract of employment or any other legal ties creating the relationship of employer and employee as regards working conditions, remuneration and the employer's liability.

A2.4 - ...on a Regular basis...

The economic activity cannot be isolated. Such regularity has to be kept throughout time (e.g., renting activities) or by means of repetition (e.g., maintenance services).

This includes any activity of producers, traders or persons supplying services, including mining and agricultural activities and activities of the liberal professions and the exploitation of tangible or intangible property for the purposes of obtaining income therefrom on a continuing basis.

There are, however, exceptions to the regularity concept, where despite being occasional, some transactions remain within the VAT scope. An example of that would be a person who, on an occasional basis, supplies a new means of transport, which is dispatched or transported to the customer by the vendor or the customer, or on behalf of the vendor or the customer, to a destination outside the territory of a Member State but within the territory of the Community. In such case, despite the non-regular basis of the activity, the person would still be qualified as a Taxable Person. Another example would be, for some countries only (as this is one of the "may" clauses mentioned above), that of a person who carries out, on an occasional basis, the supply, before first occupation, of a building or parts of a building and of the land on which the building stands or anyone who carries out, on an occasional basis, the supply of building land (also a "may" clause).

A2.5 - ...carries out any Economic activity...

Economic activity is any activity of producers, traders or persons supplying services, including:

- Mining activities
- Agricultural activities
- Activities of liberal professions or similar
- Exploitation of tangible property for the purposes of obtaining income therefrom
- Exploitation of intangible property for the purposes of obtaining income therefrom
- Supplies a new means of transport - when dispatched or transported to the customer by the vendor or the customer, or on behalf of the vendor or the customer, to a destination outside the territory of a Member State but within the territory of the Community.

When defining transactions that are subject to VAT the RVD makes them dependent on the existence of Consideration. Furthermore, and in order to be deemed as Economic Activity, the ECJ in its case law, has established a direct link between the activities and a consideration of some kind, i.e. anything of value promised to another when making a contract. It can take the form of money, physical objects, services, promised actions, abstinence from a future action, etc. Meaning that payment in form money is not a key element. For more information on this, check the following Case Law: ECJ, Case 154/80, Staatssecretaris van Financiën v. Coöperatieve Aardappelenbewaarplaats GA, 05.02.1982 ; ECJ, Case 50/87, Commission of the European Communities v. French Republic, 21.09.1988; ECJ, Case 102/86, Apple and Pear Development Council v. Commissioners of Customs and Excise, 08.03.1986; ECJ, Case C-215/94, Jürgen Mohr v. Finanzamt Bad Segeberg, 29.02.1996; ECJ,Case C-174/00, Kennemer Golf & Country Club v. Inspecteur Belastingdienst Particulieren / Ondernemingen Haarlem, 21.03.2002; ECJ, C-267/08, SPÖ Landesorganisation Kärnten v Finanzamt Klagenfurt, 06.10.2009, etc.

A2.6 - ...whatever the Purpose or Results of that activity

Meaning that even though the taxable Person needs to be carrying out an economic activity, and that a direct connection with a consideration needs to be made, that does not imply that such activity needs to be profitable; profitability is not a key element. An activity does not cease to be an economic activity (same way than an enterprise does not cease to be an enterprise) merely because it is not making a profit.

An interesting discussing is whether this disregard for purpose or result should mean that the illegality or immorality of certain activities should not exclude them from VAT scope. A literal interpretation of the corresponding article of the RVD would lead to that conclusion, however been interpreted by both the ECJ and the VAT Committee that illegal or unlawful transactions should fall outside the scope of VAT.

A3. Acting as such

As we saw above, it is not sufficient that the Person qualifies as a Taxable Person.

Even if the person qualifies as Taxable Person, in order for the transaction to fall within the scope of VAT, the person needs to be acting as such. By that it is meant that in cases where the Taxable Person that makes a supply which is not part of its' economic activity, but is a purely private transaction, the supply will not be subject to VAT.

A good example of this would be a Lawyer, independent worker, who needs to charge VAT on his services (VAT Output) and gets to deduct VAT on purchases of goods and services that are related to his activity (books, stationary, rent of the office etc). Now imagine that Lawyer leaving the office and buying a bottle of wine to share with his wife over dinner. In the present case even though the Lawyer is a taxable person, he is not acting as such and will not be allowed to offset (deduct) the input VAT he paid on the bottle of Wine to the output VAT he will receive when invoicing one of his clients. Which has as consequence that the input VAT bore with the bottle will be a cost for the Lawyer.

A second example, take the same Lawyer and imagine that he decides to sell his TV to his mother in law (as he is interested in buying a new one - a new TV, not mother in law...). Again, even tough the Lawyer is a Taxable person, when performing that sale he is not acting as such. He is, therefore, not a taxable person for the purposes of this sale and will not charge VAT on this sale.

B – Implementation measures (see Regulation 282/2011)

Article 5

A European Economic Interest Grouping (EEIG) constituted in accordance with Regulation (EEC) No 2137/85 which supplies goods or services for consideration to its members or to third parties shall be a taxable person within the meaning of Article 9(1) of Directive 2006/112/EC.

Guidance notes: This article provides that an EEIG (European Economic Interest Group) shall, for VAT purposes, be regarded as a taxable person carrying on economic activities. An EEIG can be formed by a group of traders based in different MS of the EU to facilitate or develop the economic activities of its members by a pooling of resources, activities or skills. The operation of EEIG'S in Ireland are governed by the provisions of the European Communities (European Economic Interest Groupings) Regulations 1989.

C – Guidelines VAT Committee
Meeting 4, 8, 9, 21, 22, 30, 32, 34, 39, 54, 61, 64, 75, 90, 91, 96, 98

D – Others
Annex I
List of the Activities referred to in the Third subparagraph of article 13(1)
(1) Telecommunications services;
(2) supply of water, gas, electricity and thermal energy;
(3) transport of goods;
(4) port and airport services;
(5) passenger transport;
(6) supply of new goods manufactured for sale;
(7) transactions in respect of agricultural products, carried out by agricultural intervention agencies pursuant to Regulations on the common organization of the market in those products;
(8) organization of trade fairs and exhibitions;
(9) warehousing;
(10) activities of commercial publicity bodies;
(11) activities of travel agents;
(12) running of staff shops, cooperatives and industrial canteens and similar institutions;
(13) activities carried out by radio and television bodies in so far as these are not exempt pursuant to Article 132(1)(q).

Title IV - Taxable Transactions

Chapter 1 Supply of Goods

Article 14 [Definition]

1. "**Supply of goods**" shall mean the **transfer** of the **right to dispose** of **tangible property** as **owner**.

2. **In addition** to the transaction referred to in paragraph 1, each of the following shall be regarded as a supply of goods:

    (a) the **transfer, by order** made by or in the name **of a public authority** or in **pursuance of the law**, of the **ownership of property** against payment of **compensation**;

    (b) the actual handing over of goods pursuant to a **contract for the hire of goods** for a certain period, or for the **sale of goods on deferred terms**, which provides that in the normal course of events ownership is to pass at the latest upon payment of the final installment;

    (c) the transfer of goods pursuant to a contract under which **commission** is payable on purchase or sale.

3. Member States may regard the handing over of **certain works of construction** as a supply of goods.

Article 15 [Deemed supply of goods -1]

1. **Electricity, gas, heat** or **cooling** energy and the like shall be treated as tangible property.

2. Member States may regard the following as tangible property:

    (a) certain **interests in immovable property**;

    (b) **rights** *in rem* giving the holder thereof a right of use over immovable property;

(c) **shares** or **interests** equivalent to shares giving the holder thereof de jure or de facto rights of ownership or possession over immovable property or part thereof.

Article 16 [Deemed supply of goods - 2]

The application by a taxable person of **goods forming part of his business assets** for **his private use** or for that of **his staff**, or their **disposal free of charge** or, more generally, their **application for purposes other than those of his business**, shall be treated as a supply of goods for consideration, where the VAT on those goods or the component parts thereof was wholly or partly deductible.

However, the application of goods for business use as **samples or as gifts of small value** shall not be treated as a supply of goods for consideration.

Article 17 [Deemed intra-Community supply – inventory movements]

1. The **transfer** by a taxable person of goods forming part of his business assets **to another Member State** shall be treated as a supply of goods for consideration.

"**Transfer to another Member State**" shall mean the dispatch or transport of movable tangible property by or on behalf of the taxable person, for the purposes of his business, to a destination outside the territory of the Member State in which the property is located, but within the Community.

2. The dispatch or transport of goods for the purposes of any of the following transactions **shall not be regarded as a transfer to another Member State:**

    (a) the supply of the goods by the taxable person within the territory of the Member State in which the dispatch or transport ends, in accordance with the conditions laid down in Article 33 [*Distant Sales*];

(b) the supply of the goods, for **installation** or **assembly** by or on behalf of the supplier, by the taxable person within the territory of the Member State in which dispatch or transport of the goods ends, in accordance with the conditions laid down in Article 36;

(c) the supply of the goods by the taxable person on board a **ship**, an **aircraft** or a **train** in the course of a passenger transport operation, in accordance with the conditions laid down in Article 37;

(d) the supply of **gas** through a natural gas system situated within the territory of the Community or any network connected to such a system, the supply of **electricity** or the supply of **heat** or **cooling** energy through heating or cooling networks, in accordance with the conditions laid down in Articles 38 and 39;

(e) the supply of the goods by the taxable person within the territory of the Member State, in accordance with the conditions laid down in Articles 138 [*intra-Community supplies*], 146 [*exportations*], 147 [*exportations carried in personal luggage*], 148 [*international transport*], 151 [*transactions treated as exports*] or 152 [*supply of gold to central banks*];

(f) the supply of a service performed for the taxable person and consisting in **valuations of**, or **work on**, the **goods** in question physically carried out within the territory of the Member State in which dispatch or transport of the goods ends, provided that the goods, after being valued or worked upon, are returned to that taxable person in the Member State from which they were initially dispatched or transported;

(g) the **temporary use of the goods** within the territory of the Member State in which dispatch or transport of the goods ends, **for the purposes of the supply of services** by the taxable person established within the Member State in which dispatch or transport of the goods began;

(h) the **temporary use of the goods**, for a period not exceeding **twenty-four months**, within the territory of another Member State, in which the importation of the same goods from a third country with a view to their temporary use would be covered by the arrangements for temporary importation with full exemption from import duties.

3. **If** one of the **conditions** governing eligibility under paragraph 2 **is no longer met**, the goods shall be regarded as having been transferred to another Member State. In such cases, the transfer shall be deemed to take place at the time when that condition ceases to be met.

Article 18 [Transactions that may be treated as supplies of goods]

Member States **may** treat each of the following transactions as a **supply of goods** for consideration:

(a) the **application** by a taxable person for the purposes of his business of goods produced, constructed, extracted, processed, purchased or imported in the course of such business, where the **VAT** on such goods, had they been acquired from another taxable person, **would not be wholly deductible**;

(b) the **application** of goods by a taxable person for the purposes of a **non-taxable area of activity**, where the VAT on such goods became wholly or partly deductible upon their acquisition or upon their application in accordance with point (a);

(c) with the exception of the cases referred to in Article 19, the **retention of goods** by a taxable person, or by his successors, **when** he **ceases to carry out a taxable**

economic activity, where the VAT on such goods became wholly or partly deductible upon their acquisition or upon their application in accordance with point (a).

Article 19 [Transfer of business as going concern]

In the event of a **transfer**, whether for consideration or not or as a contribution to a company, of a **totality of assets** or **part thereof**, Member States may consider that no supply of goods has taken place and that the person to whom the goods are transferred is to be treated as the successor to the transferor.

Member States may, in cases where the recipient is not wholly liable to tax, take the measures necessary to **prevent distortion of competition**. They may also adopt any measures needed to prevent tax evasion or avoidance through the use of this Article.

Chapter 2 Intra-Community Acquisition of Goods

Article 20 [Definition]

"**Intra-Community acquisition of goods**" shall mean the **[a] acquisition** of the **[b] right to dispose as owner** of **[c] movable tangible property** **[d] dispatched or transported** to the person acquiring the goods, **[e] by or on behalf of the vendor or the person acquiring the goods,** **[f] in a Member State other than that in which dispatch or transport of the goods began.**

Where goods acquired by a **non-taxable legal person** are dispatched or transported from a **third territory** or a **third country** and **imported** by that non-taxable legal person **into a Member State** other than the Member State in which dispatch or transport of the goods ends, the goods shall be **regarded as having been dispatched or transported from the Member State of importation**. That Member State shall grant the importer designated or recognized under Article 201 as liable for payment of VAT a **refund** of the VAT paid in respect of the importation of the goods, provided that the importer establishes that VAT has been applied to his acquisition in the Member State in which dispatch or transport of the goods ends.

Article 21 [Application of goods to business]

The application by a taxable person, for the purposes of his business, of goods dispatched or transported by or on behalf of that taxable person from another Member State, within which the goods were produced, extracted, processed, purchased or acquired within the meaning of Article 2(1)(b) [*intra-Community transactions*], or into which they were imported by that taxable person for the purposes of his business, shall be **treated as an intra-Community acquisition** of goods for consideration.

Article 22 [Application by armed forces party of NATO]

The application by the **armed forces of a State party to the North Atlantic Treaty**, for their use or for the use of the civilian staff accompanying them, of goods which they have not purchased subject to the general rules governing taxation on the domestic market of a Member State shall be treated as an intra-Community acquisition of goods for consideration, where the importation of those goods would not be eligible for the exemption provided for in Article 143(1)(h) [*importation of goods, into Member States party to the North Atlantic Treaty, by the armed forces of other States party to that Treaty for the use of those forces or the civilian staff accompanying them or for supplying their messes or canteens where such forces take part in the common defense effort*].

Article 23

Member States shall take the measures necessary to ensure that a transaction which would have been classed as a supply of goods if it had been carried out within their territory by a taxable person acting as such is classed as an intra-Community acquisition of goods.

Chapter 3 Supply of Services

Article 24 [Definition]

1. "**Supply of services**" shall mean any transaction which does not constitute a supply of goods.

2. "**Telecommunications services**" shall mean services relating to the transmission, emission or reception of signals, words, images and sounds or information of any nature by wire, radio, optical or other electromagnetic systems, including the related transfer or assignment of the right to use capacity for such transmission, emission or reception, with the inclusion of the provision of access to global information networks.

Article 25 [Examples of supply of services]

A supply of services may consist, inter alia, in one of the following transactions:

(a) the **assignment of intangible property**, whether or not the subject of a document establishing title;

(b) the **obligation to refrain from an act**, or **to tolerate an act** or situation;

(c) the **performance of services** in **pursuance of an order made by or in the name of a public authority** or in **pursuance of the law**.

Article 26 [Deemed supply of services]

1. Each of the following transactions shall be treated as a supply of services for consideration:

(a) the use of goods forming part of the assets of a business for the **private use** of a taxable person or of his staff or, more generally, for purposes other than those of his business, where the VAT on such goods was wholly or partly deductible;

(b) the **supply of services carried out free of charge** by a taxable person for his **private use** or for that of his staff or, more generally, for purposes other than those of his business.

2. Member States may derogate from paragraph 1, provided that such **derogation** does not lead to distortion of competition.

Article 27 [Non deductible services]

In order to **prevent distortion of competition** and after consulting the VAT Committee, Member States **may** treat as a supply of services for consideration the supply by a taxable person of a service for the purposes of his business, where the VAT on such a service, were it supplied by another taxable person, would not be wholly deductible.

Article 28 [Undisclosed commissioner]

Where a taxable person **acting in his own name** but on **behalf of another person** takes part in a supply of services, he shall be deemed to have received and supplied those services himself.

Article 29 [Transfer of business as going concern]

Article 19 shall apply in like manner to the supply of services.

Chapter 4 Importation of Goods

Article 30 [Definition]

"**Importation of goods**" shall mean the entry into the Community of goods which are not in free circulation within the meaning of Article 24 of the Treaty I*[see comments to Title IV]*.

In addition to the transaction referred to in the first paragraph, the entry into the Community of goods which are in free circulation, coming from a third territory forming part of the customs territory of the Community, shall be regarded as importation of goods.

Comments to Title IV RVD: Taxable Transactions

A - Comments

A1. General Considerations

The main question here is determining if the transaction is a supply of goods, services or something else. Together with taxable person, the question regarding taxable transaction allows to determine whether the transaction is within or outside the VAT scope.

If the transaction is not subject to VAT, then it will be outside the VAT scope and, therefore, nothing is required from a VAT standpoint (e.g., the entity does not have to register for VAT nor issue invoices). On the other hand, in case it is subject to VAT, the supply will fall within the VAT scope and it can trigger different VAT compliance obligations (e.g. VAT registration and issuance of invoices).

The RVD lists what transactions are to be regarded as taxable transactions. They are:

1. The supply of goods for consideration, within the territory of the Member State concerned, carried out by a taxable person acting as such
2. The importation of goods
3. The exportation of goods
4. The intra-community acquisition of goods for consideration, within the territory of the Member State concerned, carried out by a taxable person acting as such or by a nontaxable legal person
5. The intra-community supply of goods dispatched or transported to a destination outside their respective territory but within the Community, by or on behalf of the vendor or the person acquiring the goods, for another taxable person, or for a nontaxable legal person acting as such in a Member State other than that in which dispatch or transport of the goods began.
6. The supply of services for consideration, within the territory of the Member State concerned, carried out by a taxable person acting as such

A2. Supply of Goods

A2.1 Five Conditions

The first taxable transaction listed in the RVD is the "supply of goods for consideration, within the territory of the Member State concerned, carried out by a taxable person acting as such".

To fully determine whether a specific transaction is considered a VAT taxable transaction, it is necessary to see if 5 cumulative conditions are met:

- It must adequate to the concept of supply of goods;
- The transaction must be effected for consideration;
- The transaction must have its consequences within the territory of the Member State concerned;

- The transaction must be carried out by a taxable person; and
- The taxable person must be acting as such.

A2.2 The Concept of Supply of Goods

I - Definition

Supply of goods is defined in the RVD as "the transfer of the right to dispose of tangible property as owner".

A "transfer of a right to dispose of tangible property" needs to take place.

The reference to "dispose" clearly indicates that the concept does not only involve "sales" but any disposal (disposal de facto) independently of the juridical name attributed to such act within the domestic law of the member-States.

"...of tangible property..." where it is necessary to consider that the RVD has its own view on what should be qualified as tangible property (see A.3 Extension to others).

"...as owner" meaning that a transfer of ownership needs to occur. This excludes renting from the qualification as supply of goods (as we will see in a subsequent section, it is qualified as supply of services). Important to notice that this transference does not, however, need to be made by the owner himself. The transference rights made by third parties on behalf of the owner are also valid.

II - Also qualified as Supply of Goods

The RVD extends the qualification as Supply of Goods to the following:

- The transfer, by order made by or in the name of a public authority or in pursuance of the law, of the ownership of property against payment of compensation;
- The actual handing over of goods pursuant to a contract for the hire of goods for a certain period, or for the sale of goods on deferred terms, which provides that in the normal course of events ownership is to pass at the latest upon payment of the final installment;
- The transfer of goods pursuant to a contract under which a commission is payable on purchase or sale. Regarding this point, Ben Terra & Julie Kajus defend that "the VAT Directive should be read as follows "where a taxable person acting in his own name but on behalf of another takes part in a supply of goods, he must be considered to have received and supplied those goods". Without these provisions an agent should always be required to reveal the name of his principal, which would have been necessary for correct invoicing procedures. The Directive therefore introduces the fiction of a supply to and by the undisclosed agent, to whom and by whom proper invoices must be issued, i.e. mentioning the full price of the goods or services supplied rather than a separate invoice for the commission." (see *Commentary – A Guide to the Recast VAT Directive* - Chapter 4 – Taxable Transactions - Topical Analyses , in IBFD Tax Research Platform). The authors fully subscribe this understanding.

III- Extension to others

The RVD allows (a "may" clause, as defined above) the qualification as a supply of goods to the "handing over of certain works of construction as a supply of goods" to member-States that wish to do so.

Further, the RVD also extends the qualification as supply of goods by characterizing as tangible property:

- Electricity, gas, heat or cooling energy and the like should be treated as tangible property;
- Certain interests in immovable property;
- Rights in rem giving the holder thereof a right of use over immovable property;
- Shares - or interests equivalent to shares - giving the holder thereof rights of ownership or possession (de jure or de facto) over immovable property or part thereof.

IV - Exclusion

On the other hand, the RVD states that the transfer of samples and gifts of small value shall not be treated as supply of good for consideration.

Also the application of goods for business use as samples or as gifts of small value shall not be treated as a supply of goods for consideration.

Important to note that despite this, the VAT paid on the acquisition of gifts and samples is fully deductible (in case the Taxable person has full deduction rights).

A2.3 - For consideration

Consideration was already summarized in Chapter 2, Section 2 above.

It is a broad conception, meaning anything of value promised to another when making a contract. It can take the form of money, physical objects, services, promised actions, abstinence from a future action, etc. The payment in form money is not a key element.

The RVD extends the notion of Consideration and treats the fas supply of goods for consideration the transaction whereby business assets are used for any other purposes than the business. An example of this are business assets allocated for private use or for that of his staff, or their disposal free of charge or, more generally, their application for purposes other than those of his business, shall be treated as a supply of goods for consideration, where the VAT on those goods or the component parts thereof was wholly or partly deductible.

A2.4 - Within the territory of the Member State concerned

I - Territorial scope

The transaction must have its consequences within the territory of the Member State concerned. Example: supplies of goods carried out within Germany are not regarded as taxable transaction in France and, therefore, are outside French VAT scope.

It is important to understand that any supply of goods (as well as services) could involve three different geographic areas from an EU VAT perspective:

- The territory of the EU Member State concerned.
- The EU territory. As there are no borders regarding supplies of goods within the EU, the concepts of importation and exportation between EU member-States do not apply. Instead the supplies of goods between different EU member-States are called intra-community transaction, being the sales named intra-community supply and the purchases intra-community acquisitions. We will deal with these type of transactions

a subsequent Section

- Transaction with Non-EU countries which are characterized as importation and exportation and which will be dealt with in a subsequent Section.

II - List of EU member-States in April 2014 (year of entry)

Austria (1995), Belgium (1952), Bulgaria (2007), Croatia (2013), Cyprus (2004), Czech Republic (2004), Denmark (1973), Estonia (2004), Finland (1995), France (1952), Germany (1952), Greece (1981), Hungary (2004), Ireland (1973), Italy (1952), Latvia (2004), Lithuania (2004), Luxembourg (1952), Malta (2004), Netherlands (1952), Poland (2004), Portugal (1986), Romania (2007), Slovakia, (2004), Slovenia (2004), Spain (1986), Sweden (1995), United Kingdom (1973).

III- Territories not regarded as territory of the EU for VAT purposes - (member-State) - Excluded territories/countries

(Cyprus) - Areas of Cyprus not under the effective control of the Government of the Republic of Cyprus;

(Germany) - The Island of Heligoland and the territory of Büesingen;

(Greece) - Mount Athos;

(Spain) - The Canary Islands, Ceuta and Melilla;

(France) - The Overseas Departments (DOM);

(Italy) - Livigno, Campione d'Italia, the Italian waters of Lake Lugano;

(Finland) - Åland Islands;

(United Kingdom) - The Channel Islands and Gibraltar;

IV - States not considered as territory of the EU for VAT purposes

Andorra; Faroe Islands; Greenland; French Overseas territories; Netherlands Antilles; San Marino; Vatican City.

A2.5 - Carried out by a Taxable Person

The definition of Taxable Person is analyzed above, pg. 29 and following. In summary Taxable person is any person who, independently and on a regular basis, carries out any economic activity, whatever the purpose or results of that activity.

A2.6 - As such

The meaning of "as such" is tackled above, pg. 29 and following. In summary this means that in cases where the Taxable Person that makes a supply which is not part of its' economic activity, but is a purely private transaction, the supply will not be subject to VAT.

A3 – intra-Community transactions

A3.1 - Intra-community supply and acquisition

An intra-Community transaction of goods is transfer and acquisition of the right to dispose as owner of movable tangible property dispatched or transported to the person acquiring the goods, by or on behalf of the vendor or the person acquiring the goods, in a

Member State other than that in which dispatch or transport of the goods began.

In an intra-community transaction two points of view have to be considered. Take an example where Company "A" sells goods to Company B. The goods are in Italy, but Company B wants to receive them in the Netherlands. Both companies agree that Company A will transport the goods into the Netherlands.

From a **supplier** perspective, the transaction is an intra-Community supply. Such transaction takes place where the goods are located when dispatch or transport begins (Italy on the example).

From a **purchaser** perspective, the transaction is an intra-Community acquisition. Such transaction takes place where the goods are located when dispatch or transport ends (NL on the example).

Note: whatever transaction which would have been qualified as a supply of goods if it had been carried out within a particular Member State has to be qualified an intra-Community acquisition of goods when carried out between EU member-States.

A3.2 Derogations

The RVD foresees, however, a derogation to the Intra-community rule. According to this derogation an Intra-community transaction is regarded as outside of the VAT scope if:

1. The person doing the transaction is either: (i) a nontaxable legal person, an agricultural business subject to the common flat-rate scheme; or (ii) a person who carries out only supplies of goods or services which the VAT is not deductible

a) The following conditions are met: (a) Goods supplied are not new means of transport nor products subject to excise duty, and (b) in the current or previous calendar year, the total net amount (VAT exclusive) of the ICA does not exceed EUR 10,000 or the equivalent in national currency.

Being that products subject to excise duty are: energy products, alcohol and alcoholic beverages and manufactured tobacco, but not gas supplied through a natural gas system situated within the territory of the Community or any network connected to such a system.

Do consider that the threshold changes depending on the EU Member State concerned

A3.3 - Deemed transactions

Take the following example: Company "A" owns 30 boxes of smoothies in a warehouse in France. The company transfers 20 of such boxes to a warehouse in Germany.

In the given example, there is no transfer or acquisition of the right to dispose as owner of the 20 boxes of smoothies. In fact the owner does not change at all (it is company "A"); it just transports goods from one warehouse to another warehouse in a different country.

Although this transaction would not, by definition, be qualified as an Intra-community transfer, the RVD directs us to treat it as such.

The consequence of this is that contrary to what would be the normal commercial intuition (that there is no commercial transaction, just a movement from left pocket to right pocket, no VAT obligations would exist), "Company A" will have to comply with the same VAT declarative obligations as if a real intra-community transaction had taken place (the transaction needs to be declared in the EC Sales list and in the Intrastat form).

Please do note, that in the case of a similar transaction but under a fully domestic context (for example, "Company A" transfers 20 boxes of smoothies from one warehouse in France to another warehouse in France) the transaction has no VAT impact and is out of VAT scope (from the VAT perspective is a non event).

A3.4 - Special case 1: new means of transport

An intra-community sale of new means of transport receives an exceptional treatment, as per comparison to a regular intra-community transaction.

While a standard intra-community transaction, as we saw before, is seen in two steps: the first from the perspective of the seller, where the transaction takes place in the country where the dispatch or transport begins (which will be exempt, as we will see in a subsequent chapter) and the acquisition will take place in the country where the dispatch or transport ends (which will be "reverse-charged" as we will see in another subsequent chapter); the intra-community sale of new means of transport will be seen as a transaction located in the country of destination.

This may seem like a small nuance but has deep implications in what concerns the compliance and tax collection obligations of the companies involved.

Please note that the RVD provides with the following specific definition of what are to be understood as "Means of Transport" and as "New".

The following qualify as "means of transport":

- Motorized land vehicles the capacity of which exceeds 48 cubic centimeters or the power of which exceeds 7,2 kilowatts;

- Vessels exceeding 7,5 meters in length, with the exception of vessels used for navigation on the high seas and carrying passengers for reward, and of vessels used for the purposes of commercial, industrial or fishing activities, or for rescue or assistance at sea, or for inshore fishing;

- Aircraft the takeoff weight of which exceeds 1,550 kilograms, with the exception of aircraft used by airlines operating for reward chiefly on international routes.

- And means of transport are "new" if:

- For motorized land vehicles, where the supply takes place within six months of the date of first entry into service or where the vehicle has travelled for no more than 6,000 kilometers;

- For vessels, where the supply takes place within three months of the date of first entry into service or where the vessel has sailed for no more than 100 hours;

- For aircrafts, where the supply takes place within three months of the date of first entry into service or where the aircraft has flown for no more than 40 hours.

A3.5 - Special case 2: triangulation simplification measures

See our comments to title XI under, on pgs. 208 and following.

A4 – Importation and Exportation

A4.1 - Importation

Importation of goods means, according to the RVD, the entry into the Community, of goods:

1. Which are not in free circulation
2. Which are in free circulation, coming from a third territory forming part of the customs territory of the Community.

Being that products shall be considered to be in free circulation in a Member State if the import formalities have been complied with and any customs duties or charges having equivalent effect which are payable have been levied in that Member State, and if they have not benefited from a total or partial drawback of such duties or charges.

A4.2 - Exportation

Exportation is a transaction on which goods are dispatched or transported by the supplier, or by the customer, or by a third person, from the EU to a third country

From a supplier perspective, the place of supply in an exportation will be the place where the goods are located when dispatch or transport begins.

A5 – Supply of services

A5.1 - Definition

I- Definition of supply of services

Supply of services is, for VAT purposes, a residual term. A service is as any transaction which does not constitute a supply (domestic, intra-community or import/export) of goods.

In other words, all that is not a supply of goods is, for VAT purposes, a supply of a service.

II - Also qualified as supply of Services

The RVD expressly states (in case the residual definition was not sufficient) that the following should be included in the definition of service:

- The assignment of intangible property, whether or not the subject of a document establishing title;
- The obligation to refrain from an act, or to tolerate an act or situation;

- The performance of services in pursuance of an order made by or in the name of a public authority or in pursuance of the law;
- Telecommunications services, i.e. services relating to the transmission, emission or reception of signals, words, images and sounds or information of any nature by wire, radio, optical or other electromagnetic systems, including the related transfer or assignment of the right to use capacity for such transmission, emission or reception, with the inclusion of the provision of access to global information networks.
- Assembling, i.e., if a taxable person only assembles the various parts of a machine all of which were provided to him by his customer, that transaction shall be a supply of services.

III - Extension to others

The following transactions are, according to the RVD, to be treated as supply of services for consideration:

- Use of business assets used for any other purposes than the business. e.g.: use of business assets for private use or for that of his staff, or their disposal free of charge or, more generally, their application for purposes other than those of his business, shall be treated as a supply of goods for consideration, where the VAT on those goods or the component parts thereof was wholly or partly deductible.
- The supply of services carried out free of charge by a taxable person for his private use or for that of his staff or, more generally, for purposes other than those of his business.

III - Specific cases

Some specific cases deserve attention:

- Issuance of new shares is not a taxable transaction;
- Undisclosed agents: where a taxable person acting in his own name but on behalf of another person takes part in a supply of services, he shall be deemed to have received and supplied those services himself.
- Restaurant and catering services: services consisting of the supply of prepared or unprepared food or beverages or both, for human consumption, accompanied by sufficient support services allowing for the immediate consumption thereof. The provision of food or beverages or both is only one component of the whole in which services shall predominate. Restaurant services are the supply of such services on the premises of the supplier, and catering services are the supply of such services off the premises of the supplier.

IV - Electronic supplied services

Electronic supplied services: are services which are delivered over the Internet or an electronic network and the nature of which renders their supply essentially automated and involving minimal human intervention, and impossible to ensure in the absence of information technology.

It includes:

- Website supply, web-hosting, distance maintenance of programs and equipment,
- Supply of software and updating thereof;
- Supply of images, text and information and making available of databases;
- Supply of music, films and games, including games of chance and gambling games, and of political, cultural, artistic, sporting, scientific and entertainment broadcasts and events;
- Supply of distance teaching.
- The supply of digitized products generally, including software and changes to or upgrades of software;
- Services providing or supporting a business or personal presence on an electronic network such as a website or a webpage;
- Services automatically generated from a computer via the Internet or an electronic network, in response to specific data input by the recipient;
- The transfer for consideration of the right to put goods or services up for sale on an Internet site operating as an online market on which potential buyers make their bids by an automated procedure and on which the parties are notified of a sale by electronic mail automatically generated from a computer;
- Internet Service Packages (ISP) of information in which the telecommunications component forms an ancillary and subordinate part (i.e. packages going beyond mere Internet access and including other elements such as content pages giving access to news, weather or travel reports; play- grounds; website hosting; access to online debates, etc.);

Some **practical examples** of Electronic Supplied Services

- Website hosting and webpage hosting;
- Automated, online and distance maintenance of programs;
- Remote systems administration;
- Online data warehousing where specific data is stored and retrieved electronically;
- Online supply of on-demand disc space;
- Accessing or downloading software (including procurement/accountancy programs and antivirus software) plus updates;
- Software to block banner adverts showing, otherwise known as Banner-blockers;
- Download drivers, such as software that interfaces computers with peripheral equipment (such as printers);
- Online automated installation of filters on websites;
- Online automated installation of firewalls;
- Accessing or downloading desktop themes;

- Accessing or downloading photographic or pictorial images or screen-savers;
- The digitized content of books and other electronic publications;
- Subscription to online newspapers and journals;
- Weblogs and website statistics;
- Online news, traffic information and weather reports;
- Online information generated automatically by software from specific data input by the customer, such as legal and financial data, (in particular such data as continually updated stock market data, in real time);
- The provision of advertising space including banner ads on a website/web page;
- Use of search engines and Internet directories;
- Accessing or downloading of music on to computers and mobile phones;
- Accessing or downloading of jingles, excerpts, ringtones, or other sounds;
- Accessing or downloading of films;
- Downloading of games on to computers and mobile phones;
- Accessing automated online games which are dependent on the Internet, or other similar electronic networks, where players are geographically remote from one another;
- Automated distance teaching dependent on the Internet or similar electronic network to function and the supply of which requires limited or no human intervention, including virtual classrooms, except where the Internet or similar electronic network is used as a tool simply for communication between the teacher and student;
- Workbooks completed by pupils online and marked automatically, without human intervention.

Examples of supplies which do **NOT** qualify as Electronic Supplied Services:

- Radio and television broadcasting services;
- Telecommunications services;
- Goods, where the order and processing is done electronically;
- CD-ROMs, floppy disks and similar tangible media;
- Printed matter, such as books, newsletters, newspapers or journals;
- CDs and audiocassettes;
- Video cassettes and DVDs;
- Games on a CD-ROM;
- Services of professionals such as lawyers and financial consultants, who advise clients by e-mail;
- Teaching services, where the course content is delivered by a teacher over the

Internet or an electronic network (namely via a remote link);

- Offline physical repair services of computer equipment;
- Offline data warehousing services;
- Advertising services, in particular as in newspapers, on posters and on television;
- Telephone help-desk services;
- Teaching services purely involving correspondence courses, such as postal courses;
- Conventional auctioneers' services reliant on direct human intervention, irrespective of how bids are made;
- Telephone services with a video component, otherwise known as videophone services;
- Access to the Internet and World Wide Web;
- Telephone services provided through the Internet.

A5.2 - For consideration

Same principles as for the supply of goods apply. See the respective Section above.

A5.3 - Within the territory of the Member State concerned

Same principles as for the supply of goods apply. See the respective Section above.

A5.4 - Carried out by a Taxable Person

Same principles as for the supply of goods apply. See the respective Section above.

A5.5 - As such

Same principles as for the supply of goods apply. See the respective Section above.

B – Implementation measures (see Regulation 282/2011)

Article 6

1. Restaurant and catering services mean services consisting of the supply of prepared or unprepared food or beverages or both, for human consumption, accompanied by sufficient support services allowing for the immediate consumption thereof. The provision of food or beverages or both is only one component of the whole in which services shall predominate. Restaurant services are the supply of such services on the premises of the supplier, and catering services are the supply of such services off the premises of the supplier.

2. The supply of prepared or unprepared food or beverages or both, whether or not including transport but without any other support services, shall not be considered restaurant or catering services within the meaning of paragraph 1.

Guidance notes: This article defines the circumstances under which restaurant and catering services qualify as 'services'.

Para. 1 provides that restaurant and catering services mean services consisting of the supply of prepared or unprepared food or beverages or both, for human consumption, accompanied by sufficient support services allowing for the immediate consumption thereof.

In the case of a restaurant, support services would include the provision of facilities to eat-e.g. cutlery, plates, table service, drinking glasses etc. Restaurants include canteens and cafeterias.

In the case of a catering service, support services would include the provision of food (both hot and cold), the supply of staff to serve the food, the provision of cutlery, plates, napkins, tables etc, and cleaning services.

Para. 2 provides that the supply of prepared or unprepared food or beverages or both, whether or not including transport, but without any other support services, shall not be considered restaurant or catering services (unless such food is supplied above the ambient temperature, in which case it is taxable at the relevant reduced rate, in line with Schedule 3 Para 3(3)).

However, if connected parties provide the service element as a separate supply to the supply of food, all supplies are to be treated as supplies of catering or restaurant services.

Article 7

1. 'Electronically supplied services' as referred to in Directive 2006/112/EC shall include services which are delivered over the Internet or an electronic network and the nature of which renders their supply essentially automated and involving minimal human intervention, and impossible to ensure in the absence of information technology.

2. Paragraph 1 shall cover, in particular, the following:

(a) the supply of digitized products generally, including software and changes to or upgrades of software;

(b) services providing or supporting a business or personal presence on an electronic network such as a website or a webpage;

(c) services automatically generated from a computer via the Internet or an electronic network, in response to specific data input by the recipient;

(d) the transfer for consideration of the right to put goods or services up for sale on an Internet site operating as an online market on which potential buyers make their bids by an automated procedure and on which the parties are notified of a sale by electronic mail automatically generated from a computer;

(e) Internet Service Packages (ISP) of information in which the telecommunications component forms an ancillary and subordinate part (i.e. packages going beyond mere Internet access and including other elements such as content pages giving access to news, weather or travel reports; playgrounds; website hosting; access to online debates etc.);

(f) the services listed in Annex I.

3. Paragraph 1 shall not, in particular, cover the following:

(a) radio and television broadcasting services;

(b) telecommunications services;

(c) goods, where the order and processing is done electronically;

(d) CD-ROMs, floppy disks and similar tangible media;

(e) printed matter, such as books, newsletters, newspapers or journals;

(f) CDs and audio cassettes;

(g) video cassettes and DVDs;

(h) games on a CD-ROM;

(i) services of professionals such as lawyers and financial consultants, who advise clients by e-mail;

(j) teaching services, where the course content is delivered by a teacher over the Internet or an electronic network (namely via a remote link);

(k) offline physical repair services of computer equipment;

(l) offline data warehousing services;

(m) advertising services, in particular as in newspapers, on posters and on television;

(n) telephone helpdesk services;

(o) teaching services purely involving correspondence courses, such as postal courses;

(p) conventional auctioneers' services reliant on direct human intervention, irrespective of how bids are made;

(q) telephone services with a video component, otherwise known as videophone services;

(r) access to the Internet and World Wide Web;

(s) telephone services provided through the Internet.

Guidance notes: This article defines 'electronically supplied services', as referred to in the VAT Directive. The article also lists services that constitute 'electronically supplied services' and services that are not regarded as 'electronically supplied services'

Article 8

If a taxable person only assembles the various parts of a machine all of which were provided to him by his customer, that transaction shall be a supply of services within the meaning of Article 24(1) of Directive 2006/112/EC.

Guidance notes: This article confirms that where a taxable person is solely involved in the assembly of various parts of a machine, all of which were provided to him by his customer, such a transaction is a supply of services. (See also Article 34)

Article 9

The sale of an option, where such a sale is a transaction falling within the scope of point (f) of Article 135(1) of Directive 2006/112/EC, shall be a supply of services within the meaning of Article 24(1) of that Directive. That supply of services shall be distinct from the underlying transactions to which the services relate.

Guidance notes: This article confirms that the sale of an option that is traded within the financial markets is a supply of services, which is a distinct supply from the underlying transactions to which it relates. The sale is treated as an exempt financial transaction.

C – Guidelines VAT Committee
Meetings regarding supply of goods: 6,8,9,28,29,38,39,41,48,52,60,67,80,83
Meetings regarding supply of services: 6,8,9,24,25,29,38,51,53,80,83,90,93,97

D – Others

Article 24 Treaty
Products coming from a third country shall be considered to be in free circulation in a Member State if the import formalities have been complied with and any customs duties or charges having equivalent effect which are payable have been levied in that Member State, and if they have not benefited from a total or partial drawback of such duties or charges.

Title V - Place of Taxable Transactions

Chapter 1 Place of Supply of Goods

Section 1: Supply of Goods without Transport

Article 31 [Rule]

Where goods are not dispatched or transported, the place of supply shall be deemed to be the **place where the goods are located at the time when the supply takes place.**

Section 2: Supply of Goods with Transport

Article 32 [Rule]

Where goods are dispatched or transported by the supplier, or by the customer, or by a third person, the place of supply shall be deemed to be **the place where the goods are located at the time when dispatch or transport of the goods to the customer begins.**

However, **if dispatch or transport** of the goods **begins in a third territory or third country**, both the **place of supply** by the importer designated or recognized under Article 201 as liable for payment of VAT **and the place of any subsequent supply** shall be **deemed to be within the Member State of importation of the goods.**

Article 33 [Distant Sales – Rule]

1. By way of derogation from Article 32, the place of supply of goods dispatched or transported by or on behalf of the supplier

from a Member State other than that in which dispatch or transport of the goods ends shall be deemed to be the **place where the goods are located at the time when dispatch or transport of the goods to the customer ends**, where the following conditions are met:

(a) the supply of goods is carried out for <u>a taxable person</u>, or a <u>non-taxable legal person</u>, whose intra-Community acquisitions of goods are <u>not subject to VAT</u> pursuant to Article 3(1) or for any other non-taxable person;

(b) the goods supplied are <u>neither new means of transport nor goods supplied after assembly or installation</u>, with or without a trial run, by or on behalf of the supplier.

2. Where the goods supplied are **dispatched or transported from a third territory or a third country** and **imported by the supplier** into a Member State other than that in which dispatch or transport of the goods to the customer ends, they shall be regarded as having been **dispatched or transported from the Member State of importation**.

Article 34 [Distant sales – conditions & thresholds]

1. Provided the **following conditions are met**, Article 33 shall not apply to supplies of goods all of which are dispatched or transported to the same Member State, where that Member State is the Member State in which dispatch or transport of the goods ends:

(a) the goods supplied are **not** products **subject to excise duty**;

(b) the total value, exclusive of VAT, of such supplies effected under the conditions laid down in Article 33 within that Member State **does not** in any one calendar year **exceed EUR 100,000** or the equivalent in national currency;

(d) the **total value**, exclusive of VAT, of the supplies of goods, other than products subject to excise duty, effected under the conditions laid down in Article 33 within that Member State d**id not in the previous calendar year exceed EUR 100,000** or the equivalent in national currency.

2. The **Member State** within the territory of which the goods are located at the time when their dispatch or transport to the customer ends **may** limit the threshold referred to in paragraph 1 to **EUR 35,000** or the equivalent in national currency, where that Member State fears that the threshold of EUR 100,000 might cause serious **distortion of competition**.

Member States which exercise the option under the first subparagraph shall take the measures necessary to inform accordingly the competent public authorities in the Member State in which dispatch or transport of the goods begins.

3. The Commission shall present to the Council at the earliest opportunity a report on the operation of the special EUR 35,000 threshold referred to in paragraph 2, accompanied, if necessary, by appropriate proposals.

4. The Member State within the territory of which the goods are located at the time when their dispatch or transport begins shall grant those taxable persons who carry out supplies of goods eligible under paragraph 1 the right to opt for the place of supply to be determined in accordance with Article 33.

The Member States concerned shall lay down the detailed rules governing the exercise of the option referred to in the first subparagraph, which shall in any event cover two calendar years.

Article 35 [Distant sales – exceptions]

Articles 33 and 34 shall not apply to supplies of **second-hand goods, works of art, collectors' items** or **antiques**, as defined in points (1) to (4) of Article 311(1), nor to supplies of **second-hand means of transport**, as defined in Article 327(3), subject to VAT in accordance with the relevant special arrangements.

Article 36 [Installed or assembled Goods]

Where goods dispatched or transported by the supplier, by the customer or by a third person are installed or assembled, with or without a trial run, by or on behalf of the supplier, the place of supply shall be deemed to be the place where the goods are installed or assembled.

Where the installation or assembly is carried out in a Member State other than that of the supplier, the Member State within the territory of which the installation or assembly is carried out shall take the measures necessary to ensure that there is no double taxation in that Member State.

Section 3: Supply of goods on board ships, aircraft or trains

Article 37 [Supply during passenger transport]

1. Where goods are supplied on board ships, aircraft or trains **during the section of a passenger transport** operation effected **within the Community**, the place of supply shall be deemed to be at the **point of departure of the passenger transport operation.**

2. For the purposes of paragraph 1, "**section of a passenger transport operation effected within the Community**" shall mean the section of the operation effected, without a stopover

outside the Community, between the point of departure and the point of arrival of the passenger transport operation.

"**Point of departure of a passenger transport operation**" shall mean the first scheduled point of passenger embarkation within the Community, where applicable after a stopover outside the Community.

"**Point of arrival of a passenger transport operation**" shall mean the last scheduled point of disembarkation within the Community of passengers who embarked in the Community, where applicable before a stopover outside the Community.

In the case of a **return trip**, the return leg shall be regarded as a separate transport operation.

3. The Commission shall, at the earliest opportunity, present to the Council a report, accompanied if necessary by appropriate proposals, on the place of taxation of the supply of goods for consumption on board and the supply of services, including restaurant services, for passengers on board ships, aircraft or trains.

Pending adoption of the proposals referred to in the first subparagraph, Member States may exempt or continue to exempt, with deductibility of the VAT paid at the preceding stage, the supply of goods for consumption on board in respect of which the place of taxation is determined in accordance with paragraph 1.

Section 4: Supplies of gas through a natural gas system, of electricity and of heat or cooling energy through heating and cooling networks

Article 38 [Supply in EU to a taxable dealer]

In the case of the supply of gas through a natural gas system situated within the territory of the Community or any network connected to such a system, the supply of electricity, or the supply of heat or cooling energy through heating or cooling networks to a taxable dealer, the place of supply shall be deemed to be the **place** where that taxable dealer **has established his business or** has a **fixed establishment** for which the goods are supplied **or,** in the absence of such a place of business or fixed establishment, the place where he has his **permanent address or usually resides**.

For the purposes of paragraph 1, "**taxable dealer**" shall mean a taxable person whose principal activity in respect of purchases of gas, electricity, heat or cooling energy is reselling those products and whose own consumption of those products is negligible.

Article 39 [Supply in EU – residual rule]

In the case of the supply of gas through a natural gas system situated within the territory of the Community or any network connected to such a system, the supply of electricity or the supply of heat or cooling energy through heating or cooling networks, where such a supply is not covered by Article 38, the place of supply shall be deemed to be the **place where the customer effectively uses and consumes the goods.**

Where all or part of the gas, electricity or heat or cooling energy is **not effectively consumed by the customer**, those non-consumed goods shall be deemed to have been used and consumed at the place where the customer has **established his business** or has a

fixed establishment for which the goods are supplied. In the absence of such a place of business or fixed establishment, the customer shall be deemed to have used and consumed the goods at the place where he has his **permanent address** or **usually resides**.

Chapter 2 Place of an Intra-Community Acquisition of Goods

Article 40 [Rule 1]

The place of an intra-Community acquisition of goods shall be deemed to be the **place where dispatch or transport of the goods to the person acquiring them ends**.

Article 41 [Rule 2]

Without prejudice to Article 40, the place of an intra-Community acquisition of goods as referred to in Article 2(1)(b)(i) shall be deemed to be within the **territory of the Member State which issued the VAT identification number** under which the person acquiring the goods made the acquisition, **unless** the person acquiring the goods establishes that VAT has been applied to that acquisition in accordance with Article 40.

If VAT is applied to the acquisition in accordance with the first paragraph and subsequently applied, pursuant to Article 40, to the acquisition in the Member State in which dispatch or transport of the goods ends, the taxable amount shall be reduced accordingly in the Member State which issued the VAT identification number under which the person acquiring the goods made the acquisition.

Article 42 [Triangulation]

The first paragraph of Article 41 shall not apply and VAT shall be deemed to have been applied to the intra-Community acquisition of goods in accordance with Article 40 **where the following conditions are met** [Exception to Rule 2 - also refer to articles, 138(1), 141 and 187]:

(a) the person acquiring the goods establishes that he has made the intra-Community **acquisition for the purposes of a subsequent supply**, within the territory of the Member State identified in accordance with Article 40, for which the person to whom the supply is made has been designated in accordance with Article 197 [reverse charge] as liable for payment of VAT;

(b) the person acquiring the goods has satisfied the obligations laid down in Article 265 relating to submission of the **recapitulative statement**.

Chapter 3 Place of Supply of Services

Section 1: Definitions

Article 43 [Assumptions]

For the purpose of applying the rules concerning the place of supply of services:

1. a taxable person who also carries out activities or transactions that are not considered to be taxable supplies of goods or services in accordance with Article 2(1) shall be regarded as a taxable person in respect of all services rendered to him;
2. a non-taxable legal person who is identified for VAT purposes shall be regarded as a taxable person.

Section 2: General rules

Article 44 [General rule for B2B Transactions]

The place of supply of services to a taxable person acting as such shall be the place where that person [*the customer*] has **established his business**. However, if those services are provided to a fixed establishment of the taxable person located in a place other than the place where he has established his business, the place of supply of those services shall be the place where that **fixed establishment** is located. In the absence of such place of establishment or fixed establishment, the place of supply of services shall be the place where the taxable person who receives such services has his **permanent address** or **usually resides**.

Article 45 [General rule for B2C Transactions]

The place of supply of services to a non-taxable person shall be the place where **the supplier has established his business**. However, if those services are provided from a fixed establishment of the supplier located in a place other than the place where he has established his business, the place of supply of those services shall be the place where that **fixed establishment** is located. In the absence of such place of establishment or fixed establishment, the place of supply of services shall be the place where the supplier has his **permanent address** or **usually resides**.

Section 3: Particular provisions

Subsection 1: Supply of services by intermediaries

Article 46 [Disclosed commissioner]

The place of supply of services rendered to a non-taxable person by an intermediary acting in the name and on behalf of another person shall be the **place where the underlying transaction is supplied** in accordance with this Directive.

Subsection 2: Supply of services connected with immovable property

Article 47 [What is included]

The place of supply of services connected with immovable property, **including** the services of **experts** and estate **agents**, the provision of **accommodation** in the **hotel** sector or in sectors with a similar function, such as **holiday camps** or sites developed for use as **camping sites**, the granting of rights to use immovable property and services for the **preparation and coordination of construction work**, such as the services of **architects** and of firms providing **on-site supervision**, shall be the **place where the immovable property is located**.

Subsection 3: Supply of transport

Article 48 [Passenger Transport]

The place of supply of passenger transport shall be the place where the **transport takes place**, proportionate to the distances covered.

Article 49 [Domestic Transport of Goods B2C]

The place of supply of the transport of goods, other than the intra-Community transport of goods, to non-taxable persons shall be the **place where the transport takes place**, proportionate to the distances covered.

Article 50 [Intra-Community Transport Goods B2C]

The place of supply of the intra-Community transport of goods to non-taxable persons shall be the place of departure.

Article 51 [Definitions]

"**Intra-Community transport of goods**" shall mean any transport of goods in respect of which the place of departure and the place of arrival are situated within the territories of two different Member States.

"**Place of departure**" shall mean the place where transport of the goods actually begins, irrespective of distances covered in order to reach the place where the goods are located and "**place of arrival**" shall mean the place where transport of the goods actually ends.

Article 52 [Part of transport taking place over waters]

Member States need not apply VAT to that part of the intra-Community transport of goods to non-taxable persons taking place over waters which do not form part of the territory of the Community.

Subsection 4: Supply of cultural, artistic, sporting, scientific, educational, entertainment and similar services, ancillary transport services and valuations of and work on movable property

Article 53 [B2B Supply - Rule]

The place of supply of services in respect of admission to cultural, artistic, sporting, scientific, educational, entertainment or similar events, such as fairs and exhibitions, and of ancillary services related to the admission, supplied to a taxable person, shall be the **place where those events actually take place**.

Article 54 [B2C Supply - Rule]

1. The place of supply of services and ancillary services, relating to cultural, artistic, sporting, scientific, educational, entertainment or similar activities, such as fairs and exhibitions, including the supply of services of the organizers of such activities, supplied to a non-taxable person shall be the **place where those activities actually take place**.

2. The place of supply of the following services to a non-taxable person shall be the place where the **services are physically carried out**:

(a) **ancillary transport** activities such as **loading, unloading, handling** and **similar** activities

(b) **valuations** of and **work** on movable tangible property.

Subsection 5: Supply of restaurant and catering services

Article 55 [Rule]

The place of supply of restaurant and catering services other than those physically carried out on board ships, aircraft or trains during the section of a passenger transport operation effected within the Community, shall be the **place where the services are physically carried out.**

Subsection 6: Hiring of means of transport

Article 56 [Rules and definitions]

1. The place of **short-term hiring** of a means of transport shall be the place where the means of transport is actually **put at the disposal of the customer.**

2. The place of hiring, **other than short-term** hiring, of a means of transport **to a non-taxable person** shall be the place where the **customer is established,** has his **permanent address** or **usually resides.**

3. However, the place of hiring a **pleasure boat** to **a non-taxable person, other than short-term hiring,** shall be the place where the pleasure boat is actually **put at the disposal** of the customer, where this **service is actually provided** by the supplier from his place of business or a **fixed establishment** situated in that place.

4. For the purposes of paragraphs 1 and 2, "**short-term**" shall mean the continuous possession or use of the means of transport throughout a period of not more than thirty days and, in the case of vessels, not more than 90 days.

Subsection 7: Supply of restaurant and catering services for consumption on board ships, aircraft or trains

Article 57 [Rules and definitions]

1. The place of supply of restaurant and catering services which are physically carried out on board ships, aircraft or trains during the section of a passenger transport operation effected within the Community, shall be at the **point of departure** of the passenger transport operation.

2. For the purposes of paragraph 1, "**section of a passenger transport operation effected within the Community**" shall mean the section of the operation effected, without a stopover outside the Community, between the point of departure and the point of arrival of the passenger transport operation.

"**Point of departure of a passenger transport operation**" shall mean the first scheduled point of passenger embarkation within the Community, where applicable after a stopover outside the Community.

"**Point of arrival of a passenger transport operation**" shall mean the last scheduled point of disembarkation within the Community of passengers who embarked in the Community, where applicable before a stopover outside the Community.

In the case of a **return trip**, the return leg shall be regarded as a separate transport operation.

Subsection 8: Supply of electronic services to non-taxable persons

Article 58 [B2C supply to the EU]

The place of supply of electronically supplied services, in particular those referred to in Annex II, when supplied to non-taxable persons who are established in a Member State, or who have their permanent address or usually reside in a Member State, by a taxable person who has established his business outside the Community or has a fixed establishment there from which the service is supplied, or who, in the absence of such a place of business or fixed establishment, has his permanent address or usually resides outside the Community, shall be the **place where the non-taxable person is established**, or where he has his **permanent address** or **usually resides**.

Where the supplier of a service and the customer communicate via electronic mail, that shall not of itself mean that the service supplied is an electronically supplied service.

Subsection 9: Supply of services to non-taxable persons outside the Community

Article 59 [B2C supply to outside the EU]

The place of supply of the **following services** to a non-taxable person who is established or has his permanent address or usually resides outside the Community, shall be the place where that person is **established**, has his **permanent address** or usually **resides**:

(a) transfers and assignments of **copyrights, patents, licenses, trade marks** and **similar** rights;

(b) **advertising** services;

(c) the services of **consultants, engineers, consultancy firms, lawyers, accountants** and other **similar** services, as well as **data processing** and the **provision of information**;

(d) obligations to **refrain from pursuing or exercising**, in whole or in part, **a business activity or** a **right** referred to in this Article;

(e) **banking, financial** and **insurance** transactions including reinsurance, with the exception of the hire of safes;

(f) the **supply of staff**;

(g) the **hiring** out of movable tangible property, with the exception of all means of transport;

(h) the provision of **access to a natural gas** system situated within the territory of the Community or to any network connected to such a system, to the **electricity system** or to **heating or cooling** networks, or the transmission or distribution through these systems or networks, and the provision of other services directly linked thereto;

(i) **telecommunications** services;

(j) **radio** and **television** broadcasting services;

(k) electronically supplied services, in particular those referred to in **Annex II**.

Where the supplier of a service and the customer communicate via electronic mail, that shall not of itself mean that the service supplied is an electronically supplied service.

Subsection 10: Prevention of double taxation or non-taxation

Article 59a [Effective Use & Enjoyment]

In order to prevent double taxation, non-taxation or distortion of competition, Member States may, with regard to services the place of supply of which is governed by Articles 44, 45, 56 and 59:

(a) consider the place of supply of any or all of those services, if situated within their territory, as being situated outside the Community if the effective use and enjoyment of the services takes place outside the Community;

(b) consider the place of supply of any or all of those services, if situated outside the Community, as being situated within their territory if the effective use and enjoyment of the services takes place within their territory.

However, this provision shall not apply to the electronically supplied services where those services are rendered to non-taxable persons not established within the Community.

Article 59b

Member States shall apply Article 59a(b) to telecommunications services and radio and television broadcasting services, as referred to in point (j) of the first paragraph of Article 59, supplied to non-taxable persons who are established in a Member State, or who have their permanent address or usually reside in a Member State, by a taxable person who has established his business outside the Community or has a fixed establishment there from which the services are supplied, or who, in the absence of such a place of business or fixed establishment, has his permanent address or usually resides outside the Community.

Chapter 4 Place of Importation of Goods

Article 60 [Rule]

The place of importation of goods shall be the Member State within whose territory the goods are **located when they enter the Community**.

Article 61 [Exceptions]

By way of derogation from Article 60, where, on entry into the Community, goods which are not in free circulation are placed under one of the arrangements or situations referred to in Article 156, or under temporary importation arrangements with total exemption from import duty, or under external transit arrangements, the place of importation of such goods shall be the **Member State within whose territory the goods cease to be covered by those arrangements or situations**.

Similarly, where, on entry into the Community, goods which are in free circulation are placed under one of the arrangements or situations referred to in Articles 276 and 277, the place of importation shall be the **Member State within whose territory the goods cease to be covered by those arrangements or situations**.

Comments to Title V RVD: Place of Taxable Transactions

A - Comments

A1. – General Considerations

The main question here is determining the territorial scope of a given transaction.

In a transaction involving 2 countries, the determination of the place of supply of goods or services is important because it is the place of supply that will determine the VAT rules to be applicable. For example if a transaction is considered to take place in the UK, the VAT rules of the UK will apply (UK VAT rate, UK rules about reverse charge, UK regulations concerning compliance, etc).

This location rules serve to:

- Identify if the transaction takes place within or outside the European Union ("EU"),
- In case the transaction is within the EU, identify which is the EU Member State concerned,
- Avoid double taxation (or non taxation).

The place of supply rules need to be considered not only by the supplier but also by the acquirer whom, if certain conditions are met, may be liable for the VAT (in reverse charge).

The place of supply rules change depending on whether you are supplying goods or services. We will therefore look in the next section into the rules that define the place of supply for goods and in the subsequent section into the rules that define the place of supply for services.

A2. – Place of supply of goods

A2.1 - Introduction

In order to determine the place of supply of goods, it is key to follow the physical flow of the supply of goods. Therefore it is very important to identify following:

1. Where are the goods at the time of the supply?
2. Will the goods be transported? If yes, from which country (Ship from) to which country (Ship to)?
3. Are they going to be supplied with installation or assembly?

It is also import to keep in mind that, as mentioned before, the supply of goods could involve three different geographic areas from an EU VAT perspective:

- The territory of the EU Member State concerned.
- The EU territory. As there are no borders regarding supplies of goods within the EU, the concepts of importation and exportation between EU MS do not apply. Instead the supply of goods between EU MS are called intra-community transaction, being the sales named intra-community supply and the purchases intra-community

acquisitions.

- Transaction with NON-EU countries. The concept of importation and exportation applies in such case.

Finally, it is important to understand that the place of supply rules vary depending on certain circumstances. Thus we have divided the different rules of place of supply of goods as follows:

1. Supply without transportation
2. Supply with transportation within the EU
3. Supply with transportation outside the EU
4. Supply with installation or assembly
5. Importation
6. Supply on Board Ships, Planes or Trains
7. Supply of Gas, Electricity and Heat or Cooling
8. Triangulation - simplification measure

Please note that in some particular member-States (as Portugal or Greece) where you have regions with a different VAT rate than the mainland, the location rules can vary. We will not focus on such specific cases in this book.

Within the next pages we will take you through each of the rules listed above.

A2.2 - Supply without transportation

When there is a transaction where goods are not transported or dispatched, the supply is situated in the place where the goods are located when the supply occurs.

Take as an example, Supermarket "A" located in Germany. Mr B acquirers a bottle of milk in the referred to supermarket. Place of supply is Germany.

A2.3 - Supply with transportation within the EU

I - Rule

Where goods are dispatched or transported by the supplier, or by the customer, or by a third person, the location rule is different depending on whether you taking the supplier or the purchaser's perspective.

From the supplier's perspective, place of supply is the place where the goods are located when dispatch or transport begins.

From the purchaser's perspective, place of supply is the place where the goods are located when dispatch or transport ends.

As an example, if Company "D" sells 100 boxes of shoes to Company "E". The boxes are in a warehouse of Company "D" in Luxembourg. Company "E" sends a truck to Luxembourg to pick up the boxes and transports them to it's own warehouse in Belgium.

From the perspective of Company "D", the supply takes place in Luxembourg (and as we will see in a subsequent chapter, is exempt). From the perspective of Company "E", the supply takes place in Belgium (and as we will also see in a subsequent chapter, is reverse-charged).

II - Derogation

Place of supply will be the place where the goods are located when dispatch or transport ends, whenever the following conditions are met:

1. The goods are: (i) goods other than new means of transport, (ii) goods supplied after assembly or installation, (iii) second-hand goods, (iv) works of art, collector's items or antiques or (v) second hand-hand means of transport,
2. The goods are dispatched or transported by the supplier or on its behalf; and
3. The customer is a nontaxable legal person (e.g. public bodies, agricultural business subject to the common flat-rate scheme), or any other nontaxable person (e.g., an individual).

This derogation means that contrary to the rule, the place of supply will be for both seller and purchaser the place where the transport ends. This implies different compliance and tax collection obligations.

III - Exception to derogation: Distant Sales

As an exception to the referred to derogation we have the case of distant sales.

In such case, the derogation will not apply, i.e., the place of supply will remain the place where the transport begins.

However the following conditions need be met, for this exception to apply:

- Goods supplied are not products subject to excise duty,
- The supply occurs in the current or previous calendar year;
- The total net amount (VAT exclusive) of the supplies made to the MS which would be regarded the place of supply according to the derogation rules does not exceed EUR 100,000 or the equivalent in national currency. Do note that this threshold changes depending on the EU MS concerned

A2.4 - Supply with transportation outside the EU

Where goods are dispatched or transported by the supplier, or by the customer, or by a third person, from the EU to a third country, the place of supply, from the perspective of the EU Member State, is the place where the goods are located when dispatch or transport begins.

As we will see in the comments to title IX (pgs 157 and following), even though subject to VAT and considered located in the Member State where the transport begins, the export transaction will exempt of VAT.

Please note that for sake of completeness, you need to check whether there are Sales Tax or similar rules on the Third Country where the importation will take place. Non EU VAT is not part of the scope of this book we will not further dig into that.

A2.5 - Supply with installation or assembly

In cases where the goods dispatched or transported by the supplier, by the customer or by a third person are installed or assembled, with or without a trial run, by or on behalf of the supplier, the place of supply shall be deemed to be the place where the goods are installed or assembled.

A2.6 - Importation

As we saw in the previous chapter, Importation of goods means the entry into the Community of goods coming from abroad or which are in free circulation, coming from a third territory forming part of the customs territory of the Community. When such transactions take place the place of supply is considered to be the Member State of importation of the goods.

Please note that the goods are considered imported when release for free circulation (i.e. when the import formalities have been complied with and any customs duties or charges having equivalent effect which are payable have been levied in that Member State, and if they have not benefited from a total or partial drawback of such duties or charges).

Consider the following example: Company "A", a Spanish Company that sells T-shirts in the French Market, imports 100 boxes of T-shirts from the US. The boxes are discharged from a Vessel in the port of Lisbon (Portugal) and taken under a suspensive regime to the Company "A"'s warehouse in France. In this case, the T-shirts are only imported in France as the transport (inside the EU territory) is done under a suspensive regime (in principle the regime know as T1).

In the scenario of our example, the place of supply for a VAT perspective will be France. Thus French VAT rules will apply.

A2.6 - Supply on Board Ships, Planes or Trains

Where goods are supplied on board ships, planes or trains during the section of a passenger transport operation effected within the Community, the place of supply shall be deemed to be at the point of departure of the passenger transport operation

Important note: In the case of a return trip, the return leg shall be regarded as a separate transport operation.

You need to consider that:

- A "Section of a passenger transport operation effected within the Community" means a section of the operation effected, without a stopover outside the Community, between the point of departure and the point of arrival of the passenger transport operation
- The "Point of departure of a passenger transport operation" means the first scheduled point of passenger embarkation within the Community, where applicable after a stopover outside the Community.
- The "Point of arrival of a passenger transport operation" means the last scheduled point of disembarkation within the Community of passengers who embarked in the

Community, where applicable before a stopover outside the Community.

A.2.7 - Supply of Gas, Electricity and Heat or Cooling

I - Products in scope

This location rule applies only to the supply of:

- Gas through a natural gas system situated within the territory of the Community or any network connected to such a system
- Electricity, or
- Heat or cooling energy through heating or cooling networks

II - Location Rule

In the case of the referred to supplies to a taxable dealer, the place of supply shall be deemed to be the place where that taxable dealer has established his business or has a fixed establishment for which the goods are supplied or, in the absence of such a place of business or fixed establishment, the place where he has his permanent address or usually resides.

III - Exception 1

However, if the mentioned products are not covered by the above rule (H.2), the place of supply shall be deemed to be the place where the customer effectively uses and consumes the goods.

IV - Exception 2

In case the products listed are not effectively consumed by the customer, the non-consumed goods shall be deemed to have been used and consumed at the place where the customer has established his business or has a fixed establishment for which the goods are supplied. In the absence of such a place of business or fixed establishment, the customer shall be deemed to have used and consumed the goods at the place where he has his permanent address or usually resides.

V - Taxable dealer

Taxable dealer is defined taxable person whose principal activity in respect of purchases of gas, electricity, heat or cooling energy is reselling those products and whose own consumption of those products is negligible.

A3. Place of supply of services

A3.1 - Introduction

In this chapter we will examine the rules concerning the place of supply of services. Depending on the type of services, the following place of supply rules will apply:

- The Business-to-business ("B2B") general rule,
- The Business-to-customer ("B2C") general rule,

- Exceptions to the general rules.

There are a number of exceptions. Meaning that, in practice, the exceptions have to be checked first. In case they do not apply, then one of the 2 general rules will take place.

A3.2 - General rule for B2B

The basic rule tells us that:

1. The place of supply of services is the place where the acquirer has established his business, as long as the acquirer is a taxable person acting as such.
2. However, if those services are provided to a fixed establishment of the taxable person located in a place other than the place where he (the acquirer) has established his business.

In these cases the place of supply is where the fixed establishment of the acquirer is located.

3. Furthermore, in the absence of place of establishment or fixed establishment, the supply of services is where the acquirer has his permanent address or usually resides.

A3.3 - General rules for B2C

The basic rule tells us that:

1. The place of supply of services is the place where the supplier has established his business, as long as the acquirer is a nontaxable person.
2. If those services are provided from a fixed establishment of the supplier located in a place other than where the supplier has established his business, the supply is located where the fixed establishment of the supplier is located.
3. In the absence of place of establishment or fixed establishment, the supply of services is where the supplier has his permanent address or usually resides.

A3.4 - Supply by intermediaries (B2C)

Exception for B2C only. When services are supplied by intermediaries to nontaxable persons and as long as the intermediary is acting in the name and on behalf of another person, the place of supply is the place where the underlying transaction is supplied.

A3.5 - Supply of services connected with immovable property (B2B and B2C)

I - The exception

Exception for both B2B and B2C. In case of these type of services, the supply is considered located in the place where the immovable property is located.

II- Services connected with immovable property

Services connected with immovable property includes:

- Service of experts and estate agents,
- The provision of accommodation in the hotel sector,
- The provision of accommodation in sectors with similar function such as: (a) holiday camps and (b) sites developed for use as camping sites,
- The granting of rights to use immovable property,
- Services for the preparation and coordination of construction work such as: (a) Architects and (b) Firms providing on-site supervision.

A3.6 - Transport services (B2B and B2C)

I - Passenger transport (B2B and B2C):

In case of passenger transport, the exception applies to B2B and B2C both.

In these cases, the place of supply is the place where the transport takes place, proportionate to the distances covered.

II - Transport of goods (B2C)

In case of transport of goods, the exception applies to B2C only (for B2B you should apply the main B2B rule)

Thus for a Transport of goods to nontaxable persons:

1. Other than intra-Community: the supply takes place where the transport takes place, proportionate to the distances covered;
2. Intra-community: the supply takes place at the place of departure.

Please note that if part of the intra-Community transport of goods to nontaxable persons takes place over territory which is not part of the EU, for that part of the transport no VAT is applicable.

III - Applicable definitions

Intra-Community transport of goods is any transport of goods in respect of which the place of departure and the place of arrival are situated within the territories of two different MS.

Place of departure is place where the transport of goods actually begins, irrespective of distances covered in order to reach the place where the goods are located

Place of arrival is place where the transport of goods actually ends.

A3.7 - Ancillary transport services (B2C)

I - Rule

This exception applies to B2C only. In such cases, the place of supply for the referred to services is place where the services are physically carried out.

II - What are ancillary transport services

Are considered as ancillary transport services: loading, unloading, handling and similar activities.

A3.8 - Hiring of means of transport (B2B and B2C)

This exception applies to B2B and B2C cases. It varies depending on whether the hiring is short term or other than short term.

I - Short term hiring

In case of short-term hiring, the supply is considered located at the place where it is actually put at the disposal of the customer.

II - Hiring, other than short-term

Only applies to B2C. In these cases the supply is considered to take place where the customer is established.

III - Special case - B2C hiring of pleasure boats other than short-term

A specific treatment is foreseen for the case of B2C hiring of pleasure boats (other than short term).

In such cases the supply is considered to take place where it is actually put at the disposal of the customer if:

1. The service is actually provided by the supplier from his place of business or

2. There is fixed establishment situated in that place.

IV - Definitions

Means of transport: cars, motorcycles, bicycles, caravans, trailers and semi-trailers, railway wagons, vessels, aircraft. Please note that Vehicles which are permanently immobilized and containers are not considered to be means of transport.

Short-term: is defined as continuous possession or use of the means of transport throughout a period of no more than 30 days and, in case of vessels, no more than 90 days.

A3.9 - Cultural, artistic, sporting, scientific, entertainment & similar services (B2B and B2C)

I - Scope

The exception applies to the following events and their ancillary services: cultural, scientific, artistic, educational, sporting and entertainment or similar (such as fairs or exhibitions).

I.2 - Rule

Exception applies to both B2B and B2C.

The exception for B2B regards only the admission. And the place of supply is considered to be where the events take place.

In what concerns B2C the place of supply is considered to be the place where the activities actually take place.

A3.10 - Valuation of, and work on, movable property (B2C)

Regarding supplies that consist of the valuations of movable tangible property and work on movable tangible property, the supply is considered to take place where the services are physically carried out.

A3.11 - Supply of restaurant and catering services (B2B and B2C)

Place of supply of restaurant and catering services other than those physically carried out on board ships, aircraft or trains during the section of a passenger transport operation within the community, is place where services are physically carried out.

A3.12 Restaurant and catering on board ships, aircrafts or trains (B2B and B2C)

I - Rule

This exception applies to B2B and B2C both.

The place of supply of restaurant and catering services which are carried out on board ships, aircrafts or trains during the section of a passenger transport operation effected within the Community is the point of departure of the passenger transport operation.

In case of return trip, the return leg shall be regarded as separate transport operation.

II - Definitions

- Section of passenger transport within the community is defined as section of the operation effected, without stopover, outside the Community, between the point of departure and the point of arrival of the passenger transport operation.

- Point of departure of a passenger transport operation is defined as the first scheduled point of passenger embarkation within the Community where applicable after a stopover outside the Community.

- Point of arrival of a passenger transport operation is defined as last scheduled point of disembarkation within the Community of passengers who embarked in the Community, where applicable before a stopover outside the Community.

A3.12 - Electronic services (B2C)

I - Rule

This exception applies only in cases of B2C supplies.

The supply of such transactions are considered to take place where the customer is established or where he has his permanent address or usually resides as long as the following conditions are met:

The supplier is:

- A taxable person; and
- Established outside the EU; or
- With fixed establishment from which service is supplied outside the EU; or, if not,
- With permanent address or usually residence outside the EU; AND

The customer is:

- Non taxable person; and
- Established in a Member State; or
- With permanent address or usual residence in a Member State

II - Electronic services

Electronic services are listed in the RVD. In order to understand what are and what are not Electronic supplied services, please refer to the previous chapter.

A3.13 - Telecom, radio and TV broadcasting services(B2C)

This exception applies only in cases of B2C supplies.

The supply of these is considered to take place where the services are effectually used, as long as the following conditions are met:

The supplier is:

- A taxable person; and
- Established outside the EU; or
- With fixed establishment from which service is supplied outside the EU; or, if not,
- With permanent address or usually residence outside the EU; AND

The customer is:

- Non taxable person; and
- Established in a Member State; or
- With permanent address or usual residence in a Member State.

A3.14 - Intangible services to non-EU clients (B2C)

I - Rule

In case of B2C intangible services, the supply is considered to take place where the customer is established or where he has his permanent address or usually resides if the Customer is:

- Non taxable person; and
- Established or with permanent address or usual residence outside the EU

II - Intangible services

Intangible services for this purpose, are listed in the RVD as follows:

- Transfers and assignments of copyrights, patents, licenses, trade marks and similar rights;
- Advertising services;
- The services of consultants, engineers, consultancy firms, lawyers, accountants and other similar services, as well as data processing and the provision of information
- Obligations to refrain from pursuing or exercising, in whole or in part, a business activity or a right referred in this Section;
- Banking, financial and insurance transactions including reinsurance, with the exception of the hire of safes;
- The supply of staff;
- The hiring out of movable tangible property, with the exception of all means of transport;
- The provision of access to a natural gas system situated within the territory of the Community or to any network connected to such a system, to the electricity system or to heating or cooling networks, or the transmission or distribution through these systems or networks, and the provision of other services directly linked thereto;
- Telecommunications services;
- Radio and television broadcasting services;
- Electronically supplies services (refer to examples in related Section)

B – Implementation measures (see Regulation 282/2011)

SECTION 1

Concepts

Article 10

1. For the application of Articles 44 and 45 of Directive 2006/112/EC [*Rule - place supply of services B2B and B2C*], the place where the **business** of a taxable person is established shall be the place where the functions of the business's central administration are carried out.

2. In order to determine the place referred to in paragraph 1, account shall be taken of the place where **essential decisions** concerning the general management of the business are taken, the place where the **registered office** of the business is located and the place where management meets.

Where these criteria do not allow the place of establishment of a business to be determined with certainty, the place where essential decisions concerning the general management of the business are taken shall take precedence.

3. The mere presence of a **postal address** may not be taken to be the place of establishment of a business of a taxable person.

Guidance notes: This article deals with the **establishment rules** for the application of Articles 44 and 45 of the VAT Directive. These relate to the place of supply of services for Business to Business (B2B) and Business to Consumer (B2C) supplies respectively.

The article confirms that the place of establishment is the place where the functions of the business's central administration are carried out i.e. the place where:

- the essential decisions concerning the general management of the business are taken (primary criteria),

- the registered office is located, and

- management meets.

A postal address is not sufficient for determining the place of establishment.

Article 11

1. For the application of Article 44 of Directive 2006/112/EC [*Rule - place supply of services B2B*], a '**fixed establishment**' shall be any establishment, other than the place of establishment of a business referred to in Article 10 of this Regulation, characterized by a sufficient degree of permanence and a suitable structure in terms of human and technical resources to enable it to receive and use the services supplied to it for its own needs.

2. For the application of the following Articles, a '**fixed establishment**' shall be any establishment, other than the place of establishment of a business referred to in Article 10 of this Regulation, characterized by a sufficient degree of permanence and a suitable structure in terms of human and technical resources to enable it to provide the services which it supplies:

(a) Article 45 of Directive 2006/112/EC[*Rule - place supply of services B2C*];

(b) from 1 January 2013, the second subparagraph of Article 56(2) of Directive 2006/112/EC [*Hiring means of transport B2C*];

(c) until 31 December 2014, Article 58 of Directive 2006/112/EC [*Supply of electronic services B2C*];

(d) Article 192a of Directive 2006/112/EC [*Intervention of the Fixed Establishment*].

3. The fact of having a **VAT identification** number shall not in itself be sufficient to consider that a taxable person has a fixed establishment.

Guidance notes: This article deals with the rules relating to **fixed establishments**. Generally, under Article 442 of the VAT Directive, a B2B supply is taxed at the place of establishment of the taxable person receiving the service, unless it is supplied to a fixed establishment.

For the application of Article 44 of the VAT Directive, a fixed establishment requires a **sufficient degree of permanence and a suitable structure** in terms of human and technical resources to enable it to receive and use the service supplied to it for its own needs. For example, if a fixed establishment were to receive software licenses, it would require sufficient numbers of employees and IT equipment to use such licenses. This primarily relates to B2C supplies, where the place of supply is the establishment supplying the services. This rule will not apply to electronic supplies of services as and from 1 January 2015, when these supplies will be taxable where the customer is located.

Having a VAT number is not sufficient, in itself, to evidence the place of establishment of a taxable person.

Article 21 of the Regulation provides guidance for determining whether the place where a taxable person has established his business, or the fixed establishment, received the service.

Article 12

For the application of Directive 2006/112/EC, the '**permanent address**' of a natural person, whether or not a taxable person, shall be the address entered in the population or similar register, or the address indicated by that person to the relevant tax authorities, unless there is evidence that this address does not reflect reality.

Article 13

The place where a natural person '**usually resides'**, whether or not a taxable person, as referred to in Directive 2006/112/EC shall be the place where that natural person usually lives as a result of personal and occupational ties.

Where the occupational ties are in a country different from that of the personal ties, or where no occupational ties exist, the place of usual residence shall be determined by **personal ties** which show close links between the natural person and a place where he is living.

Guidance notes (arts.12&13): These articles provide rules for determining the permanent address or usual residence of a person. The rules are not specific to any article and apply to both taxable and non-taxable persons.

The permanent address is the address entered in the population or similar register, or the address indicated to the tax authority.

In respect of a taxable person the business address provided to Revenue will be considered the permanent address, unless there is evidence that the address does not reflect reality e.g. the address is that of the business's accountant or tax practitioner. In respect of non-taxable persons, the address will be the principal private residence.

The place where a person usually resides will be the place where that person usually lives as a result of personal and occupational ties. Where occupational ties are in a country different from personal ties, the place of usual residence will be determined by personal ties, which show close links between the natural person and the place where he/she is living.

SECTION 2
Place of supply of goods
(Articles 31 to 39 of Directive 2006/112/EC)

Article 14

Where in the course of a calendar year the threshold applied by a Member State in accordance with Article 34 of Directive 2006/112/EC [*Threshold for distant sales*] is exceeded, Article 33 of that Directive [*Distant sales*] shall not modify the place of supplies of goods other than products subject to excise duty carried out in the course of the same calendar year which are made before the threshold applied by the Member State for the calendar year then current is exceeded provided that all of the following conditions are met:

(a) the supplier has not exercised the option provided for under Article 34(4) of that Directive;

(b) the value of his supplies of goods did not exceed the threshold in the course of the preceding calendar year.

However, Article 33 of Directive 2006/112/EC shall modify the place of the following supplies to the Member State in which the dispatch or transport ends:

(a) the supply of goods by which the threshold applied by the Member State for the calendar year then current was exceeded in the course of the same calendar year;

(b) any subsequent supplies of goods within that Member State in that calendar year;

(c) supplies of goods within that Member State in the calendar year following the calendar year in which the event referred to in point (a) occurred.

Guidance notes: This article clarifies the application of the distance sales regime.

Article 15

The section of a **passenger transport operation** effected within the Community referred to in Article 37 of Directive 2006/112/EC [*Supply during passenger transport*], shall be determined by the journey of the means of transport and not by the journey completed by each of the passengers.

Guidance notes: This article deals with the application of Article 37 of the VAT Directive. The 'section of a passenger transport operation effected within the Community' shall be determined by the journey of the means of transport and not by the journey completed by each of the passengers.

SECTION 3
Place of intra-Community acquisitions of goods
(Articles 40, 41 and 42 of Directive 2006/112/EC)

Article 16

Where an **intra-Community acquisition** of goods within the meaning of Article 20 of Directive 2006/112/EC [*Definition of intra-Community acquisitions*] has taken place, the

Member State in which the dispatch or transport ends shall exercise its power of taxation **irrespective of the VAT treatment applied to the transaction in the Member State in which the dispatch or transport began.**

Any request by a supplier of goods for a **correction in the VAT invoiced** by him and reported by him to the Member State where the dispatch or transport of the goods began shall **be treated by that Member State in accordance with its own domestic rules.**

Guidance notes: This article Community acquisition of movable goods is the Member State where the transportation ends. Any request by a supplier of goods for a correction in the VAT invoiced by him/her and reported by him/her to the Member State where the dispatch or transport of the goods began shall be treated by that Member State in accordance with its own domestic rules.

SECTION 4

Place of supply of services

(Articles 43 to 59 of Directive 2006/112/EC)

Subsection 1

Status of the Customer

Article 17

1. If the place of supply of services depends on whether the customer is a taxable or non-taxable person, the **status of the customer** shall be **determined** on the basis of Articles 9 [*Definition of Taxable Person*] to 13 [*exceptions*] and Article 43 [*Deemed taxable persons and non-taxable persons*] of Directive 2006/112/EC.

2. A **non-taxable legal person** who is **identified** or required to be identified for VAT purposes under point (b) of Article 214(1) of Directive 2006/112/EC [*VAT number rules*] because his intra-Community acquisitions of goods are subject to VAT or because he has exercised the option of making those operations subject to VAT **shall be a taxable person** within the meaning of Article 43 of that Directive.

Guidance notes: The place of supply rules for services will depend on whether the person is a taxable or non-taxable person i.e. whether it is a B2B or B2C supply. Essentially this means that a person who carries on activities in the course or furtherance of business will be considered a taxable person. Non-taxable legal persons who are obliged to register for VAT in respect of services received from a supplier established outside the State are considered to be 'a business' for the purposes of the place of supply rules for services.

Article 18

1. Unless he has information to the contrary, the supplier may regard a **customer established** within the Community as a **taxable person**:

(a) where the customer has **communicated his individual VAT identification** number to him, and the supplier obtains confirmation of the **validity** of that identification number and of the associated name and address in accordance with Article 31 of Council Regulation (EC) No 904/2010 of 7 October 2010 [*see D- Others*] on administrative cooperation and combating fraud in the field of value added tax ;

(b) where the customer has not yet received an individual VAT identification number, but informs the supplier that he has applied for it and the supplier obtains any other proof which demonstrates that the customer is a taxable person or a non-taxable legal person required to be identified for VAT purposes and carries out a reasonable level of verification of the accuracy of the information provided by the customer, by normal commercial security measures such as those relating to identity or payment checks.

2. Unless he has information to the contrary, the supplier may regard a customer established within the Community as a non-taxable person when he can demonstrate that the customer has not communicated his individual VAT identification number to him.

3. Unless he has information to the contrary, the supplier may regard a customer established outside the Community as a taxable person:

(a) if he obtains from the customer a certificate issued by the customer's competent tax authorities as confirmation that the customer is engaged in economic activities in order to enable him to obtain a refund of VAT under Council Directive 86/560/EEC of 17 November 1986 on the harmonization of the laws of the Member States relating to turnover taxes – Arrangements for the refund of value added tax to taxable persons not established in Community territory;

(b) where the customer does not possess that certificate, if the supplier has the VAT number, or a similar number attributed to the customer by the country of establishment and used to identify businesses or any other proof which demonstrates that the customer is a taxable person and if the supplier carries out a reasonable level of verification of the accuracy of the information provided by the customer, by normal commercial security measures such as those relating to identity or payment checks.

Subsection 2

Capacity of the Customer

Guidance notes: This Article provides detailed rules to enable suppliers identify the status of the customer.

Para. 1 states that a supplier may determine that a customer established within the Community is a taxable person where the customer has provided a VAT number and the supplier obtains confirmation of the validity of the number and the associated name and address through the EU Commission VAT verification portal (http://ec.europa.eu/taxation_customs/vies/). The Regulation recognizes that in a small number of cases the recipient of the service, while clearly engaged in an economic activity, may not yet have received a VAT number from the tax authority in the relevant Member State. In such cases, the recipient business will be required to provide evidence that it is in business. Proof may include an alternative tax identification number or a letter from the tax authority in the recipient's Member State confirming that he/she is in business. For practical purposes, a supplier should ask the recipient to indicate whether he or she is a 'business' or 'private customer'. This is particularly relevant for electronic sales, where there is little human intervention in a supply. Where the recipient indicates that he/she is in 'business', the VAT number should be obtained and the number verified. Where there is no VAT number yet assigned, the alternative checks can be undertaken. This is to prevent non-taxation with regard to supplies of services. The supplier will be required to obtain a VAT number from the recipient at a later date in order to fulfill his/her requirements regarding the completion of the recapitulative VIES statement of intra-Community supplies.

Para. 2 provides that, unless there is information to the contrary, a supplier may regard a customer established within the Community as a non-taxable person, and therefore subject to the B2C rules, if the customer does not quote/produce a VAT number.

Instances may arise where a business customer in another MS may not be able to supply a VAT number. This may be because the customer does not carry on any taxable activities in his/her own MS and the services he/she has received from the Irish supplier are exempt from VAT there. In such cases the supply should be treated as a B2B supply and no Irish VAT should be charged. The supplier in Ireland should ensure that appropriate evidence is obtained from the customer to verify his/her tax status. The VAT exempt status of the transaction should also be verified. Where similar transactions involve Irish customers the foreign supplier should be notified that the Irish customer does not have a VAT number because he/she does not make any taxable supplies. Evidence should be given to the foreign supplier to verify that the services received are exempt from VAT in Ireland.

Para. 3 deals with supplies to persons outside the Community. A supplier may consider a customer established outside the Community as a taxable person if the customer produces a certificate from his/her tax authority (Non-Community), which has been issued in accordance with the VAT refund scheme under the 13th Directive. In the absence of this certificate, a supplier is required to obtain a tax identification number from the country of establishment of the supplier, or any other documentary proof, which demonstrates that the recipient is established outside the Community. From a practical perspective, alternative proof may include printouts from the customer's website, a letter from his/her tax authority, company registration documents etc. Where a supply is a B2C supply, and has been incorrectly treated as a B2B supply with no VAT charged, then in accordance with the VAT Consolidation Act the supplier will be liable to pay the VAT at the appropriate rate, together with appropriate interest and penalties.

Article 19

For the purpose of applying the rules concerning the place of supply of services laid down in Articles 44 [*Rule - place supply of services B2B*] and 45 [*Rule - place supply of services B2B*] of Directive 2006/112/EC, a taxable person, or a non-taxable legal person deemed to be a taxable person, who receives services exclusively for private use, including use by his staff, shall be **regarded as a non-taxable person**.

Unless he has information to the contrary, such as information on the nature of the services provided, the **supplier may consider that the services are for the customer's business use** if, for that transaction, the customer has **communicated** his individual **VAT identification** number.

Where one and the same service is intended for both private use, including use by the customer's staff, and business use, the supply of that service shall be covered exclusively by Article 44 of Directive 2006/112/EC, provided there is no abusive practice.

Guidance notes: Where a service is intended in part for the personal use of the customer (or staff) and in part for professional use, the supply of that service will be treated as B2B. Supplies to a taxable person or staff of that taxable person for private use, shall be considered as B2C. In determining the place of supply of a service, only the circumstances existing at the time of the supply will be taken into account. Where there are reasonable indications that the service supplied is intended for the customer's own personal use or that of the staff of a business, and he/she has communicated a VAT number or provided other proof of being a taxable person, the supplier should seek a self-declaration from the customer on the planned purpose of the acquired service. Reasonable indications would be that the nature of the supply is not consistent with the nature of the business.

Subsection 3

Location of the Customer

Article 20 [*Customer in one Country*]

Where a supply of services carried out for a taxable person, or a non-taxable legal person deemed to be a taxable person, falls within the scope of Article 44 of Directive 2006/112/EC [*Rule - place supply of services B2B*], and where that taxable person is **established in a single country**, or, in the absence of a place of establishment of a business or a fixed establishment, has his **permanent address** and **usually resides** in a single country, that supply of services shall be **taxable in that country**.

The supplier shall establish that place based on **information from the customer**, and **verify** that information by normal commercial security measures such as those relating to identity or payment checks.

The information may include the **VAT identification** number attributed by the Member State where the customer is established.

Guidance notes: Supplies to a taxable person established in one country will be taxed in that country. The supplier should verify this based on information supplied by the customer. The supplier may consider the VAT identification number attributed to that person (see note for guidance above on Article 18) in determining the location of the customer.

Article 21 [*Customer established in several Countries*]

Where a supply of services to a taxable person, or a non-taxable legal person deemed to be a taxable person, falls within the scope of Article 44 of Directive 2006/112/EC [*Rule - place supply of services B2B*], and the taxable person is **established in more than one country**, that supply shall be **taxable in the country where that taxable person has established his business**.

However, where the service is provided to a **fixed establishment** of the taxable person located in a place other than that where the customer has established his business, that supply shall be **taxable at the place of the fixed establishment receiving that service and using it for its own needs**.

Where the taxable person does not have a place of establishment of a business or a fixed establishment, the supply shall be taxable at his **permanent address or usual residence**.

Article 22

1. In order to identify the customer's fixed establishment to which the service is provided, the **supplier shall examine the nature and use of the service provided.**

Where the nature and use of the service provided do not enable him to identify the fixed establishment to which the service is provided, the supplier, in identifying that fixed establishment, shall pay particular attention to whether **the contract**, the **order form** and the **VAT identification** number attributed by the Member State of the customer and communicated to him by the customer **identify the fixed establishment** as the customer of the service and whether the **fixed establishment is the entity paying for the service.**

Where the customer's fixed establishment to which the service is provided **cannot be determined** in accordance with the first and second subparagraphs of this paragraph or where services covered by Article 44 of Directive 2006/112/EC are supplied to a taxable person under a contract covering one or more services used in an unidentifiable and non-quantifiable manner, the **supplier may legitimately consider that the services have been supplied at the place where the customer has established his business.**

2. The application of this Article shall be without prejudice to the customer's obligations.

Guidance notes (arts. 21&22): Supplies to a taxable person who has establishments in more than one country will be taxed at the place where that taxable person has established his/her business. However, if the supply is being made to a fixed establishment and that establishment is receiving the service for its own needs, then the supply will be taxable in the country of that fixed establishment. In identifying the customer's fixed establishment, the supplier is required to examine the nature and the use of the service provided. If a supplier can identify that a fixed establishment is receiving and using a service for its own needs, then that service will be taxed at the place of the fixed establishment. However, if this cannot be established, a supplier can consider that the place of establishment of the customer is the place of supply.

Example: If an Irish transport company provides services to a UK establishment with a fixed establishment in Ireland, and such services are used for the operation of the fixed establishment, then the place of supply of that service will be the State. This will apply irrespective of whether the administration/accounting/billing etc. is centralized at the place of establishment in another Member State- e.g. EU headquarters.

Article 23

1. From 1 January 2013, where, in accordance with the first subparagraph of Article 56(2) of Directive 2006/112/EC [*Rule for B2C Hiring of means of transport services*], a supply of services is taxable at the place where the customer is established, or, in the absence of an establishment, where he has his permanent address or usually resides, the supplier shall establish that place based on factual **information provided by the customer**, and **verify** that information by **normal commercial security measures** such as those relating to identity or payment checks.

2. Where, in accordance with Articles 58 [*Supply electronic services B2C*] to and 59 [*Supplies B2C to outside EU*] of Directive 2006/112/EC, a supply of services is taxable at the **place where the customer is established**, or, in the absence of an establishment, where he has his **permanent address** or **usually resides**, the supplier shall establish that place based on **factual information** provided by the customer, and verify that information by normal commercial security measures such as those relating to identity or payment checks.

Article 24

1. From 1 January 2013, where services covered by the first subparagraph of Article 56(2) of Directive 2006/112/EC [*Rule for B2C Hiring of means of transport services*], are supplied to a non-taxable person who is **established in more than one country** or has his **permanent address in one** country and his **usual residence in another**, **priority** shall be given **to the place that best ensures taxation at the place of actual consumption** when determining the place of supply of those services.

2. Where services covered by Articles 58 [*Supply electronic services B2C*] to and 59 [*Supplies B2C to outside EU*] of Directive 2006/112/EC are supplied to a non-taxable person who is established in **more than one country** or has his permanent **address in one country** and his **usual residence in another**, **priority** shall be given to the **place that best ensures taxation at the place of actual consumption** when determining the

place of supply of those services.

Guidance notes (arts. 21&22): These articles relate to the place of supply rules and obligations of suppliers in respect of:

a) supplies (from 1 January 2013) of long-term hiring-out of a means of transport (other than pleasure boats), and

b) supplies to non-taxable persons in the Community by suppliers established outside the Community and supplies from suppliers established within the Community to non-taxable persons established outside the Community.

These supplies are taxed at the place of the customer. Suppliers verify the place of establishment and keep documentary proof. Measures may include checking the address associated with the credit card, asking for proof of address etc. For the majority of e-service supplies, the IP address, together with the address given by the customer (and verified), should be sufficient to determine the place of establishment of the customer.

Where a person has more than one residence, priority will be given to the place of actual consumption in determining the place of supply. E.g. If an Irish person has a residence in another Member State, and hires out a vehicle in that Member State for use there on a long-term basis, then the place of taxation shall be that Member State.

Subsection 4

Common provisions regarding determination of the status, the capacity and the location of the Customer

Article 25

For the application of the rules governing the place of supply of services, only the circumstances existing at the time of the **chargeable event shall be taken into account**. Any subsequent changes to the use of the service received shall not affect the determination of the place of supply, provided there is no abusive practice.

Guidance notes: This article provides that only the circumstances existing at the time of supply can be taken into account in determining the place of supply. As long as there is no abusive practice, any change in the use of a service subsequent to a supply will not affect the original determination i.e. a supply initially for B2C use cannot be subsequently determined as a B2B service if the use changes.

Subsection 5

Supply of services governed by the general rules

Article 26

A transaction whereby a body assigns **television broadcasting** rights in respect of **football matches** to taxable persons, shall be covered by Article 44 of Directive 2006/112/EC [*Rule - place supply of services B2B*].

Guidance notes: This article deals with the place of supply of the assignment of television broadcasting rights in respect of football matches. It provides that the assignment of such rights will be taxable under the general rule in Article 44 of the VAT Directive i.e. where the assignee is established. If he/she is established in a different MS to the assignor then the assignee will account for VAT under the reverse charge mechanism.

Article 27

The supply of services which consist in applying for or receiving **refunds of VAT** under Council Directive 2008/9/EC of 12 February 2008 laying down detailed rules for the refund of value added tax, provided for in Directive 2006/112/EC, to taxable persons not established in the Member State of refund but established in another Member State shall be covered by Article 44 of Directive 2006/112/EC *Rule - place supply of services B2B*].

Guidance notes: This article provides that the place of supply of services consisting of processing applications for Intra-Community VAT refunds (provided for by Directive 2008/9/EC) to taxable persons not established in the Member State of refund but established in another Member State is the place where that person has established his or her business or where that person has his or her fixed establishment.

Article 28

In so far as they constitute a single service, the supply of services made in the framework of organizing a **funeral** shall fall within the scope of Articles 44 [*Rule - place supply of services B2B*] and 45 [*Rule - place supply of services B2C*] of Directive 2006/112/EC.

Guidance notes: This article provides that the place of supply of a single service of the organization of a funeral to a taxable person is the place where that person has established his or her business or where that person has his or her fixed establishment. The place of supply of such a service to non-taxable persons (B2C) is the place where the supplier has established his or her business or where that supplier has his or her fixed establishment.

Article 29

Without prejudice to Article 41 of this Regulation, the supply of **services of translation** of texts shall fall within the scope of Articles 44 [*Rule - place supply of services B2B*] and 45 [*Rule - place supply of services B2C*] of Directive 2006/112/EC.

Guidance notes: This article provides that the place of supply of translation services when supplied to a taxable person is the place where that person has established his or her business or where that person has his or her fixed establishment. The place of supply of such services to non-taxable persons (B2C) is the place where the supplier has established his or her business or where that supplier has his or her fixed establishment. This is without prejudice to Article 41 below.

Subsection 6

Supply of services by intermediaries

Article 30

The supply of services of **intermediaries** as referred to in Article 46 of Directive 2006/112/EC shall cover the services of intermediaries acting in the **name and on behalf of the recipient** of the service procured and the services performed by intermediaries acting in the **name and on behalf of the provider** of the services procured.

Guidance notes: Article 46 of the VAT Directive provides that the place of supply of intermediary services to a non-taxable person is the place where the underlying transaction takes place. Article 30 confirms that such treatment applies where the intermediary is supplying his/her services to a non-taxable person, be it for transactions where he/she is acting in the name and on behalf of the person receiving the service (usually the same non-taxable person) or be it for transactions where he/she is acting in the name and on behalf of the person supplying the service.

Article 31

Services supplied by intermediaries acting in the **name and on behalf of another person** consisting of the intermediation in the provision of accommodation in the **hotel sector** or in sectors having a **similar** function shall fall within the scope of:

(a) Article 44 of Directive 2006/112/EC EC [*Rule - place supply of services B2B*] if supplied to a taxable person acting as such, or a non-taxable legal person deemed to be a taxable person;

(b) Article 46 of that Directive [*Services by intermediaries B2C*], if supplied to a non-taxable person.

Guidance notes: This article deals with intermediary services in respect of hotel (or similar)accommodation.

Intermediary services supplied to a taxable person in respect of hotel accommodation are covered under the general B2B rule (Article 44 of the VAT Directive). Where an intermediary is engaged by a business customer to arrange for the provision of intermediary services on behalf of that business customer, and is paid a fee by the business customer, the place of supply of the intermediary's services is the place where the business customer is established. If the business customer is established in a different Member State from the intermediary, the business customer will account for the VAT involved under the reverse charge procedure.

Intermediary services supplied to a non-taxable person in respect of hotel accommodation are covered under Article 46 of the VAT Directive. Where an intermediary provides a service to a traveler, while acting in the name and on behalf of that traveler, the place of supply of the intermediary service is the place where the underlying transaction is supplied. The intermediary is required to register and account for VAT in each Member State where the intermediary arranges the service for the customer. If a customer requires services to be arranged in 2 or 3 Member States in respect of one journey, the intermediary is obliged to apportion VAT on the fee and account appropriately on each portion of that fee in each Member State.

Example: An Irish intermediary acts on behalf of an Irish non-taxable customer and arranges accommodation for that customer in a Spanish hotel.

• Irish intermediary charges the Irish customer a commission.

• Place of supply of the underlying service (accommodation) is Spain.

• The Irish intermediary is required to account for VAT in Spain on the commission charge.

Subsection 7

Supply of cultural, artistic, sporting, scientific, educational, entertainment and similar services

Article 32

1. Services in respect of **admission** to cultural, artistic, sporting, scientific, educational, entertainment or similar events as referred to in Article 53 of Directive 2006/112/EC shall include the supply of **services of which the essential characteristics are the**

granting of the right of admission to an event in exchange for a ticket or payment, including payment in the form of a **subscription**, a **season ticket** or a **periodic fee**.

2. Paragraph 1 shall apply in particular to:

(a) the right of admission to shows, theatrical performances, circus performances, fairs, amusement parks, concerts, exhibitions, and other similar cultural events;

(b) the right of admission to sporting events such as matches or competitions;

(c) the right of admission to educational and scientific events such as conferences and seminars.

3. Paragraph 1 shall **not cover** the use of facilities such **as gymnastics halls** and **suchlike**, in exchange for the payment of a fee.

Article 33

The **ancillary services** referred to in Article 53 of Directive 2006/112/EC shall include services which are **directly related** to admission to cultural, artistic, sporting, scientific, educational, entertainment or similar events and which are **supplied separately** for a consideration to a person attending an event.

Such ancillary services shall **include** in particular the use of **cloakrooms** or **sanitary facilities** but shall **not include** mere **intermediary** services relating to the sale of tickets.

Guidance notes (arts 32&33): These articles confirm that Article 535 of the VAT Directive (B2B supplies) covers admission to cultural, artistic, sporting, scientific, educational, entertainment and similar events.

In particular, Article 53 of the VAT Directive applies to the right of admission (including season tickets, subscriptions or periodic fees) to:

• Shows, theatrical performances, fairs, amusement parks, concerts, exhibitions etc.

• Sporting events such as matches or competitions.

• Educational and scientific events such as conferences or competitions.

Access to gymnastic halls, etc., in exchange for payment, are not covered by Article 53 of the VAT Directive.

Ancillary services referred to in Article 53 of the VAT Directive are those, which are directly related to admission to the event, although for a separate consideration. This includes cloakroom facilities etc, but does not include intermediary services relating to the sale of tickets.

Please see Revenue leaflet on admissions to cultural, artistic, sporting, scientific, educational, entertainment and similar events.

Subsection 8

Supply of ancillary transport services and valuations of and work on movable property

Article 34

Except where the **goods being assembled become part of immovable property**, the place of the supply of services to a non-taxable person consisting only of the assembly by a taxable person of the various parts of a machine, all of which were provided to him by his customer, shall be established in accordance with Article 54 of Directive

2006/112/EC.

Guidance notes: This article deals with the place of supply of the assembly of a machine. A transaction, which consists solely of assembly of a machine, the various parts of which are provided by a customer, is considered a supply of services. Where this service is supplied to a non-taxable person, the place of supply is where it is physically carried out (in accordance with Article 54 (2)(b) of the VAT Directive).

Example: if an Irish supplier carries out a machine assembly service for a non-taxable person (B2C supply) which does not become part of a building or structure in another MS of the EU, then the place of supply of that service will be in that other MS.

Subsection 9

Supply of restaurant and catering services on board means of transport

Article 35

The section of a passenger transport operation effected within the Community as referred to in Article 57 of Directive 2006/112/EC shall be **determined by the journey of the means of transport** and not by the journey completed by each of the passengers.

Article 36

Where restaurant services and catering services are supplied during the section of a passenger transport operation effected within the Community, that supply shall be covered by Article 57 of Directive 2006/112/EC.

Where restaurant services and catering services are supplied **outside such a section** but on the territory of a Member State or a third country or third territory, that supply shall be covered by Article 55 of that Directive [*Restaurant and Catering Services*].

Article 37

The place of supply of a restaurant service or catering service carried out within the Community **partly** during a section of a passenger transport operation effected within the Community, and **partly** outside such a section but on the territory of a Member State, shall be **determined** in its **entirety** according to the rules for determining the place of supply applicable at the **beginning of the supply** of the restaurant or catering service.

Guidance notes (arts. 35, 36 & 37): These articles concern the supply of restaurant and catering services on board vessels, aircraft and trains during intra-Community transport. The 'section of a passenger transport operation effected within the Community' is determined by the journey of the means of transport and not by the journey completed by each of the passengers. Where restaurant and catering services are supplied during 'the section of transport within the Community' the place of supply is the point of departure of the transport operation. However, where those services are supplied outside such a 'section' the place of supply is where the services are physically carried out. The place of supply of restaurant or catering services carried out within the Community, partly during a section of a passenger transport operation effected within the Community, and partly outside such a section but on the territory of a Member State, shall be determined in its entirety according to the rules for determining the place of supply applicable at the beginning of the supply of the restaurant or catering service.

Subsection 10

Hiring of means of transport

Article 38

1. **'Means of transport'** as referred to in Article 56 [*Rule for B2C Hiring of means of transport services*] and point (g) of the first paragraph of Article 59 [*B2C Services to outside EU*] of Directive 2006/112/EC shall include vehicles, whether motorized or not, and other equipment and devices designed to transport persons or objects from one place to another, which might be pulled, drawn or pushed by vehicles and which are normally designed to be used and actually capable of being used for transport.

2. The **means of transport** referred to in paragraph 1 shall include, in particular, the following vehicles:

(a) land vehicles, such as cars, motor cycles, bicycles, tricycles and caravans;

(b) trailers and semi-trailers;

(c) railway wagons;

(d) vessels;

(e) aircraft;

(f) vehicles specifically designed for the transport of sick or injured persons;

(g) agricultural tractors and other agricultural vehicles;

(h) mechanically or electronically propelled invalid carriages.

3. Vehicles which are **permanently immobilized** and **containers** shall not be considered to be means of transport as referred to in paragraph 1.

Guidance notes: This article provides a definition for a means of transport for the purposes of Articles 56 and 59(g) of the VAT Directive. It lists the types of vehicles, which are covered under the definition of a means of transport, and excludes permanently immobilized vehicles and containers as a means of transport.

Article 39

1. For the application of Article 56 of Directive 2006/112/EC [*Rule for B2C Hiring of means of transport services*], the duration of the **continuous possession** or use of a **means of transport** which is the subject of hiring shall be determined on the basis of the **contract** between the parties involved.

The contract shall serve as a **presumption** which **may be rebutted** by any means in fact or law in order to establish the actual duration of the continuous possession or use.

The fact that the contractual period of short-term hiring within the meaning of Article 56 of Directive 2006/112/EC is **exceeded** on grounds of **force majeure** shall have no bearing on the determination of the duration of the continuous possession or use of the means of transport.

2. Where **hiring of one and the same means of transport** is covered by **consecutive contracts** between the same parties, the duration shall be that of the continuous possession or use of the means of transport provided for under the contracts as a whole.

For the purposes of the first subparagraph a contract and its extensions shall be consecutive contracts.

However, the duration of the short-term hire contract or contracts preceding a contract which is regarded as long-term shall not be called into question provided there is no abusive practice

3. Unless there is abusive practice, consecutive contracts between the same parties for **different means of transport** shall not be considered to be consecutive contracts for the purposes of paragraph 2.

Guidance notes: This article provides the rules for determining the length of a contract. The relevance of this is that the place of supply for the short-term hiring-out of a means of transport is where the means of transport is actually put at the disposal of the customer. The place of supply of long-term hiring-out out of a means of transport for both B2B and B2C supplies are covered by the general rules. Short-term hire means up to 30 days for means of transport such as cars, vans etc. and up to 90 days for vessels.

Para. 1 provides that the place of supply will be determined based on the duration of the possession or use and will be assessed on the basis of the contractual agreement between the parties involved, unless this does not reflect the real intentions of the parties to the contract.

When a short-term contract is subject to an extension, which has the effect of causing it to exceed the 30 or 90-day limits, a reassessment of the contract will be required. However, when the prolongation is due to clearly established circumstances outside the control of the parties involved (force majeure), no reassessment of the contract will take place.

Para. 2 provides that where there are consecutive contracts between the same parties for the same means of transport, the duration will be the total period. However, the duration of a short-term contract before a subsequent contract, which qualifies as long-term by means of the previous contracts, will not be reassessed retrospectively provided no evidence of abuse of law exists.

Example: a person hires a car for a period of 25 days, which would qualify as a short-term hiring-out of a vehicle. This will be taxed at the place where the vehicle is put at the disposal of the customer. Subsequent to this, the person decides to enter into a separate contract for an additional period of 10 days. As the total period would now be 35 days, this second contract will be considered long-term and therefore follow the general B2B and B2C rules as appropriate. As the original contract of 25 days was made in good faith, this will remain as short-term and not be revisited.

Article 40

The place where the means of transport is actually put at the disposal of the customer as referred to in Article 56(1) of Directive 2006/112/EC, shall be the place where the customer or a third party acting on his behalf **takes physical possession of it.**

Guidance notes: A means of transport will be considered as "actually put at the disposal of the customer" at the place where the means of transport is situated when the customer actually takes physical possession of it. Legal control (signature of contract, taking possession of the keys) is not in itself sufficient to determine the place where the means of transport was put at the disposal of the customer.

Subsection 11

Supply of services to non-taxable persons outside the Community

Article 41

The supply of services of **translation** of texts to a non-taxable person established outside the Community shall be covered by point (c) of the first paragraph of Article 59 of Directive 2006/112/EC.

Guidance notes: This article provides that the place of supply of translation services to a non-taxable person established outside the Community is the place where that person is established, has his permanent address or usually resides. This service is covered by Article 59(c) of the VAT Directive.

C – Guidelines VAT Committee
Place of supply of goods
Meeting: 14,52,54,57,58,60,64,80,86,98

Place of supply of services
Meeting: 5, 8, 9, 10, 11, 12, 14, 15, 16, 17, 18, 21, 22, 23, 24, 26, 28, 31, 34, 38, 48, 51, 52, 53, 54, 56, 58, 60, 61, 62, 65, 67, 69, 75, 80, 83, 86, 88, 89, 91, 92, 93, 96, 97

Place of i/c acquisition of goods
Meeting: 80

D – Others

Council Regulation (EC) No 904/2010 of 7 October 2010

Article 31

1. The competent authorities of each Member State shall ensure that persons involved in the intra-Community supply of goods or of services and non-established taxable persons supplying telecommunication services, broadcasting services and electronically supplied services, in particular those referred to in Annex II to Directive 2006/112/EC, are allowed to obtain, for the purposes of such transactions, confirmation by electronic means of the validity of the VAT identification number of any specified person as well as the associated name and address. This information shall correspond to the data referred to in Article 17.

2. Each Member State shall provide confirmation by electronic means of the name and address of the person to whom the VAT identification number has been issued in accordance with its national data protection rules.

3. During the period provided for in Article 357 of Directive 2006/112/EC, paragraph 1 of this Article shall not apply to non-established taxable persons supplying telecommunication services and radio and television broadcasting services.

Title VI - Chargeable Event and chargeability of VAT

Chapter 1 General Provisions

Article 62 [Definitions]

For the purposes of this Directive:

(1) **"chargeable event"** shall mean the occurrence by virtue of which the legal conditions necessary for VAT to become chargeable are fulfilled;

(2) VAT shall become **"chargeable"** when the tax authority becomes entitled under the law, at a given moment, to claim the tax from the person liable to pay, even though the time of payment may be deferred.

Chapter 2 Supply of Goods or Services

Article 63 [Rule]

The **chargeable event** shall occur and VAT shall become **chargeable** when the **goods or the services are supplied**.

Article 64 [Successive statements or payments & continuous supplies]

1. Where it gives rise to **successive statements of account** or **successive payments**, the supply of goods, other than that consisting in the hire of goods for a certain period or the sale of goods on deferred terms, as referred to in point (b) of Article 14(2), or the supply of services shall be regarded as being completed on expiry of the periods to which such statements of account or payments relate.

2. **Continuous supplies** of goods over a period of more than one calendar month which are dispatched or transported to a Member State other than that in which the dispatch or transport of those goods begins and which are supplied VAT-exempt or which are transferred VAT-exempt to another Member State by a taxable person for the purposes of his business, in accordance with the conditions laid down in Article 138, shall be regarded as being **completed on expiry of each calendar month** until such time as the supply comes to an end.

Supplies of services for which VAT is payable by the customer pursuant to Article 196 [*Reverse charge*], which are supplied **continuously** over a period of more than one year and which do not give rise to statements of account or payments during that period, shall be regarded as being completed on **expiry of each calendar year** until such time as the supply of services comes to an end.

Member States may provide that, in certain cases other than those referred to in the first and second subparagraphs, the continuous supply of goods or services over a period of time is to be regarded as being completed at least at intervals of one year.

Article 65 [Payments on account]

Where a **payment is to be made on account** before the goods or services are supplied, VAT shall become chargeable on **receipt of the payment** and on the amount received.

Article 66 [*Options of MS*]

By way of derogation from Articles 63, 64 and 65, **Member States may** provide that VAT is to become chargeable, in respect of certain transactions or certain categories of taxable person at one of the following times:

(a) no later than the time the **invoice is issued**;

(b) no later than the time the **payment is received**;

(c) where an invoice is not issued, or is issued late, within a specified time no later than on expiry of the time-limit for issue of invoices imposed by Member States pursuant to the second paragraph of Article 222 or where no such time-limit has been imposed by the Member State, within a specified period from the date of the chargeable event.

The derogation provided for in the first paragraph shall not, however, apply to supplies of services in respect of which VAT is payable by the customer pursuant to Article 196 and to supplies or transfers of goods referred to in Article 67.

Article 67 [Triangulations & exempt i/c transfer]

Where, in accordance with the conditions laid down in Article 138[*Triangulations*], goods dispatched or transported to a Member State other than that in which dispatch or transport of the goods begins are supplied VAT-exempt or where goods are transferred VAT-exempt to another Member State by a taxable person for the purposes of his business, VAT shall become **chargeable on issue of the invoice**, or on **expiry of the time limit** [*fifteenth day of the month following that in which the chargeable event occurs*] referred to in the first paragraph of Article 222 if no invoice has been issued by that time.

Article 64(1), [*Successive payments*] the third subparagraph of Article 64(2) [*Continuous payments*] and Article 65 [*Payments on account*] shall not apply with respect to the supplies and transfers of goods referred to in the first paragraph.

Chapter 3 Intra-Community Acquisition of Goods

Article 68 [Chargeable event - Rule]

The **chargeable event** shall occur when the intra-Community acquisition of goods is made.

The **intra-Community acquisition** of goods shall be regarded as **being made** when the supply of similar goods is regarded as being effected within the territory of the relevant Member State.

Article 69 [VAT is chargeable – Rule]

In the case of the intra-Community acquisition of goods, VAT shall **become chargeable** on issue of the invoice, or on expiry of the **time limit** *[fifteenth day of the month following that in which the chargeable event occurs]* referred to in the first paragraph of Article 222 if no invoice has been issued by that time.

Chapter 4 Importation of Goods

Article 70 [Chargeable event - Rule]

The **chargeable event** shall occur and VAT shall become chargeable when the goods are imported.

Article 71 [*Exceptions*]

1. Where, on entry into the Community, goods are placed under one of the **arrangements** or situations referred to in Articles 156, 276 and 277, or under **temporary importation arrangements** with total exemption from import duty, or under **external transit arrangements**, the **chargeable event** shall occur and **VAT shall become chargeable** only **when the goods cease to be covered by those arrangements or situations.**

However, where imported goods are subject to **customs duties**, to **agricultural levies** or to charges having **equivalent** effect established under a common policy, the chargeable event shall occur and VAT shall become chargeable **when the chargeable event in respect of those duties occurs and those duties become chargeable**.

2. Where imported goods are not subject to any of the duties referred to in the second subparagraph of paragraph 1, Member States shall, as regards the chargeable event and the moment when VAT becomes chargeable, apply the provisions in force governing customs duties.

Comments to Title VI RVD: Chargeable event and Chargeability

A - Comment

A1. - Chargeable event v. Chargeability

A1.1 - Chargeable event

Chargeable event is the occurrence by virtue of which the legal conditions necessary for VAT to become chargeable are fulfilled.

In practice, it is relevant in determining which rate applies in case of VAT rate changes or when a vat exemption becomes subject to VAT.

A1.2 Chargeability

Chargeability is the moment when the tax authority becomes entitled under the law, at a given moment, to claim the tax from the person liable to pay, even though the time of payment may be deferred.

A1.3 Chargeable Event v. Chargeability

Normally, the chargeable event and chargeability occur at the same time. However some exceptions apply.

In practice, payment is due by the time of the submission of the VAT return.

A2. - Supply of goods and services

The chargeable event shall occur and VAT shall become chargeable when the goods or the services are supplied.

Where a payment is to be made on account before the goods or services are supplied, VAT shall become chargeable on receipt of the payment and on the amount received.

A3. - Intra-community transactions

The chargeable event shall occur when the intra-Community acquisition of goods is made.

The intra-Community acquisition of goods shall be regarded as being made when the supply of similar goods is regarded as being effected within the territory of the relevant Member State.

A4. - Importation

The chargeable event shall occur and VAT shall become chargeable when the goods are imported.

Title VII - Taxable Amount

Chapter 1 Definition

Article 72 [Arm's length Rule]

For the purposes of this Directive, "**open market value**" shall mean the full amount that, in order to obtain the goods or services in question at that time, a customer at the same marketing stage at which the supply of goods or services takes place, would have to pay, under **conditions of fair competition**, to a supplier at **arm's length** within the territory of the Member State in which the supply is subject to tax.

Where **no comparable** supply of goods or services can be ascertained, "open market value" shall mean the following:

(1) in respect of **goods**, an amount that is **not less than the purchase price** of the goods or of similar goods or, in the absence of a purchase price, the **cost price**, determined at the time of supply;

(2) in respect of **services**, an amount that is not less than the **full cost** to the taxable person of providing the service.

Chapter 2 Supply of Goods or Services

Article 73 [Rule]

In respect of the supply of goods or services, other than as referred to in Articles 74 to 77 [*Disposal or retaining of business assets, use of business assets, transfer to another Member State and special deemed supply*] , the taxable amount shall include **everything** which constitutes **consideration** obtained or to be obtained by the supplier, in return for the supply, from the customer or a third party, including subsidies directly linked to the price of the supply.

Article 74 [Disposal or retaining of Business assets]

Where a taxable person applies or disposes of goods forming part of his business assets, or where goods are retained by a taxable person, or by his successors, when his taxable economic activity ceases, as referred to in Articles 16 and 18, the taxable amount shall be **the purchase price of the goods** or of **similar goods** or, in the absence of a purchase price, the **cost price**, determined at the time when the application, disposal or retention takes place.

Article 75 [Usage of Business assets]

In respect of the supply of services, as referred to in Article 26, where goods forming part of the assets of a business are used for private purposes or services are carried out free of charge, the taxable amount shall be the **full cost** to the taxable person of providing the services.

Article 76 [transfer to another Member State]

In respect of the supply of goods consisting in transfer to another Member State, the taxable amount shall be the **purchase price** of the goods or of **similar goods** or, in the absence of a purchase price, the **cost price**, determined at the time the transfer takes place.

Article 77 [special deemed supply]

In respect of the supply by a taxable person of a service for the purposes of his business, as referred to in Article 27, the taxable amount shall be the **open market value** of the service supplied.

Article 78 [Also part of taxable amount]

The taxable amount shall **include** the following factors:

(a) **taxes, duties, levies** and **charges**, excluding the VAT itself;

(b) **incidental expenses**, such as commission, packing, transport and insurance costs, charged by the supplier to the customer.

For the purposes of point (b) of the first paragraph, Member States may regard expenses covered by a separate agreement as **incidental** expenses.

Article 79 [Not included in taxable amount]

The taxable amount shall **not include** the following factors:

(a) price reductions by way of **discount** for **early payment**;

(b) **price discounts** and **rebates** granted to the customer and obtained by him **at the time of the supply**;

(c) amounts received by a taxable person from the customer, as **repayment of expenditure** incurred in the name and on behalf of the customer, and entered in his books in a **suspense account**.

The taxable person must furnish **proof** of the actual amount of the expenditure referred to in point (c) of the first paragraph and may not deduct any VAT which may have been charged.

Article 80 [Open market value, if special relations]

1. In order to prevent tax evasion or avoidance, Member States may in any of the following cases take measures to ensure that, in respect of the supply of goods or services involving **family** or other close **personal ties, management, ownership,**

membership, financial or **legal ties** as defined by the Member State, the taxable amount is to be the **open market value**:

(a) where the **consideration is lowe**r than the open **market value** and the recipient of the supply does not have a full right of deduction under Articles 167 to 171 and Articles 173 to 177;

(b) where the **consideration is lower** than the open **market value** and the supplier does not have a full right of deduction under Articles 167 to 171 and Articles 173 to 177 and the supply is subject to an exemption under Articles 132, 135, 136, 371, 375, 376, 377, 378(2), 379(2) or Articles 380 to 390c;

(c) where the **consideration is higher** than the open **market value** and the supplier does not have a full right of deduction under Articles 167 to 171 and Articles 173 to 177.

For the purposes of the first subparagraph, **legal ties** may include the **relationship between an employer and employee or the employee's family**, or any **other** closely connected persons.

2. Where Member States exercise the option provided for in paragraph 1, they may restrict the categories of suppliers or recipients to whom the measures shall apply.

3. Member States shall inform the VAT Committee of national legislative measures adopted pursuant to paragraph 1 in so far as these are not measures authorized by the Council prior to 13 August 2006 in accordance with Article 27 (1) to (4) of Directive 77/388/EEC, and which are continued under paragraph 1 of this Article.

Article 81

Member States which, at 1 January 1993, were not availing themselves of the option under Article 98 of applying a reduced rate may, if they avail themselves of the option under Article 89, provide that in respect of the supply of **works of art**, as referred to in Article 103(2), the taxable amount is to be equal to a fraction of the amount determined in accordance with Articles 73, 74, 76, 78 and 79.

The fraction referred to in the first paragraph shall be determined in such a way that the VAT thus due is equal to at least 5 % of the amount determined in accordance with Articles 73, 74, 76, 78 and 79.

Article 82 [Investment Gold]

Member States may provide that, in respect of the supply of goods and services, the taxable amount is to include the value of exempt **investment gold** within the meaning of Article 346, which has been provided by the customer to be used as basis for working and which as a result, loses its VAT exempt investment gold status when such goods and services are supplied. The value to be used is the open market value of the investment gold at the time that those goods and services are supplied.

Chapter 3 Intra-Community Acquisition of Goods

Article 83 [Rule]

In respect of the intra-Community acquisition of goods, the taxable amount shall be established on the basis of the **same factors as are used in** accordance with Chapter1 [Arm's length Rule] determine the taxable amount for the supply of the same goods within the territory of the Member State concerned.

In the case of the transactions, to be **treated as intra-Community** acquisitions of goods, referred to in Articles 21 and 22 [Deemed i/c community acquisitions], the taxable amount shall be the **purchase price** of the **goods** or of **similar goods** or, in the absence of a purchase price, the **cost price**, determined at the time of the supply.

Article 84 [Excise duties]

1. Member States shall take the measures necessary to ensure that the **excise duty** due from or paid by the person making the intra-Community acquisition of a product subject to excise duty is **included** in the taxable amount in accordance with point (a) of the first paragraph of Article 78.

2. Where, after the intra-Community acquisition of goods has been made, the person acquiring the goods obtains a **refund** of the excise duty paid in the Member State in which dispatch or transport of the goods began, the taxable amount shall be reduced accordingly in the Member State in the territory of which the acquisition was made.

Chapter 4 Importation of Goods

Article 85 [Rule]

In respect of the importation of goods, the taxable amount shall be the **value for customs purposes**, determined in accordance with the Community provisions in force.

Article 86 [Also to be included]

1. The taxable amount shall **include** the following factors, in so far as they are not already included:

    (a) **taxes, duties, levies** and **other charges** due outside the Member State of importation, and those due by reason of importation, excluding the VAT to be levied;

    (b) **incidental expenses**, such as commission, packing, transport and insurance costs, incurred up to the first place of destination within the territory of the Member State of importation as well as those resulting from transport to another place of destination within the Community, if that other place is known when the chargeable event occurs.

2. For the purposes of point (b) of paragraph 1, "**first place of destination**" shall mean the place mentioned on the consignment note or on any other document under which the goods are imported into the Member State of importation. If no such mention is made, the first place of destination shall be deemed to be the place of the first transfer of cargo in the Member State of importation.

Article 87 [Not included]

The taxable amount shall **not include** the following factors:

   (a) price reductions by way of **discount** for **early** payment;

   (b) price **discounts** and **rebates** granted to the customer and obtained by him at the **time of importation**.

Article 88 [Re-importations after repair, etc]

Where goods temporarily exported from the Community are re-imported after having undergone, outside the Community, **repair, processing, adaptation, making up** or **re-working**, Member States shall take steps to ensure that the tax treatment of the goods for VAT purposes is **the same** as that which would have been applied had the repair, processing, adaptation, making up or re-working been carried out within their territory.

Article 89

Member States which, at 1 January 1993, were not availing themselves of the option under Article 98 of applying a reduced rate may provide that in respect of the importation of works of art, collectors' items and antiques, as defined in points (2), (3) and (4) of Article 311(1), the taxable amount is to be equal to a fraction of the amount determined in accordance with Articles 85, 86 and 87.

The fraction referred to in the first paragraph shall be determined in such a way that the VAT thus due on the importation is equal to at least 5 % of the amount determined in accordance with Articles 85, 86 and 87.

Chapter 5 Miscellaneous Provisions

Article 90 [Credit note, Cancelation, refusal, non-payment or a posteriori price reduction]

1. In the case of **cancellation, refusal** or total or partial **non-payment**, or where the **price is reduced after** the supply takes place, the **taxable amount shall be reduced accordingly** under conditions which shall be determined by the Member States.

2. In the case of total or partial non-payment, Member States may derogate from paragraph 1.

Article 91 [Exchange Rate]

1. Where the factors used to determine the taxable amount on importation are expressed in a **currency** other than that of the Member State in which assessment takes place, the **exchange rate** shall be determined in accordance with the Community provisions governing the calculation of the value for customs purposes.

2. Member States shall accept instead the use of the latest exchange rate published by the **European Central Bank** at the time the tax becomes chargeable. Conversion between currencies other than the euro shall be made by using the euro exchange rate of each currency. Member States may require that they be notified of the exercise of this option by the taxable person.

However, for some of the transactions referred to in the first subparagraph or for certain categories of taxable persons, Member States may use the exchange rate determined in accordance with the Community provisions in force governing the calculation of the value for customs purposes.

Article 92 [Returnable packing material]

As regards the costs of **returnable packing material**, Member States may take one of the following measures:

(a) **exclude** them from the taxable amount and take the measures necessary to ensure that this amount is adjusted if the packing material is not returned;

(b) **include** them in the taxable amount and take the measures necessary to ensure that this amount is adjusted if the packing material is in fact returned.

Comments to Title VII RVD: Taxable amount

A - Comment

A1. General Rule

The taxable basis is the amount that will be used to compute the VAT to be paid (by multiplying it against the applicable VAT rate).

The taxable amount includes everything which constitutes consideration obtained or to be obtained by the supplier, from the customer or a third party (including subsidies directly linked to the price of the supply) in return for the supply.

One important detail: VAT is never part of its taxable basis. Nevertheless, within consideration shall be included:

- Taxes, duties, levies and charges, excluding the VAT itself;
- Incidental expenses, such as commission, packing, transport and insurance costs, charged by the supplier to the customer.

The RVD allows member-States to regard expenses covered by a separate agreement as incidental expenses (may Clause).

On the other hand, the taxable amount needs to be netted of the following factors:

- Price reductions by way of discount for early payment;
- Price discounts and rebates granted to the customer and obtained by him at the time of the supply;
- Amounts received by a taxable person from the customer, as repayment of expenditure incurred in the name and on behalf of the customer, and entered in his books in a suspense account (i.e., disbursements).

Which means that the if the price is EUR100 and there is a discount of EUR20, the taxable amount will only be EUR80.

A2. - Debt/credit card

In the case where a supplier of goods or services, as a condition of accepting payment by credit or debit card,

- Requires the customer to pay an amount to himself or another undertaking, and
- Where the total price payable by that customer is unaffected irrespective of how payment is accepted,

that amount shall constitute an integral part of the taxable amount for the supply of the goods or services.

A3. Exception 1 - Taxable basis on Certain Supply goods and services

A3.1 - Certain supplies of goods

Where a taxable person applies or disposes of goods forming part of his business assets, or where goods are retained by a taxable person, or by his successors, when his taxable economic activity ceases, the taxable amount shall be:

- The purchase price of the goods or of similar goods or,
- In the absence of a purchase price, the cost price, determined at the time when the application, disposal or retention takes place.

A3.2 - Certain supplies of services

In case of supply of a service for the purposes of his business, the taxable amount shall be the open market value of the service supplied.

In respect of the supply of services, where goods forming part of the assets of a business are used for private purposes or services are carried out free of charge, the taxable amount shall be the full cost to the taxable person of providing the services.

A3.3 - Deemed intra-Community supplies

In respect of the supply of goods consisting in transfer to another Member State (deemed intra-community supply), the taxable amount shall be:

- The purchase price of the goods or of similar goods or
- In the absence of a purchase price, the cost price, determined at the time the transfer takes place.

A4. - Taxable basis in Intra-community transactions

In respect of Intra-community transactions, the taxable amount shall be established on the basis of the same factors as are used to determine the taxable amount for the supply of the same goods within the territory of the Member State concerned.

A5 - Exception 2 - Taxable basis on Importation

A5.1 - Rule

In respect of the importation of goods, the taxable amount shall be the value for customs purposes, determined in accordance with the Community Custom's provisions in force.

The taxable amount shall include the following factors, in so far as they are not already included:

- Taxes, duties, levies and other charges due outside the Member State of importation, and those due by reason of importation, excluding the VAT to be levied;
- Incidental expenses, such as: commission, packing, transport and insurance costs, incurred up to the first place of destination within the territory of the Member State of importation as well as those resulting from transport to another place of destination within the Community, if that other place is known when the chargeable event occurs.

The taxable amount shall be netted of the following factors:

- Price reductions by way of discount for early payment;
- Price discounts and rebates granted to the customer and obtained by him at the time of

importation.

A5.2 - First place of destination

First place of destination the place mentioned on the consignment note or on any other document under which the goods are imported into the Member State of importation. If no such mention is made, the first place of destination shall be deemed to be the place of the first transfer of cargo in the Member State of importation.

A5.3 Value for customs purposes

The value for customs purposes is determined in accordance with the Community Custom's provisions in force. You can find this value the Single Administrative Document (SAD) which documents the import.

Please note that in some countries the Customs' value does not necessarily match the custom's invoice value but is a value predetermined in the country's customs regulations (for example "x" EUR per "x" KG or Tons).

A6 - Concept of Open Market Value

A6.1 - Transactions between related parties need to be arms' length

For the purpose of the determination of the taxable basis, the RVD foresees a clause which establishes an arms' length principle similar to the one used for Transfer Pricing Purposes.

Thus, in order to prevent tax evasion or avoidance, the RVD allows (may clause) the member-States to take measures to ensure that, in respect of the supply of goods or services involving related parties the taxable amount is to be the open market value:

A6.2 - Open market

By open market value the RVD means he full amount that, in order to obtain the goods or services in question at that time, a customer at the same marketing stage at which the supply of goods or services takes place, would have to pay, under conditions of fair competition, to a supplier at arm's length within the territory of the Member State in which the supply is subject to VAT.

In case no comparable supply of goods or services can be ascertained, 'open market value' shall mean:

In respect of goods, an amount that is not less than the purchase price of the goods or of similar goods or, in the absence of a purchase price, the cost price, determined at the time of supply;

In respect of services, an amount that is not less than the full cost to the taxable person of providing the service.

A6.3 - Related parties

Related parties are defined in the RVD as family or other close personal ties, management, ownership, membership, financial or legal ties as defined by the Member State.

A7 - Credit Notes

In the case of cancellation, refusal or total or partial non-payment, or where the price is reduced after the supply takes place, the taxable amount shall be reduced accordingly.

A8 - Foreign currency

A8.1 - On importation

Where the factors used to determine the taxable amount on importation are expressed in a currency other than that of the Member State in which importation, the exchange rate shall be determined in accordance with the Community provisions governing the calculation of the value for customs purposes.

A8.2 - On other transactions (not Importations)

On other transactions, where the factors used to determine the taxable amount of the transaction are expressed in a currency other than that of the Member State in which assessment takes place, the exchange rate applicable shall be:

The latest selling rate recorded, at the time VAT becomes chargeable, on the most representative exchange market or markets of the Member State concerned, or

A rate determined by reference to that or those markets, in accordance with the rules laid down by that Member State.

Moreover, the RVD foresees that member-States shall accept instead the use of the latest exchange rate published by the European Central Bank at the time the tax becomes chargeable.

B – Implementation measures (see Regulation 282/2011)

Article 42

Where a supplier of goods or services, as a condition of accepting payment by **credit** or **debit card**, requires the customer to pay an amount to himself or another undertaking, and where the total price payable by that customer is unaffected irrespective of how payment is accepted, that amount shall constitute an integral part of the taxable amount for the supply of the goods or services, under Articles 73 to 80 of Directive 2006/112/EC.

Guidance notes: This article provides a definition of the taxable amount in case of payment with a credit or debit card. Where a supplier of goods or services, as a condition of accepting payment by credit or debit card, requires the customer to pay an amount to himself/herself or another undertaking, and where the total price payable by that customer is unaffected irrespective of how payment is accepted, that amount shall constitute an integral part of the taxable amount for the supply of the goods or services.

Example: a retail jeweler offers for sale a bracelet for €100. If a customer pays €100 for the bracelet by credit card, the tax-inclusive consideration for the sale of the bracelet is €100 even if the jeweler bills the customer €98 for the bracelet and €2 for the credit card charge.

B – Guidelines VAT Committee
Meeting 91

Title VIII - Rates

Chapter 1 Application of Rates

Article 93 [Application in time]

The rate applicable to taxable transactions shall be that **in force** at the time of the **chargeable event**.

However, in the following situations, the rate applicable shall be that in force when **VAT becomes chargeable**:

(a) in the cases referred to in Articles 65 *[payment on account]* and 66*[derogations allowed to MS]*;

(b) in the case of an **intra-Community acquisition** of goods;

(c) in the cases, concerning the **importation** of goods, referred to in the second subparagraph of Article 71(1) and in Article 71(2).

Article 94 [Rate applicable to I/C acquisition and Importations]

1. The **rate** applicable to the **intra-Community acquisition** of goods shall be that applied to the supply of like goods within the territory of the Member State.

2. Subject to the option under Article 103(1) of applying a reduced rate to the importation of works of art, collectors' items or antiques, the rate applicable to the **importation of goods** shall be that applied to the supply of like goods within the territory of the Member State.

Article 95 [Change of rates – adjustments]

Where rates are changed, Member States may, in the cases

referred to in Articles 65 and 66, effect adjustments in order to take account of the rate applying at the time when the goods or services were supplied.

Member States may also adopt all appropriate transitional measures.

Chapter 2 Structure and level of Rates

Section 1: Standard Rate

Article 96 [Rule]

Member States shall apply a **standard rate** of VAT, which shall be fixed by each Member State as a percentage of the taxable amount and which shall be the same for the supply of goods and for the supply of services.

Article 97 [Minimum standard rate]

From 1 January 2011 until 31 December 2015, the standard rate may not be lower than **15 %**

Section 2: Reduced Rates

Article 98 [Rule]

1. Member States may apply either **one or two** reduced rates.
2. The reduced rates shall apply only to supplies of **goods** or **services** in the categories set out **in Annex III**.

The reduced rates shall **not apply to electronically supplied services**.

3. When applying the reduced rates provided for in paragraph 1 to categories of goods, Member States **may use the Combined Nomenclature** to establish the precise coverage of the category concerned.

Article 99 [Minimum reduced rate]

1. The reduced rates shall be fixed as a percentage of the taxable amount, which may not be less than **5 %**.
2. Each reduced rate shall be so fixed that the amount of VAT resulting from its application is such that the VAT deductible under Articles 167 to 171 and Articles 173 to 177 can normally be deducted in full.

Article 100 [review of scope of reduced rates]

On the basis of a report from the Commission, the Council shall, starting in 1994, review the scope of the reduced rates every two years.

The Council may, in accordance with Article 93 of the Treaty, decide to alter the list of goods and services set out in Annex III.

Article 101

By 30 June 2007 at the latest the Commission shall present to the European Parliament and the Council an overall assessment report on the impact of reduced rates applying to locally supplied services, including restaurant services, notably in terms of job creation, economic growth and the proper functioning of the internal market, based on a study carried out by an independent economic think-tank.

Section 3: Particular Provisions

Article 102 [Gas, electricity & heating]

After consultation of the VAT Committee, each Member State may apply a reduced rate to the supply of **natural gas, electricity** or **district heating**.

Article 103 [Works of art, collectors' items and antiques]

1. Member States may provide that the reduced rate, or one of the reduced rates, which they apply in accordance with Articles 98 and 99 is also to apply to the **importation of works of art, collectors' items** and **antiques**, as defined in points (2), (3) and (4) of Article 311(1).

2. If Member States avail themselves of the option under paragraph 1, they may also apply the reduced rate to the following transactions:

    (a) the **supply** of **works of art**, by their creator or his **successors** in title;

    (b) the **supply of works of art**, on an **occasional** basis, by a taxable person other than a taxable dealer, where the works of art have been imported by the taxable person himself, or where they have been supplied to him by their creator or his successors in title, or where they have entitled him to full deduction of VAT.

Article 104 [Jungholz & Mittelberg (Austria)]

Austria may, in the communes of Jungholz and Mittelberg (Kleines Walsertal), apply a **second standard rate** which is lower than the corresponding rate applied in the rest of Austria but not less than 15 %.

Article 104a [LPG in Cyprus]

Cyprus may apply one of the two reduced rates provided for in Article 98 to the supply of liquid petroleum gas (**LPG**) in cylinders.

Article 105 [Portugal: Lisbon bridges, Madeira & Azores]

1. Portugal may apply one of the two reduced rates provided for in Article 98 to the tolls on **bridges** in the Lisbon area.

2. Portugal may, in the case of transactions carried out in the autonomous regions of the **Azores** and **Madeira** and of direct importation into those regions, apply **rates lower than those applying on the mainland**.

Chapter 3

Article 106-108 [Deleted].

Chapter 4 Special Provisions applying until the Adoption of Definitive Arrangements

Article 109 [Application of provisory provisions]

Pending introduction of the definitive arrangements referred to in Article 402, the provisions laid down in this Chapter shall apply.

Article 110 [Grandfathering rule 1]

Member States which, at 1 January 1991, were granting exemptions with deductibility of the VAT paid at the preceding stage or applying reduced rates lower than the minimum laid down in Article 99 may continue to grant those exemptions or apply those reduced rates.

The exemptions and reduced rates referred to in the first paragraph must be in accordance with Community law and must have been adopted for clearly defined social reasons and for the benefit of the final consumer.

Article 111 [Grandfathering rule 2]

Subject to the conditions laid down in the second paragraph of Article 110, exemptions with deductibility of the VAT paid at the preceding stage may continue to be granted in the following cases:

(a) by **Finland** in respect of the supply of newspapers and periodicals sold by subscription and the printing of publications distributed to the members of corporations for the public good;

(b) by **Sweden** in respect of the supply of newspapers, including radio and cassette newspapers for the visually impaired, pharmaceutical products supplied to hospitals or on prescription, and the production of, or other related services concerning, periodicals of non-profit-making organizations.

(c) by **Malta** in respect of the supply of foodstuffs for human consumption and pharmaceuticals.

Article 112 [Ireland: energy]

If the provisions of Article 110 cause for **Ireland** distortion of competition in the supply of **energy products** for **heating** and **lighting**, Ireland may, on specific request, be authorized by the Commission to apply a reduced rate to such supplies, in accordance with Articles 98 and 99.

In the case referred to in the first paragraph, Ireland shall submit a request to the Commission, together with all necessary information. If the Commission has not taken a decision within three months of receiving the request, Ireland shall be deemed to be authorized to apply the reduced rates proposed.

Article 113 [Grandfathering rule 3]

Member States which, at 1 January 1991, in accordance with Community law, were granting exemptions with deductibility of the VAT paid at the preceding stage or applying reduced rates lower than the minimum laid down in Article 99, in respect of goods and services other than those specified in Annex III, may apply the reduced rate, or one of the two reduced rates, provided for in Article 98 to the supply of such goods or services.

Article 114 [Grandfathering rule 4]

1. Member States which, on 1 January 1993, were obliged to increase their standard rate in force at 1 January 1991 by more than 2 % may apply a reduced rate lower than the minimum laid down in Article 99 to the supply of goods and services in the categories set out in Annex III.

The Member States referred to in the first subparagraph may also apply such a rate to children's clothing and children's footwear and housing.

2. Member States may not rely on paragraph 1 to introduce exemptions with deductibility of the VAT paid at the preceding stage.

Article 115 [Grandfathering rule 5]

Member States which, at 1 January 1991, were applying a reduced rate to children's clothing children's footwear or housing may continue to apply such a rate to the supply of those goods or services.

Article 116

[Deleted]

Article 117 [Austria: immovable property]

1. [Deleted].

2. **Austria** may apply one of the two reduced rates provided for in Article 98 to the letting of immovable property for residential use, provided that the rate is not lower than 10%.

Article 118 [Grandfathering rule 6]

Member States which, at 1 January 1991, were applying a reduced rate to the supply of goods or services other than those specified in Annex III may apply the reduced rate, or one of the two reduced rates, provided for in Article 98 to the supply of those goods or services, provided that the rate is not lower than 12%.

The first paragraph shall not apply to the supply of second-hand goods, works of art, collectors' items or antiques, as defined in points (1) to (4) of Article 311(1), subject to VAT in accordance with the margin scheme provided for in Articles 312 to 325 or the arrangements for sales by public auction.

Article 119 [Austria: wine]

For the purposes of applying Article 118, **Austria** may apply a reduced rate to **wines** produced on an agricultural holding by the producer-farmer, provided that the rate is not lower than 12 %.

Article 120 [Greece: special regions]

Greece may apply rates up to 30% lower than the corresponding rates applied in mainland Greece in the departments of **Lesbos, Chios, Samos,** the **Dodecanese** and the **Cyclades,** and on the islands of **Thassos,** the **Northern Sporades, Samothrace** and **Skiros.**

Article 121 [Grandfathering rule 7]

Member States which, at 1 January 1993, regarded **work under contract** as the supply of goods may apply to the delivery of work under contract the rate applicable to the goods obtained after execution of the work under contract.

For the purposes of applying the first paragraph, "**delivery of work under contract**" shall mean the handing over by a contractor to his customer of movable property made or assembled by the contractor from materials or objects entrusted to him by the customer for that purpose, whether or not the contractor has provided any part of the materials used.

Article 122 [Live Plants]

Member States may apply a reduced rate to the supply of **live plants** and other floricultural products, including bulbs, roots and the like, cut flowers and ornamental foliage, and of wood for use as firewood.

Chapter 5 Temporary Provisions

Article 123 [Czech Republic]

The **Czech Republic** may, until 31 December 2010, continue to apply a reduced rate of not less than 5 % to the supply of construction work for residential housing not provided as part of a social policy, excluding building materials.

Article 124

[Deleted]

Article 125 [Cyprus]

1. Cyprus may, until 31 December 2010, continue to grant an exemption with deductibility of VAT paid at the preceding stage in respect of the supply of pharmaceuticals and foodstuffs for human consumption, with the exception of ice cream, ice lollies, frozen yoghurt, water ice and similar products and savory food products (potato crisps/sticks, puffs and similar products packaged for human consumption without further preparation).

2. [Deleted].

Article 126

[Deleted]

Article 127

[Deleted]

Article 128 [Poland]

1. **Poland** may, until 31 December 2010, grant an exemption with deductibility of VAT paid at the preceding stage in respect of the supply of certain books and specialist periodicals.

2. [Deleted].

3. **Poland** may, until 31 December 2010, continue to apply a reduced rate of not less than 3 % to the supply of foodstuffs as referred to in point (1) of Annex III.

4. **Poland** may, until 31 December 2010, continue to apply a reduced rate of not less than 7 % to the supply of services, not provided as part of a social policy, for construction, renovation and alteration of housing, excluding building materials, and to the supply before first occupation of residential buildings or parts of residential buildings, as referred to in Article 12(1)(a).

Article 129 [Slovenia]

1. [Deleted].

2. **Slovenia** may, until 31 December 2010, continue to apply a reduced rate of not less than 5 % to the supply of construction, renovation and maintenance work for residential housing not provided as part of a social policy, excluding building materials.

Article 130

[Deleted]

Comments to Title VIII RVD: Rates

A – Comment

A1 - VAT rates

Once you know what is the Taxable amount, it is time to determine what is the VAT rate that applies, so that you can finally compute the VAT that will apply to your transaction.

The main types of VAT rates:

- Standard rate
- Reduced rate
- Super-reduced rate
- Zero rate
- Parking rate

A2 - rules

When determining their VAT rates, EU Members States have to follow certain rules. The main ones are as follows:

- (Until Dec. 31, 2015) The standard rate cannot be lower than 15%
- The (super) reduced rates cannot be lower than 5%
- MS may apply maximum of 2 reduced rates (the reduced and super-reduced rate)
- The reduced rates only apply to certain goods/services
- The reduced rates do not apply to electronically supplied services

A3 - Special cases - Parking rates

Note that there are cases where the member-States may have negotiated (when Directive 92/77/EEC was adopted or in the Accession Treaty framework) to that certain special rates would be applicable to them (intender to be a temporary period). These rates can be lower than the ones mentioned in the rules just enumerated above.

B – Implementation measures (see Regulation 282/2011)

Article 43

'**Provision of holiday accommodation**' as referred to in point (12) of Annex III to Directive 2006/112/EC shall include the hiring out of tents, caravans or mobile homes installed on camping sites and used as accommodation.

Guidance notes: This article provides that the 'provision of holiday accommodation' includes the hiring-out of tents, caravans or mobile homes installed on camping sites and used as holiday accommodation.

B – Guidelines VAT Committee
Meeting 45,54,65,86,92

Title IX - Exemptions

Chapter 1 General Provisions

Article 131

The exemptions provided for in Chapters 2 to 9 shall apply without prejudice to other Community provisions and in accordance with conditions which the Member States shall lay down for the purposes of ensuring the correct and straightforward application of those exemptions and of preventing any possible evasion, avoidance or abuse.

Chapter 2 Exemptions for Certain Activities in the Public Interest

Article 132 [also refer to article 13(2)]

1. Member States shall exempt the following transactions:

   (a) the supply by the public **postal services** of services other than passenger transport and telecommunications services, and the supply of goods **incidental** thereto;

   (b) **hospital** and **medical** care and closely **related** activities undertaken by bodies governed by public law or, under social conditions comparable with those applicable to bodies governed by public law, by hospitals, centers for medical treatment or diagnosis and other duly recognized establishments of a similar nature;

   (c) the provision of **medical care** in the exercise of the medical and paramedical professions as defined by the Member State concerned;

   (d) the supply of **human organs**, **blood** and **milk**;

(e) the supply of services by **dental** technicians in their professional capacity and the supply of dental prostheses by dentists and dental technicians;

(f) the supply of services by **independent groups of persons** [IGP], who are carrying on an activity which is **exempt** from VAT or in relation to which they are not taxable persons, for the purpose of rendering their members the services directly necessary for the exercise of that activity, where those groups merely claim from their members exact reimbursement of their share of the joint expenses, provided that such exemption is not likely to cause distortion of competition [IGP and VAT group (article 11) are two different VAT concepts];

(g) the supply of services and of goods closely linked to **welfare** and **social security** work, including those supplied **by old people's homes**, by bodies governed by public law or by other bodies recognized by the Member State concerned as being devoted to social wellbeing;

(h) the supply of services and of goods closely linked to the **protection of children and young persons** by bodies governed by public law or by other organizations recognized by the Member State concerned as being devoted to social wellbeing;

(i) the provision of **children's or young people's education**, **school** or **university** education, **vocational training** or **retraining**, including the supply of services and of goods closely related thereto, by bodies governed by public law having such as their aim or by other organizations recognized by the Member State concerned as having similar objects;

(j) **tuition** given privately by teachers and covering school or university education;

(k) the supply of staff by **religious** or **philosophical institutions** for the purpose of the activities referred to in points (b), (g), (h) and (i) and with a view to spiritual welfare;

(l) the supply of services, and the supply of goods closely linked thereto, to their members in their common interest in return for a subscription fixed in accordance with their rules by non-profit-making organizations with aims of a **political**, **trade-union**, **religious**, **patriotic**, **philosophical**, **philanthropic** or **civic nature**, provided that this exemption is not likely to cause distortion of competition;

(m) the supply of certain services closely linked to **sport** or **physical** education by **non-profit-making organizations** to persons taking part in sport or physical education;

(n) the supply of certain **cultural services**, and the supply of goods closely **linked** thereto, by bodies governed by public law or by other cultural bodies recognized by the Member State concerned;

(o) the supply of services and goods, by organizations whose activities are exempt pursuant to points (b), (g), (h), (i), (l), (m) and (n), in connection with **fund-raising events** organized exclusively for their own benefit, provided that exemption is not likely to cause distortion of competition;

(p) the supply of **transport services for sick** or **injured** persons in vehicles specially designed for the purpose, by duly authorized bodies;

(q) the activities, other than those of a commercial nature, carried out by **public radio** and **television** bodies.

2. For the purposes of point (o) of paragraph 1, Member States may introduce any restrictions necessary, in particular as regards the number of events or the amount of receipts which give entitlement to exemption.

Article 133

Member States may make the granting to bodies other than those governed by public law of each exemption provided for in points (b), (g), (h), (i), (l), (m) and (n) of Article 132(1) **subject** in each individual case to one or more of the **following conditions**:

- (a) the bodies in question must **not** systematically **aim to** make a **profit**, and any surpluses nevertheless arising must not be distributed, but must be assigned to the continuance or improvement of the services supplied;

- (b) those bodies must be **managed** and **administered** on an essentially **voluntary** basis by persons who have no direct or indirect interest, either themselves or through intermediaries, in the results of the activities concerned;

- (c) those bodies must charge **prices** which are **approved** by the **public authorities** or which do not exceed such approved prices or, in respect of those services not subject to approval, prices lower than those charged for similar services by commercial enterprises subject to VAT;

- (d) the exemptions must **not** be likely to cause **distortion** of **competition** to the disadvantage of commercial enterprises subject to VAT.

Member States which, pursuant to Annex E of Directive 77/388/EEC, on 1 January 1989 applied VAT to the transactions referred to in Article 132(1)(m) and (n) may also apply the conditions provided for in point (d) of the first paragraph of this Article when the said supply of goods or services by bodies governed by public law is granted exemption.

Article 134

The supply of goods or services **shall not be granted exemption**, as provided for in points (b), (g), (h), (i), (l), (m) and (n) of Article 132(1), in the following cases:

(a) where the supply is **not essential** to the transactions exempted;

(b) where the basic **purpose** of the supply is to **obtain additional income** for the body in question through transactions which are in direct competition with those of commercial enterprises subject to VAT.

Chapter 3 Exemptions for other Activities

Article 135

[Exemption with right do deduct incurred VAT - see and article 169(c)]

1. Member States shall **exempt** the following transactions:

    (a) **insurance** and **reinsurance** transactions, including related services performed by **insurance brokers** and **insurance agents**;

    (b) the granting and the **negotiation of credit** and the **management of credit** by the person granting it;

    (c) the negotiation of or any dealings in **credit guarantees** or any other security for money and the management of credit guarantees by the person who is granting the credit;

    (d) transactions, including negotiation, concerning **deposit** and **current accounts, payments, transfers, debts, cheques** and other negotiable **instruments**, but **excluding debt collection**;

    (e) transactions, including negotiation, concerning **currency, bank notes** and **coins** used as legal tender, with the **exception of collectors' items**, that is to say, **gold, silver** or other metal coins or **bank notes** which are **not normally used as legal tender** or coins of **numismatic interest**;

    (f) transactions, including negotiation but not management or safekeeping, in **shares, interests** in companies or associations, **debentures** and other **securities**, but excluding documents establishing title to goods, and the **rights** or **securities** referred to in Article 15(2);

(g) the **management** of special **investment funds** as defined by Member States;

(h) the supply at face value of **postage stamps** valid for use for postal services within their respective territory, fiscal stamps and other similar stamps;

(i) **betting, lotteries** and other forms of **gambling**, subject to the conditions and limitations laid down by each Member State;

(j) the supply of a **building or parts** thereof, and of the **land** on which it stands, other than the supply referred to in point (a) of Article 12(1);

(k) the supply of **land** which has not been built on other than the supply of building land as referred to in point (b) of Article 12(1);

(l) the **leasing** or **letting** of **immovable property**.

2. The following shall be excluded from the exemption provided for in point (l) of paragraph 1:

(a) the provision of **accommodation**, as defined in the laws of the Member States, in the **hotel sector** or in sectors with a **similar** function, including the provision of accommodation in **holiday camps** or on sites developed for use as camping sites;

(b) the **letting** of premises and sites for the **parking of vehicles**;

(c) the letting of **permanently installed equipment** and **machinery**;

(d) the **hire of safes**.

Member States may apply further exclusions to the scope of the exemption referred to in point (l) of paragraph 1.

Article 136 [also refer to article 13(2)]

Member States shall exempt the following transactions:

(a) the supply of goods used solely for an activity exempted under Articles 132, 135, 371, 375, 376 and 377, Article 378(2), Article 379(2) and Articles 380 to 390c, if those goods have not given rise to deductibility;

(b) the supply of goods on the acquisition or application of which VAT was not deductible, pursuant to Article 176.

Article 137 [Option for Taxation]

1. Member States may allow taxable persons a **right of option for taxation** in respect of the following transactions:

    (a) the **financial transactions** referred to in points (b) to (g) of Article 135(1) [*management of investment funds*];

    (b) the supply of a **building** or of parts thereof, and of the **land** on which the building stands, other than the supply referred to in point (a) of Article 12(1);

    (c) the supply of **land** which has not been built on other than the supply of building land referred to in point (b) of Article 12(1);

    (d) the **leasing** or **letting** of **immovable property**.

2. Member States shall lay down the detailed rules governing exercise of the option under paragraph 1.

Member States may restrict the scope of that right of option.

Chapter 4 Exemptions for Intra-Community Transactions

Section 1: Exemptions related to the Supply of Goods

Article 138 [Exemption on intra-Community supplies & others]

[Exemption with right to deduct input VAT incurred - see article 169]

1. Member States shall exempt the **supply of goods dispatched or transported** to a **destination outside their respective territory** but **within the Community, by or on behalf of the vendor** or the **person acquiring the goods**, for **another taxable person,** or for a non-taxable legal person acting as such in a **Member State other** than that in which **dispatch or transport of the goods began.**

2. In addition to the supply of goods referred to in paragraph 1, Member States shall exempt the following transactions:

   (a) the supply of **new means of transport**, dispatched or transported to the customer at a destination outside their respective territory but within the Community, by or on behalf of the vendor or the customer, for taxable persons, or non-taxable legal persons, whose intra-Community acquisitions of goods are not subject to VAT pursuant to Article 3(1), or for any other non-taxable person;

   (b) the supply of **products subject to excise duty**, dispatched or transported to a destination outside their respective territory but within the Community, to the customer, by or on behalf of the vendor or the customer, for taxable persons, or non-taxable legal persons, whose intra-Community acquisitions of goods other than products subject to excise duty are not subject to VAT pursuant to

Article 3(1), where those products have been dispatched or transported in accordance with Article 7(4) and (5) or Article 16 of Directive 92/12/EEC;/p>

(c) the supply of goods, consisting in a transfer to another Member State, which would have been entitled to exemption under paragraph 1 and points (a) and (b) if it had been made on behalf of another taxable person.

Article 139 [Exception: small enterprises]

1. The exemption provided for in Article 138(1) shall not apply to the supply of goods carried out by taxable persons who are covered by the **exemption for small enterprises** provided for in Articles 282 to 292.

Nor shall that exemption apply to the supply of goods to taxable persons, or non-taxable legal persons, whose intra-Community acquisitions of goods are not subject to VAT pursuant to Article 3(1).

2. The exemption provided for in Article 138(2)(b) shall not apply to the supply of products subject to excise duty by taxable persons who are covered by the exemption for small enterprises provided for in Articles 282 to 292.

3. The exemption provided for in Article 138(1) and (2)(b) and (c) shall not apply to the supply of goods subject to VAT in accordance with the margin scheme provided for in Articles 312 to 325 or the special arrangements for sales by public auction.

The exemption provided for in Article 138(1) and (2)(c) shall not apply to the supply of second-hand means of transport, as defined in Article 327(3), subject to VAT in accordance with the transitional arrangements for second-hand means of transport.

Section 2 Exemptions for Intra-Community Acquisitions of Goods

Article 140

Member States shall exempt the following transactions:

(a) the intra-Community acquisition of goods the supply of which by taxable persons **would in all circumstances be exempt** within their respective territory;

(b) the intra-Community acquisition of goods the importation of which would in **all circumstances be exempt** under points (a), (b) and (c) and (e) to (l) of Article 143(1)

(c) the intra-Community acquisition of goods where, pursuant to Articles 170 and 171, the person acquiring the goods **would in all circumstances be entitled to full reimbursement** of the VAT due under Article 2(1)(b).

Article 141 [Triangulation]

Each Member State shall take specific measures to ensure that VAT is not charged on the intra-Community acquisition of goods within its territory, made in accordance with Article 40, where the following conditions are met *[also refer to articles 42 and 197]*:

(a) the **acquisition** of goods is made by a **taxable person** who is **not established** in the Member State concerned **but is identified** for VAT purposes **in another Member State**;

(b) the acquisition of goods is made for the **purposes of the subsequent supply of those goods**, in the Member State concerned, by the taxable person referred to in point (a);

(c) the **goods** thus acquired by the taxable person referred to in point (a) are **directly dispatched or transported**, from a Member State other than that in which he is identified for VAT purposes, to the person for whom he is to carry out the subsequent supply;

(d) the **person** to whom the **subsequent supply** is to be made is another taxable person, or a non-taxable legal person, who is **identified for VAT purposes in the Member State concerned**;

(e) the **person** referred to in point (d) has been **designated** in accordance with Article 197 as **liable for payment** of the VAT due on the supply carried out by the taxable person who is not established in the Member State in which the tax is due.

Section 3 Exemptions for Certain Transport Services

Article 142 [Madeira and Azores]

[Exemption with right to deduct input VAT incurred - see article 169]

Member States shall exempt the supply of intra-Community transport of goods **to and from the islands** making up the autonomous regions of the **Azores** and **Madeira**, as well as the supply of transport of goods between those islands.

Chapter 5: Exemptions on Importation

Article 143

1. Member States shall exempt the following transactions:

   (a) the **final importation** of goods of which the supply by a **taxable person** would in all circumstances be **exempt** within their respective territory;

   (b) the **final importation** of goods governed by Council Directives 69/169/EEC, 83/181/EEC and 2006/79/EC;

   (c) the **final importation** of goods, **in free circulation** from a third territory forming part of the Community customs territory, which would be entitled to exemption under point (b) if they had been imported within the meaning of the first paragraph of Article 30;

   (d) the **importation** of goods **dispatched** or **transported from a third territory** or a third country into a Member State other than that in which the dispatch or transport of the goods ends, where the supply of such goods by the importer designated or recognized under Article 201 as liable for payment of VAT is exempt under Article 138;

   (e) the **re-importation**, by the person who exported them, of goods in the state in which they were exported, where those goods are exempt from customs duties;

   (f) the **importation**, under **diplomatic** and **consular** arrangements, of goods which are exempt from customs duties;

   (fa) the **importation** of goods **by the European Community**, the **European Atomic Energy Community**, the **European Central Bank** or the **European Investment** Bank, or by the bodies set up by the Communities to which the Protocol of 8 April 1965 on the privileges and immunities of the European Communities applies, within the limits and under the conditions of that Protocol and the agreements for its implementation or the headquarters agreements, in so far as it does not lead to distortion of competition;

(g) the importation of goods by **international bodies**, other than those referred to in point (fa), recognized as such by the public authorities of the host Member State, or by members of such bodies, within the limits and under the conditions laid down by the international conventions establishing the bodies or by headquarters agreements;

(h) the importation of goods, into **Member States party** to the **North Atlantic Treaty**, by the **armed forces** of other States party to that Treaty for the use of those forces or the civilian staff accompanying them or for supplying their messes or canteens where such forces take part in the common defense effort;

(i) the importation of goods by the **armed forces** of the United Kingdom stationed in the island of Cyprus pursuant to the Treaty of Establishment concerning the Republic of Cyprus, dated 16 August 1960, which are for the use of those forces or the civilian staff accompanying them or for supplying their messes or canteens;

(j) the importation into ports, by **sea fishing undertakings,** of their catches, unprocessed or after undergoing preservation for marketing but before being supplied;

(k) the importation of gold by **central banks**;

(l) the importation of gas through a **natural gas system** or any network connected to such a system or fed in from a vessel transporting gas into a natural gas system or any upstream pipeline network, of electricity or of heat or cooling energy through heating or cooling networks.

2. The exemption provided for in paragraph 1(d) shall apply in cases when the importation of goods is followed by the supply of goods exempted under Article 138(1) and (2)(c) only if at the time of importation the importer has provided to the competent authorities of the Member State of importation at least the following information:

   (a) his VAT identification number issued in the Member State of importation or the VAT identification number of his tax representative, liable for payment of the VAT, issued in the Member State of importation;

   (b) the VAT identification number of the customer, to whom the goods are supplied in accordance with Article 138(1), issued in another Member State, or his own VAT identification number issued in the Member State in which the dispatch or transport of the goods ends when the goods are subject to a transfer in accordance with Article 138(2)(c);

   (c) the evidence that the imported goods are intended to be transported or dispatched from the Member State of importation to another Member State.

However, Member States may provide that the evidence referred to in point (c) be indicated to the competent authorities only upon request.

Article 144 [services relating to the importation]

[Exemption with right to deduct input VAT incurred - see article 169]

Member States shall exempt the supply of services relating to the importation of goods where the value of such services is included in the taxable amount in accordance with Article 86(1)(b).

Article 145

1. The Commission shall, where appropriate, as soon as possible, present to the Council proposals designed to delimit the scope of the exemptions provided for in Articles 143 and 144 and to lay down the detailed rules for their implementation.

2. Pending the entry into force of the rules referred to in paragraph 1, Member States may maintain their national provisions in force.

Member States may adapt their national provisions so as to minimize distortion of competition and, in particular, to prevent non-taxation or double taxation within the Community.

Member States may use whatever administrative procedures they consider most appropriate to achieve exemption.

3. Member States shall notify to the Commission, which shall inform the other Member States accordingly, the provisions of national law which are in force, in so far as these have not already been notified, and those which they adopt pursuant to paragraph 2.

Chapter 6 Exemptions on Exportation

Article 146 [Exemption on Exportation]

[Exemption with right to deduct input VAT incurred - see article 169]

1. Member States shall exempt the following transactions:

    (a) the supply of goods dispatched or transported to a destination outside the Community by or on behalf of the vendor;

    (b) the supply of goods dispatched or transported to a destination outside the Community by or on behalf of a customer not established within their respective territory, with the exception of goods transported by the customer himself for the equipping, fuelling and provisioning of pleasure boats and private aircraft or any other means of transport for private use;

    (c) the supply of goods to approved bodies which export them out of the Community as part of their humanitarian, charitable or teaching activities outside the Community;

    (d) the supply of services consisting in work on movable property acquired or imported for the purpose of undergoing such work within the Community, and dispatched or transported out of the Community by the supplier, by the customer if not established within their respective territory or on behalf of either of them;

    (e) the supply of services, including transport and ancillary transactions, but excluding the supply of services exempted in accordance with Articles 132 and 135, where these are directly connected with the exportation or importation of goods covered by Article 61 and Article 157(1)(a).

2. The exemption provided for in point (c) of paragraph 1 may be granted by means of a refund of the VAT.

Article 147 [Goods carried in personal luggage]

[Exemption with right to deduct input VAT incurred - see article 169]

1. Where the supply of goods referred to in point (b) of Article 146(1) relates to goods to be carried in the personal luggage of travelers, the exemption shall apply only if the following conditions are met:

    (a) the traveler is not established within the Community;

    (b) the goods are transported out of the Community before the end of the third month following that in which the supply takes place;

    (c) the total value of the supply, including VAT, is more than EUR 175 or the equivalent in national currency, fixed annually by applying the conversion rate obtaining on the first working day of October with effect from 1 January of the following year.

    However, Member States may exempt a supply with a total value of less than the amount specified in point (c) of the first subparagraph.

2. For the purposes of paragraph 1, "a traveler who is not established within the Community" shall mean a traveler whose permanent address or habitual residence is not located within the Community. In that case "permanent address or habitual residence" means the place entered as such in a passport, identity card or other document recognized as an identity document by the Member State within whose territory the supply takes place.

    Proof of exportation shall be furnished by means of the invoice or other document in lieu thereof, endorsed by the customs office of exit from the Community.

Each Member State shall send to the Commission specimens of the stamps it uses for the endorsement referred to in the second subparagraph. The Commission shall forward that information to the tax authorities of the other Member States.

Chapter 7 Exemptions Related to International Transport

Article 148 [Vessels, fighting ships and aircrafts]

[Exemption with right to deduct input VAT incurred - see article 169]

Member States shall exempt the following transactions:

- (a) the supply of goods for the **fuelling** and **provisioning** of **vessels** used for navigation on the high seas and **carrying passengers** for reward or used for the purpose of **commercial, industrial** or **fishing activities**, or for **rescue** or **assistance** at sea, or for inshore **fishing**, with the exception, in the case of vessels used for inshore fishing, of ships' provisions;

- (b) the supply of goods for the **fuelling** and **provisioning** of **fighting ships**, falling within the combined nomenclature (CN) code 8906 10 00, leaving their territory and bound for ports or anchorages outside the Member State concerned;

- (c) the **supply, modification, repair, maintenance, chartering** and **hiring** of the **vessels** referred to in point (a) and the **supply, hiring, repair** and **maintenance** of **equipment**, including fishing equipment, incorporated or used therein;

- (d) the supply of services other than those referred to in point (c), to meet the direct needs of the **vessels** referred to in point (a) or of their cargoes;

- (e) the supply of goods for the fuelling and provisioning of **aircraft** used by airlines operating for reward chiefly on international routes;

(f) the **supply, modification, repair, maintenance, chartering** and **hiring** of the **aircraft** referred to in point (e), and the **supply, hiring, repair** and **maintenance** of **equipment** incorporated or used therein;

(g) the supply of services, other than those referred to in point (f), to meet the direct needs of the aircraft referred to in point (e) or of their cargoes.

Article 149 [Portugal]

[Exemption with right to deduct input VAT incurred - see article 169]

Portugal may treat **sea** and **air transport** between the islands making up the autonomous regions of the **Azores** and **Madeira** and between those regions and the **mainland** as international transport.

Article 150

1. The Commission shall, where appropriate, as soon as possible, present to the Council proposals designed to delimit the scope of the exemptions provided for in Article 148 and to lay down the detailed rules for their implementation.

2. Pending the entry into force of the provisions referred to in paragraph 1, Member States may limit the scope of the exemptions provided for in points (a) and (b) of Article 148.

Chapter 8 Exemptions Relating to Certain Transactions treated as Exports

Article 151 [Personal exemptions]

[Exemption with right to deduct input VAT incurred - see article 169]

1. Member States shall exempt the following transactions:

    (a) the supply of goods or services under **diplomatic** and **consular** arrangements;

    (aa) the supply of goods or services to the European Community, the European Atomic Energy Community, the European Central Bank or the European Investment Bank, or to the bodies set up by the Communities to which the Protocol of 8 April 1965 on the privileges and immunities of the European Communities applies, within the limits and under the conditions of that Protocol and the agreements for its implementation or the headquarters agreements, in so far as it does not lead to distortion of competition;

    (b) the supply of goods or services to **international bodies**, other than those referred to in point (aa), recognized as such by the public authorities of the host Member States, and to members of such bodies, within the limits and under the conditions laid down by the international conventions establishing the bodies or by headquarters agreements;

    (c) the supply of goods or services within a Member State which is a party to the **North Atlantic Treaty**, intended either for the armed forces of other States party to that Treaty for the use of those forces, or of the civilian staff accompanying them, or for supplying their messes or canteens when such forces take part in the common defense effort;

(d) the supply of goods or services to another Member State, intended for the **armed forces** of any State which is a party to the North Atlantic Treaty, other than the Member State of destination itself, for the use of those forces, or of the civilian staff accompanying them, or for supplying their messes or canteens when such forces take part in the common defense effort;

(e) the supply of goods or services to the **armed forces** of the United Kingdom stationed in the island of Cyprus pursuant to the Treaty of Establishment concerning the Republic of Cyprus, dated 16 August 1960, which are for the use of those forces, or of the civilian staff accompanying them, or for supplying their messes or canteens.

Pending the adoption of common tax rules, the exemptions provided for in the first subparagraph shall be subject to the limitations laid down by the host Member State.

2. In cases where the goods are not dispatched or transported out of the Member State in which the supply takes place, and in the case of services, the exemption may be granted by means of a refund of the VAT.

Article 152 [Gold to Central Banks]

[Exemption with right to deduct input VAT incurred - see article 169]

Member States shall exempt the supply of **gold** to **central banks**.

Chapter 9 Exemptions for the Supply of Services by Intermediaries

Article 153 [Services by intermediaries]

[Exemption with right to deduct input VAT incurred - see article 169]

Member States shall exempt the supply of **services by intermediaries**, acting in the name and on behalf of another person, where they take part in the transactions referred to in Chapters 6, 7 and 8, or of transactions carried out outside the Community.

The exemption referred to in the first paragraph shall not apply to travel agents who, in the name and on behalf of travelers, supply services which are carried out in other Member States.

Chapter 10 Exemptions for Transactions relating to International Trade

Section 1: Customs warehouses, warehouses other than customs warehouses and similar arrangements

Article 154 [Definition of warehouses other than customs warehouses]

For the purposes of this Section, "**warehouses other than customs warehouses**" shall, in the case of products subject to excise duty, mean the places defined as tax warehouses by Article 4(b) of Directive 92/12/EEC and, in the case of products not subject to excise duty, the places defined as such by the Member States.

Article 155

Without prejudice to other Community tax provisions, Member States may, after consulting the VAT Committee, take special measures designed to exempt all or some of the transactions referred to in this Section, provided that those measures are not aimed at final use or consumption and that the amount of VAT due on cessation of the arrangements or situations referred to in this Section corresponds to the amount of tax which would have been due had each of those transactions been taxed within their territory.

Article 156

[Exemption with right to deduct input VAT incurred]

1. Member States may exempt the following transactions:

    (a) the supply of goods which are intended to be presented to **customs** and, where applicable, placed in **temporary storage**;

    (b) the supply of goods which are intended to be placed in a **free zone or in a free warehouse**;

    (c) the supply of goods which are intended to be placed under **customs warehousing arrangements or inward processing arrangements**;

    (d) the supply of goods which are intended to be admitted into **territorial waters** in order to be incorporated into drilling or production platforms, for purposes of the construction, repair, maintenance, alteration or fitting-out of such platforms, or to link such drilling or production platforms to the mainland;

(e) the supply of goods which are intended to be admitted into territorial waters for the fuelling and provisioning of drilling or production platforms.

2. The places referred to in paragraph 1 shall be those defined as such by the Community customs provisions in force.

Article 157

1. Member States may exempt the following transactions:

   (a) the **importation** of goods which are intended to be placed under **warehousing arrangements** other than customs warehousing;

   (b) the supply of goods which are intended to be placed, within their territory, under **warehousing** arrangements other than customs warehousing. *[Exemption with right to deduct input VAT incurred]*

2. Member States may not provide for warehousing arrangements other than customs warehousing for goods which are not subject to excise duty where those goods are intended to be supplied at the retail stage.

Article 158

[Exemption with right to deduct input VAT incurred]

1. By way of derogation from Article 157(2), Member States may provide for warehousing arrangements other than customs warehousing in the following cases:

   (a) where the goods are intended for tax-free shops, for the purposes of the supply of goods to be carried in the personal luggage of travelers taking flights or sea crossings to third territories or third countries, where that supply is exempt pursuant to point (b) of Article 146(1);

   (b) where the goods are intended for taxable persons, for the purposes of carrying out supplies to travelers on board an aircraft or a ship in the course of a flight or sea crossing where the place of arrival is situated outside the Community;

(c) where the goods are intended for taxable persons, for the purposes of carrying out supplies which are exempt from VAT pursuant to Article 151.

2. Where Member States exercise the option of exemption provided for in point (a) of paragraph 1, they shall take the measures necessary to ensure the correct and straightforward application of this exemption and to prevent any evasion, avoidance or abuse.

3. For the purposes of point (a) of paragraph 1, "**tax-free shop**" shall mean any establishment which is situated within an airport or port and which fulfills the conditions laid down by the competent public authorities.

Article 159

[Exemption with right to deduct input VAT incurred]

Member States **may** exempt the supply of services relating to the supply of goods referred to in Article 156, Article 157(1)(b) or Article 158.

Article 160

[Exemption with right to deduct input VAT incurred]

1. Member States **may** exempt the following transactions:

    (a) the supply of goods or services carried out in the locations referred to in Article 156(1), where one of the situations specified therein still applies within their territory;

    (b) the supply of goods or services carried out in the locations referred to in Article 157(1)(b) or Article 158, where one of the situations specified in Article 157(1)(b) or in Article 158(1) still applies within their territory.

2. Where Member States exercise the option under point (a) of paragraph 1 in respect of transactions effected in customs warehouses, they shall take the measures necessary to provide for warehousing arrangements other than customs warehousing under which point (b) of paragraph 1 may be applied to the same transactions when they concern goods listed in Annex V and are carried out in warehouses other than customs warehouses.

Article 161

[Exemption with right to deduct input VAT incurred]

Member States **may** exempt supply of the following goods and of services relating thereto:

(a) the supply of goods referred to in the first paragraph of Article 30 while they remain covered by arrangements for temporary importation with total exemption from import duty or by external transit arrangements;

(b) the supply of goods referred to in the second paragraph of Article 30 while they remain covered by the internal Community transit procedure referred to in Article 276.

Article 162

Where Member States exercise the option provided for in this Section, they shall take the measures necessary to ensure that the intra-Community acquisition of goods intended to be placed under one of the arrangements or in one of the situations referred to in Article 156, Article 157(1)(b) or Article 158 is covered by the same provisions as the supply of goods carried out within their territory under the same conditions.

Article 163

If the goods cease to be covered by the arrangements or situations referred to in this Section, thus giving rise to importation for the purposes of Article 61, the Member State of importation shall take the measures necessary to prevent double taxation.

Section 2: Transactions exempted with a view to export and in the framework of trade between the Member States

Article 164

[Exemption with right to deduct input VAT incurred]

1. Member States **may**, after consulting the VAT Committee, exempt the following transactions carried out by, or intended for, a taxable person up to an amount equal to the value of the exports carried out by that person during the preceding 12 months:

    (a) intra-Community acquisitions of goods made by the taxable person, and imports for and supplies of goods to the taxable person, with a view to their exportation from the Community as they are or after processing;

    (b) supplies of services linked with the export business of the taxable person.

2. Where Member States exercise the option of exemption under paragraph 1, they shall, after consulting the VAT Committee, apply that exemption also to transactions relating to supplies carried out by the taxable person, in accordance with the conditions specified in Article 138, up to an amount equal to the value of the supplies carried out by that person, in accordance with the same conditions, during the preceding 12 months.

Article 165

Member States may set a common maximum amount for transactions which they exempt pursuant to Article 164.

Section 3: Provisions common to Sections 1 and 2

Article 166

The Commission shall, where appropriate, as soon as possible, present to the Council proposals concerning common arrangements for applying VAT to the transactions referred to in Sections 1 and 2.

Comments to Title IX RVD: Exemptions

A - Comments

A1 – General

When analyzing a specific transaction in order to determine it's VAT treatment, before arriving to the present point you should have determined:

If the Persons involved in the transaction qualify Taxable Persons

If the transaction itself qualities as a Taxable Transaction

In which country the transaction is located.

Now is the moment to determine whether there is an exemption that would apply for the transaction you are analyzing. This will allow you to understand whether VAT is due or not in the supply in question. Indeed, if no VAT exemption applies then, *a contrario sensu* , VAT is due meaning that it has to be determined both the VAT rate applicable and who is liable for VAT.

It worth pointing out that the exemption also have an important effect on the VAT recoverability rights of the supplier. In this respect, the exemption can be qualified as "good" exemption and "bad" exemption. In a "good" exemption, the supplier despite doing an exempt supply (i.e. not obliged to charge VAT to the acquirer) he still is entitled to recover the input VAT he bore (e.g. VAT related to COGS or SG&A). A "bad" exemption does not allow the supplier to recover the input VAT he paid.

A2 – Good Exemptions

A2.1 - Introduction

By "good" exemptions we mean the VAT exemption that allow the supplier to keep a full deductibility right in relation to the input VAT incurred on the related cost. Meaning if the company supplies goods or services subject to good exemptions, it will be allowed to keep 100% of the input VAT incurred linked to such goods/services. Good exemptions are:

- Exportation

- Intra-community supply

- Other exemptions linked to international trades and connected services.

Please Note: This also applies to the supply of services carried out by intermediaries acting in the name and on behalf of another person taking part of the supplies above or of transactions carried out outside the Community. However it will not apply to travel agents who, in the name and on behalf of travelers, supply services which are carried out in other member-States.

A2.2 - Exemption on Exportations

This exemption includes:

- The supply of goods dispatched or transported to a destination outside the

Community by or on behalf of a customer not established within their respective territory, with the exception of goods transported by the customer himself for the equipping, fueling and provisioning of pleasure boats and private aircraft or any other means of transport for private use. Note that Where such supply is related to goods to be carried in the personal luggage of travelers, this exemption shall apply only if the traveller is not resident within the EU;

- The supply of goods to approved bodies which export them out of the Community as part of their humanitarian, charitable or teaching activities outside the Community;

- The supply of services consisting in work on movable property acquired or imported for the purpose of undergoing such work within the Community, and dispatched or transported out of the Community by the supplier, by the customer if not established within their respective territory or on behalf of either of them;

- The supply of services, including transport and ancillary transactions, but excluding the supply of services exempted as financial services or as (for instance) charity purposes, where these are directly connected with the exportation or importation of goods covered by (for instance) temporary importation arrangements.

A2.3 - Exemption on Intra-community supplies

One of the most important "shall" rules foreseen in the RVD states that member-States shall exempt the Intra-community Supplies, i.e., supply of goods dispatched or transported to a destination outside their respective territory but within the Community, by or on behalf of the vendor or the person acquiring the goods, for another taxable person, or for a nontaxable legal person acting as such in a Member State other than that in which dispatch or transport of the goods began.

This exemption rule is extended to the following (not exhaustive):

- Transfer of inventory to another EU MS,

- The supply of new means of transport, dispatched or transported to the customer at a destination outside their respective territory but within the Community, by or on behalf of the vendor or the customer, for taxable persons, or non-taxable legal persons, or any other non-taxable person,

- Under certain conditions to be met, the supply of products subject to excise duty, dispatched or trans- ported to a destination outside their respective territory but within the Community, to the customer, by or on behalf of the vendor or the customer, for taxable persons, or nontaxable legal persons, whose intra-Community acquisitions of goods other than products subject to excise duty are not subject to VAT

It does, however, not apply to:

- Supplies to taxable person covered by the special scheme for small business

- In case where the customer is and the customer is a non-taxable legal person (e.g. public bodies, agricultural business subject to the common flat-rate scheme), or any other non-taxable person (e.g., an individual)

A.2.4 - Other exemptions linked to international trade and connected service

I - General

The last "good" exemptions are related to International Trade and Connected services. This refer, specifically to the following:

- Some supplies related to vessels and aircrafts.
- Supplies to diplomatic bodies
- Supplies to EU institutions.
- Supplies to NATO.
- Supply of gold.

II - Specifically

More specifically, these exemptions can be listed as follows.

- The supply of goods for the fueling and provisioning, the supply, modification, repair, maintenance, chartering and hiring and any other supply of services to meet the direct needs of: (i) Aircraft used by airlines operating for reward chiefly on international route; (ii) Vessels used for navigation on the high seas and carrying passengers for reward or used for the purpose of commercial, industrial or fishing activities, or for rescue or assistance at sea, or for inshore fishing, with the exception, in the case of vessels used for inshore fishing, of ships' provisions;
- The supply of goods or services under diplomatic and consular arrangements,
- The supply of goods or services to the European Community,
- The supply of goods or services to the European Atomic Energy Community,
- The supply of goods or services to the European Central Bank or the European Investment Bank, or
- The supply of goods or services to the bodies set up by the Communities to which the Protocol of 8 April 1965 on the privileges and immunities of the European Communities applies, within the limits and under the conditions of that Protocol and the agreements for its implementation or the headquarters agreements, in so far as it does not lead to distortion of competition;
- The supply of goods or services to international bodies, other than those referred above, recognized as such by the public authorities of the host member-States, and to members of such bodies, within the limits and under the conditions laid down by the international conventions establishing the bodies or by head-quarters agreements;
- The supply of goods or services within a MS which is a party to the NATO;
- Supply of gold to central banks.

A3. – Bad Exemption

A3.1 - Introduction

By bad exemptions it is meant the VAT exemptions that do not allow the supplier to deduct the input VAT incurred on the related cost. Meaning if the company supplies goods or services subject to bad exemptions, it will NOT be allowed to recover the input VAT it incurred regarding to COGS and SG&A linked to the providing of such goods or services:

The RVD list the following as bad exemptions:

- Financial services
- Management of investment funds
- Insurance and reinsurance services
- Sales and letting of immovable property
- Others

Regarding the Financial services and the re-insurance services, it is important to note that in case these are provided to customers outside the EU, they are considered as an Export and fall into the "Good" exemptions category.

In some cases, the RVD authorizes the member-States to grant taxable persons the option to tax some of the above exemptions. We will deal with this further ahead in the subsequent point.

A3.2 - Option to Tax

As mentioned, the RVD includes a "may" clause, according to which member-States may grant taxable persons the option to tax some of the following "bad" exemptions:

- Financial transactions
- Management of investment funds
- Exemptions related to immovable property

In such cases (where the Member State provides the tax payer with the option to tax) the supplier, if he so wishes and fulfills the conditions the member-States determines, may treat the transaction as a non exempt transaction. This means that the supplier will collect VAT from its customer. On the other hand it also means that the input VAT, that the supplier spent in order to perform the transaction, can be offset against the VAT output of the transaction. This makes the transaction neutral for the supplier (while if this was not possible, the input VAT would be a cost for him) and is fully in line with the underlying principles of VAT.

A3.3 - Financial Services

The RVD lists the following as financial services:

- The granting and the negotiation of credit and the management of credit by the person granting it;
- The negotiation of or any dealings in credit guarantees or any other security for money and the management of credit guarantees by the person who is granting the credit;
- Transactions, including negotiation, concerning deposit and current accounts, payments, transfers, debts, cheques and other negotiable instruments, but excluding

debt collection;

- Transactions, including negotiation, concerning currency, bank notes and coins used as legal tender, with the exception of collectors' items, that is to say, gold, silver or other metal coins or bank notes which are not normally used as legal tender or coins of numismatic interest;
- Transactions, including negotiation but not management or safekeeping, in shares, interests in companies or associations, debentures and other securities, but excluding documents establishing title to goods, and the right or securities over immovable property that could be regarded as tangible property by the member-States

Do note that, as mentioned above, this is only a "bad" exemption if services are provided to customers in the EU. If these services are provided to customers outside the EU, they are considered as an Export and fall into the "Good" exemptions category.

A3.4 - Management of investment funds

The RVD makes a direct link to the legislation of the member-States, relying on their definition of what is Investment Funds.

This means that a certain transaction may be exempt in one country (at the transaction qualifies as a management of an investment fund as defined by the law of that country) while it is not exempt in another country.

Some examples of what can be considered as activity of management of investment funds is:

- Daily portfolio management;
- Investment research and advice;
- Maintenance of accounting records;
- Calculation of NAV (Net Asset Value);
- Issuance and repurchase of securities, as well as other administrative services.

A3.5 - (Re)Insurance transactions

According to the RVD, insurance and reinsurance transactions, including related services performed by insurance brokers and insurance agents are exempt.

The concept of "insurance" is a generally accepted one according to which "the insurer undertakes, in return for a prior payment of a premium, to provide the insured, in the event of materialization of the risk covered, with the service agreed when the contract was concluded"

Important to note that the exemption also applies to supplies performed by trader and insurance intermediaries. Also of relevance to note that for the purposes of VAT insurance transactions can be provided by other taxable person than insurance companies.

Also do note that, as mentioned above, this is only a "bad" exemption if services are provided to customers in the EU. If these services are provided to customers outside the

EU, they are considered as an Export and fall into the "Good" exemptions category.

A3.6 - Immovable Property

I - Rule

The definition of transactions involving immovable property, for this purpose, includes:

- The supply of a building or parts thereof, and of the land on which it stands, but not before its first occupation
- The supply of land which has not been built on other than the supply of building land
- The leasing or letting of immovable property.

II - Exceptions

Regarding the leasing or letting of immovable property, the exemption does not apply to the following (non-exhaustive):

- The provision of accommodation usually dedicated to temporary accommodation such as,
- hotel, motel or sectors with a similar function,
- in holiday camps
- camping sites
- The letting of premises and sites for the parking of vehicles;
- The letting of permanently installed equipment and machinery;
- The hire of safes.

A3.7 - Other bad exemptions

Other bad exemptions foreseen in the RVD include:

- The supply at face value of postage stamps valid for use for postal services within their respective territory, fiscal stamps and other similar stamps
- Betting, lotteries and other forms of gambling, subject to the conditions and limitations laid down by each Member State.

B – Implementation measures (see Regulation 282/2011)

SECTION 1

Exemptions for certain activities in the public interest

(Articles 132, 133 and 134 of Directive 2006/112/EC)

Article 44

Vocational training or retraining services provided under the conditions set out in point

(i) of Article 132(1) of Directive 2006/112/EC shall include instruction relating directly to a trade or profession as well as any instruction aimed at acquiring or updating knowledge for vocational purposes. The duration of a vocational training or retraining course shall be irrelevant for this purpose.

Guidance notes: This article provides that the exemption from VAT for vocational training and retraining services includes instruction relating directly to a trade or profession, as well as any instruction aimed at acquiring or updating knowledge for vocational purposes. The duration of a vocational training or retraining course is irrelevant.

SECTION 2

Exemptions for other activities

(Articles 135, 136 and 137 of Directive 2006/112/EC)

Article 45

The exemption provided for in point (e) of Article 135(1) of Directive 2006/112/EC shall not apply to platinum nobles.

Guidance notes: This article provides that the VAT exemption in respect of transactions, including negotiation, concerning currency, bank notes and coins used as legal tender does not apply to platinum nobles.

SECTION 3

Exemptions on importation

(Articles 143, 144 and 145 of Directive 2006/112/EC)

Article 46

The exemption provided for in Article 144 of Directive 2006/112/EC shall apply to transport services connected with the importation of movable property carried out as part of a change of residence.

Guidance notes: This article provides that the exemption provided for in Article 144 of the VAT Directive relating to importation of goods applies to transport services connected with the importation of movable property carried out as part of a change of residence.

SECTION 4

Exemptions on exportation

(Articles 146 and 147 of Directive 2006/112/EC)

Article 47

'Means of transport for private use' as referred to in point (b) of Article 146(1) of Directive 2006/112/EC shall include means of transport used for non-business purposes by persons other than natural persons, such as bodies governed by public law within the meaning of Article 13 of that Directive and associations.

Guidance notes: This article provides that 'means of transport for private use' as referred to in point (b) of Article 146(1) of the VAT Directive includes means of transport used for non-business purposes by persons other than natural persons, such as bodies governed by public law within the meaning of Article 13 of the VAT Directive.

Article 48

In order to determine whether, as a condition for the exemption of the supply of goods carried in the personal luggage of travellers, the threshold set by a Member State in accordance with point (c) of the first subparagraph of Article 147(1) of Directive 2006/112/EC has been exceeded, the calculation shall be based on the invoice value. The aggregate value of several goods may be used only if all those goods are included on the same invoice issued by the same taxable person supplying goods to the same customer.

Guidance notes: This article provides that in order to determine whether, as a condition for the zero rating of the supply of goods carried in the personal luggage of travellers, the threshold set by a Member State has been exceeded, the calculation shall be based on the invoice value. The aggregate value of several goods may be used only if all those goods are included on the same invoice issued by the same taxable person supplying goods to the same customer.

SECTION 5

Exemptions relating to certain transactions treated as exports

(Articles 151 and 152 of Directive 2006/112/EC)

Article 49

The exemption provided for in Article 151 of Directive 2006/112/EC shall also apply to electronic services where these are provided by a taxable person to whom the special scheme for electronically supplied services provided for in Articles 357 to 369 of that Directive applies.

Guidance notes: This article confirms that the exemptions in Article 151 of the VAT Directive also apply to electronic services covered by the special scheme for electronically supplied services (Articles 357 to 369 of the VAT Directive).

Article 50

1. In order to qualify for recognition as an international body for the application of point (g) of Article 143(1) and point (b) of the first subparagraph of Article 151(1) of Directive 2006/112/EC a body which is to be set up as a European Research Infrastructure Consortium (ERIC), as referred to in Council Regulation (EC) No 723/2009 of 25 June 2009 on the Community legal framework for a European Research Infrastructure Consortium (ERIC) (1) shall fulfill all of the following conditions:

(a) it shall have a distinct legal personality and full legal capacity;

(b) it shall be set up under and shall be subject to European Union law;

(c) its membership shall include Member States and, where appropriate, third countries and inter-governmental organizations, but exclude private bodies;

(d) it shall have specific and legitimate objectives that are jointly pursued and essentially non-economic in nature.

2. The exemption provided for in point (g) of Article 143(1) and point (b) of the first subparagraph of Article 151(1) of Directive 2006/112/EC shall apply to an ERIC referred to in paragraph 1 where it is recognized as an international body by the host Member State.

The limits and conditions of such an exemption shall be laid down by agreement between the members of the ERIC in accordance with point (d) of Article 5(1) of Regulation (EC) No 723/2009. Where the goods are not dispatched or transported out of the Member State in which the supply takes place, and in the case of services, the exemption may be granted by means of a refund of the VAT in accordance with Article 151(2) of Directive 2006/112/EC.

Guidance notes: This article sets out the conditions for which a European Research Infrastructure Consortium (ERIC) needs to satisfy in order to benefit from the VAT exemption provided for under Articles 141(1)(g) and 151(1)(b) of the VAT Directive.

Article 51

1. Where the recipient of a supply of goods or services is established within the Community but not in the Member State in which the supply takes place, the VAT and/or excise duty exemption certificate set out in Annex II to this Regulation shall, subject to the explanatory notes set out in the Annex to that certificate, serve to confirm that the transaction qualifies for the exemption under Article 151 of Directive 2006/112/EC.

When making use of that certificate, the Member State in which the recipient of the supply of goods or services is established may decide to use either a common VAT and excise duty exemption certificate or two separate certificates.

2. The certificate referred to in paragraph 1 shall be stamped by the competent authorities of the host Member State. However, if the goods or services are intended for official use, Member States may dispense the recipient from the requirement to have the certificate stamped under such conditions as they may lay down. This dispensation may be withdrawn in the case of abuse.

Member States shall inform the Commission of the contact point designated to identify the services responsible for stamping the certificate and the extent to which they dispense with the requirement to have the certificate stamped. The Commission shall inform the other Member States of the information received from Member States.

3. Where direct exemption is applied in the Member State in which the supply takes place, the supplier shall obtain the certificate referred to in paragraph 1 of this Article from the recipient of the goods or services and retain it as part of his records. If the exemption is granted by means of a refund of the VAT, pursuant to Article 151(2) of Directive 2006/112/EC, the certificate shall be attached to the request for refund submitted to the Member State concerned.

Guidance notes: This article sets out the procedures for the application of the exemptions in Article 151 of the VAT Directive.

C – Guidelines VAT Committee
Meeting 1, 2, 4, 5, 6, 7, 8, 9, 10, 11, 12, 14, 15, 17, 18, 19, 20, 21, 22, 23, 25, 26, 27, 28, 30, 31, 41, 43, 44, 46, 47, 48, 52, 54, 56, 60, 61, 63, 65, 70, 75, 80, 87, 90, 91, 93, 94, 96, 97, 98

Title X Deductions

Chapter 1 Origin and Scope of Right of Deduction

Article 167 [Timing]

A right of deduction shall arise **at the time the deductible tax becomes chargeable**.

Article 167a [Optional Scheme]

Member States may provide within an **optional scheme** that the right of deduction of a taxable person whose VAT solely becomes chargeable in accordance with Article 66(b) be **postponed** until the VAT on the goods or services supplied to him has been paid to his supplier.

Member States which apply the optional scheme referred to in the first paragraph shall set a **threshold** for taxable persons using the scheme within their territory, based on the annual turnover of the taxable person calculated in accordance with Article 288. That threshold may not be higher than EUR 500,000 or the equivalent in national currency. Member States may increase that threshold up to EUR 200,0000 or the equivalent in national currency after consulting the VAT Committee. However, such consultation of the VAT Committee shall not be required for Member States which applied a threshold higher than EUR 500,000 or the equivalent in national currency on 31 December 2012.

Member States shall inform the VAT Committee of national legislative measures adopted pursuant to the first paragraph.

Article 168 [What can be deducted]

In so far as the goods and services are used for the purposes of the taxed transactions of a taxable person, the taxable person shall be entitled, <u>in the Member State in which he carries out these transactions,</u> to **deduct** the following from the VAT which he is liable to pay:

- (a) the **VAT due** or **paid** in that Member State in respect of **supplies to him** of goods or services, carried out or to be carried out by another taxable person;

- (b) the **VAT due** in respect of **transactions treated as supplies of goods or services** pursuant to Article 18 (a)and Article 27;

- (c) the **VAT due** in respect of **intra-Community acquisitions** of goods pursuant to Article 2(1)(b)(i);

- (d) the **VAT due** on transactions **treated as intra-Community acquisitions** in accordance with Articles 21 and 22;

- (e) the **VAT due** or **paid** in respect of the **importation** of goods into that Member State.

Article 168a [Mixed use: proportional deduction]

1. In the case of **immovable property** forming part of the **business assets** of a taxable person and **used both** for purposes of the taxable **person's business** and for his **private use** or that of his staff, or, more generally, for purposes other than those of his business, VAT on expenditure related to this property shall be **deductible** in accordance with the principles set out in Articles 167, 168, 169 and 173 only **up to the proportion** of the property's use for purposes of the taxable person's business.

By way of derogation from Article 26, changes in the proportion of use of immovable property referred to in the first subparagraph shall be taken into account in accordance with the principles provided for in Articles 184 to 192 as applied in the respective Member State.

2. Member States may also apply paragraph 1 in relation to VAT on expenditure related to **other goods** forming part of the business assets as they specify.

Article 169

In addition to the deduction referred to in Article 168, the taxable person shall be entitled to deduct the VAT referred to therein in so far as the goods and services are **used** for the purposes of the following:

(a) **transactions** relating to the **activities** referred to in the second subparagraph of **Article 9(1),** carried out **outside the Member State** in which that tax is due or paid, in respect of which **VAT would be deductible** if they had been carried out within that Member State;

(b) transactions which are **exempt** pursuant to Articles 138, 142 or 144, Articles 146 to 149, Articles 151, 152, 153 or 156, Article 157(1)(b), Articles 158 to 161 or Article 164;

(c) transactions which are **exempt** pursuant to points (a) to (f) of Article 135(1), where the customer is established outside the Community or where those transactions relate directly to goods to be exported out of the Community.

Article 170 [VAT Refunds]

All taxable persons who, within the meaning of Article 1 of Directive 86/560/EEC, Article 2(1) and Article 3 of Directive 2008/9/EC and Article 171 of this Directive, are not established in the Member State in which they purchase goods and services or import goods subject to VAT shall be **entitled to obtain a refund** of that VAT insofar as the goods and services are used for the purposes of the following:

(a) transactions referred to in Article 169;

(b) transactions for which the tax is solely payable by the customer in accordance with Articles 194 to 197 or Article 199.

Article 171 [VAT Refunds]

1. VAT shall be refunded to taxable persons who are not established in the Member State in which they purchase goods and services or import goods subject to VAT but who are established in another Member State, in accordance with the detailed rules laid down in Directive 2008/9/EC.

2. VAT shall be refunded to taxable persons who are not established within the territory of the Community in accordance with the detailed implementing rules laid down in Directive 86/560/EEC.

The taxable persons referred to in Article 1 of Directive 86/560/EEC shall also, for the purposes of applying that Directive, be regarded as taxable persons who are not established in the Community where, in the Member State in which they purchase goods and services or import goods subject to VAT, they have only carried out the supply of goods or services to a person designated in accordance with Articles 194 to 197 or Article 199 as liable for payment of VAT.

3. Directive 86/560/EEC shall not apply to:

(a) amounts of VAT which according to the legislation of the Member State of refund have been incorrectly invoiced;

(b) invoiced amounts of VAT in respect of supplies of goods the supply of which is, or may be, exempt pursuant to Article 138 or Article 146(1)(b).

Article 171a [Deduction as alternative to refund]

Member States may, **instead of granting a refund** of VAT pursuant to Directives 86/560/EEC or 2008/9/EC on those supplies of goods or services to a taxable person in respect of which the taxable person is liable to pay the tax in accordance with Articles 194 to 197 or Article 199, **allow deduction** of this tax pursuant to the procedure laid down in Article 168. The existing restrictions pursuant to Article 2(2) and Article 4(2) of Directive 86/560/EEC may be retained.

To that end, Member States may exclude the taxable person who is liable to pay the tax from the refund procedure pursuant to Directives 86/560/EEC or 2008/9/EC.

Article 172 [Occasional supplies]

1. Any person who is regarded as a taxable person by reason of the fact that he supplies, on an occasional basis, a new means of transport in accordance with the conditions specified in Article 138(1) and (2)(a) shall, in the Member State in which the supply takes place, be entitled to **deduct the VAT** included in the purchase price or paid in respect of the importation or the intra-Community acquisition of this means of transport, up to an amount not exceeding the amount of VAT for which he would be liable if the supply were not exempt.

A right of deduction shall arise and may be exercised only at the **time of supply** of the new means of transport.

2. Member States shall lay down detailed rules for the implementation of paragraph 1.

Chapter 2 Proportional Deduction

Article 173 [Mixed transactions]

1. In the case of goods or services used by a taxable person both for transactions in respect of which VAT is deductible pursuant to Articles 168, 169 and 170, and for transactions in respect of which VAT is not deductible, only such **proportion of the VAT as is attributable to the former transactions shall be deductible**.

The deductible proportion shall be **determined**, in accordance with Articles 174 and 175, for all the transactions carried out by the taxable person.

2. Member States may take the following measures:

    (a) **authorize** the taxable person to **determine** a proportion for each sector of his business, provided that separate accounts are kept for each sector;

    (b) **require** the taxable person to **determine** a proportion for each sector of his business and to keep separate accounts for each sector;

    (c) **authorize or require** the taxable person to **make the deduction** on the basis of the use made of all or part of the goods and services;

    (d) **authorize or require** the taxable person to **make the deduction** in accordance with the rule laid down in the first subparagraph of paragraph 1, in respect of all goods and services used for all transactions referred to therein;

(e) **provide** that, where the VAT which is not deductible by the taxable person **is insignificant**, it is to be treated as **nil**.

Article 174 [Pro-rata]

1. The deductible proportion shall be made up of a fraction comprising the following amounts:

    (a) as numerator, the total amount, exclusive of VAT, of turnover per year attributable to transactions in respect of which VAT is deductible pursuant to Articles 168 and 169;

    (b) as denominator, the total amount, exclusive of VAT, of turnover per year attributable to transactions included in the numerator and to transactions in respect of which VAT is not deductible.

2. Member States may include in the denominator the amount of subsidies, other than those directly linked to the price of supplies of goods or services referred to in Article 73.

3. By way of derogation from paragraph 1, the following amounts shall be excluded from the calculation of the deductible proportion:

    (a) the amount of turnover attributable to supplies of capital goods used by the taxable person for the purposes of his business;

    (b) the amount of turnover attributable to incidental real estate and financial transactions;

    (c) the amount of turnover attributable to the transactions specified in points (b) to (g) of Article 135(1) in so far as those transactions are incidental.

4. 3 Where Member States exercise the option under Article 191 not to require adjustment in respect of capital goods, they may

include disposals of capital goods in the calculation of the deductible proportion.

Article 175 [Pro-rata]

1. The deductible proportion shall be determined on an **annual basis**, fixed as a **percentage** and **rounded up** to a figure not exceeding the next whole number.

2. The provisional proportion for a year shall be that calculated on the **basis of the preceding year's** transactions. In the absence of any such transactions to refer to, or where they were insignificant in amount, the deductible proportion shall be estimated provisionally, under the supervision of the tax authorities, by the taxable person on the basis of his own forecasts.

However, Member States may retain the rules in force at 1 January 1979 or, in the case of the Member States which acceded to the Community after that date, on the date of their accession.

3. Deductions made on the basis of such provisional proportions shall be **adjusted** when the final proportion is fixed during the following year.

Chapter 3 Restrictions on the Right of Deduction

Article 176 [Not deductible]

The Council, acting unanimously on a proposal from the Commission, shall determine the expenditure in respect of which VAT shall not be deductible. **VAT shall in no circumstances be deductible in respect of expenditure which is not strictly business expenditure**, such as that on **luxuries, amusements** or **entertainment**.

Pending the entry into force of the provisions referred to in the first paragraph, Member States may retain all the exclusions provided for under their national laws at 1 January 1979 or, in the case of the Member States which acceded to the Community after that date, on the date of their accession.

Article 177

After consulting the VAT Committee, each Member State may, for **cyclical economic reasons**, totally or partly exclude all or some capital goods or other goods from the system of deductions.

In order to maintain identical conditions of competition, Member States may, instead of refusing deduction, tax goods manufactured by the taxable person himself or goods which he has purchased within the Community, or imported, in such a way that the tax does not exceed the amount of VAT which would be charged on the acquisition of similar goods.

Chapter 4 Rules Governing Exercise of the Right of Deduction

Article 178 [Conditions for deduction]

In order to exercise the right of deduction, a taxable person must meet the following **conditions**:

(a) for the purposes of deductions pursuant to Article 168(a), in respect of the supply of goods or services, he must **hold an invoice** drawn up in accordance with Sections 3 to 6 of Chapter 3 of Title XI;

(b) for the purposes of deductions pursuant to Article 168(b), in respect of transactions treated as the supply of goods or services, he must **comply with the formalities** as laid down by each Member State;

(c) for the purposes of deductions pursuant to Article 168(c), in respect of the intra-Community acquisition of goods, he must **set out in the VAT return** provided for in Article 250 **all the information** needed for the amount of VAT due on his intra-Community acquisitions of goods to be calculated and he must **hold an invoice** drawn up in accordance with Sections 3 to 5 of Chapter 3 of Title XI;

(d) for the purposes of deductions pursuant to Article 168(d), in respect of transactions treated as intra-Community acquisitions of goods, he must complete the **formalities** as laid down by each Member State;

(e) for the purposes of deductions pursuant to Article 168(e), in respect of the **importation of goods**, he must hold an **import document** specifying him as **consignee** or **importer**, and stating the amount of VAT due or enabling that amount to be calculated;

(f) when required to pay VAT as a customer where Articles 194 to 197 or Article 199 apply, he must comply with the **formalities** as laid down by each Member State.

Article 179 [Computing the deduction]

The taxable person shall make the deduction by **subtracting from the total** amount of VAT **due** for a given tax period **the total amount of VAT in respect of which**, during the same period, **the right of deduction has arisen** and is exercised in accordance with Article 178.

However, Member States may require that taxable persons who carry out **occasional transactions**, as defined in Article 12, exercise their right of deduction only at the **time of supply**.

Article 180

Member States may authorize a taxable person to make a deduction which he has not made in accordance with Articles 178 and 179.

Article 181

Member States may authorize a taxable person who does **not hold an invoice** drawn up in accordance with Sections 3 to 5 of Chapter 3 of Title XI to make the deduction referred to in Article 168(c) in respect of his intra-Community acquisitions of goods.

Article 182

Member States shall determine the conditions and detailed rules for applying Articles 180 and 181.

Article 183

Where, for a given tax period, the **amount of deductions exceeds the amount of VAT due**, the Member States may, in accordance with conditions which they shall determine, either **make a refund** or **carry the excess forward** to the following period.

However, **Member States may refuse to refund or carry forward** if the amount of the excess is **insignificant**.

Chapter 5 Adjustment of Deductions

Article 184

The initial deduction shall be **adjusted** where it is higher or lower than that to which the **taxable person was entitled**.

Article 185

1. Adjustment shall, in particular, be made where, after the VAT return is made, some **change** occurs in the **factors** used to determine the amount to be deducted, for example where **purchases are cancelled or price reductions are obtained**.

2. By way of derogation from paragraph 1, **no adjustment** shall be made in the case of transactions remaining **totally or partially unpaid** or in the case of **destruction, loss** or **theft** of property duly **proved** or **confirmed**, or in the case of goods reserved for the purpose of making **gifts** of **small value** or of **giving samples**, as referred to in Article 16.

However, in the case of transactions remaining totally or partially **unpaid** or in the case of **theft**, Member States may require adjustment to be made.

Article 186

Member States shall lay down the detailed rules for applying Articles 184 and 185.

Article 187 [Fixed assets regularization]

1. In the case of **capital goods**, adjustment shall be spread over **five years** including that in which the goods were **acquired** or **manufactured**.

Member States **may**, however, base the adjustment on a period of

five full years starting from the time at which the goods are first used.

In the case of **immovable property** acquired as capital goods, the adjustment period may be **extended up to 20 years.**

2. The annual adjustment shall be made only in respect of **one-fifth of the VAT charged** on the capital goods, or, if the adjustment period has been extended, in respect of the corresponding fraction thereof.

The adjustment referred to in the first subparagraph shall be made on the basis of the variations in the deduction entitlement in subsequent years in relation to that for the year in which the goods were acquired, manufactured or, where applicable, used for the first time.

Article 188

1. If supplied during the adjustment period, **capital goods** shall be treated as if they had been applied to an **economic activity** of the taxable person up until expiry of the adjustment period.

The economic activity shall be presumed to be fully taxed in cases where the supply of the capital goods is taxed.

The economic activity shall be presumed to be fully exempt in cases where the supply of the capital goods is exempt.

2. The adjustment provided for in paragraph 1 shall be made only once in respect of all the time covered by the adjustment period that remains to run. However, where the supply of capital goods is exempt, Member States may waive the requirement for adjustment in so far as the purchaser is a taxable person using the capital goods in question solely for transactions in respect of which VAT is deductible.

Article 189

For the purposes of applying Articles 187 and 188, Member States may take the following measures:

(a) define the concept of capital goods;

(b) specify the amount of the VAT which is to be taken into consideration for adjustment;

(c) adopt any measures needed to ensure that adjustment does not give rise to any unjustified advantage;

(d) permit administrative simplifications.

Article 190

For the purposes of Articles 187, 188, 189 and 191, Member States may regard as capital goods those services which have characteristics similar to those normally attributed to capital goods.

Article 191

If, in any Member State, the practical effect of applying Articles 187 and 188 is negligible, that Member State may, after consulting the VAT Committee, refrain from applying those provisions, having regard to the overall impact of VAT in the Member State concerned and the need for administrative simplification, and provided that no distortion of competition thereby arises.

Article 192

Where a taxable person transfers from being taxed in the normal way to a special scheme or vice versa, Member States may take all measures necessary to ensure that the taxable person does not enjoy unjustified advantage or sustain unjustified harm.

Comments to Title X RVD: Deductions

A – Implementation measures (see Regulation 282/2011)
Article 52
Where the Member State of importation has introduced an electronic system for completing customs formalities, the term '**import document**' in point (e) of Article 178 of Directive 2006/112/EC shall cover electronic versions of such documents, provided that they allow for the exercise of the right of deduction to be checked.
Guidance notes: This article provides that where the Member State of importation has introduced an electronic system for completing customs formalities, the term 'import document' shall cover electronic versions of such documents, provided that they allow for the exercise of the right of deduction to be checked.
C – Guidelines VAT Committee Meeting 8, 9, 10, 11, 13, 14, 15, 16, 18, 22, 23, 24, 27, 28, 29, 32, 50, 94

Title XI - Obligations of Taxable Persons and Certain Non-Taxable Persons

Chapter 1 Obligation to Pay

Section 1 Persons liable for payment of VAT to the tax authorities

Article 192a [Deemed not established]

For the purposes of this Section, a taxable person who has a **fixed establishment** within the territory of the Member State where the tax is due shall be regarded as a taxable person who is not established within that Member State when the following conditions are met:

(a) he makes a **taxable supply** of goods or of services within the territory of that Member State;

(b) an establishment which the supplier has within the territory of that Member State **does not intervene** in that supply.

Article 193

[see article 204]

VAT shall be payable by any taxable person carrying out a taxable supply of goods or services, except where it is payable by another person in the cases referred to in Articles 194 to 199b and Article 202.

Article 194 [Reverse charge – domestic supply of goods & services]

[see article 204]

1. Where the taxable supply of goods or services is carried out by a taxable person who is not established in the Member State in which the VAT is due, Member States may provide that the **person liable for payment of VAT is the person to whom the goods or services are supplied.**

2. Member States shall lay down the conditions for implementation of paragraph 1.

Article 195 [Reverse charge – Gas, electricity & heat or cool]

[see article 204]

VAT shall be **payable** by any person who is **identified for VAT purposes** in the Member State in which the tax is due and to whom goods are supplied in the circumstances specified in Articles 38 or 39, if the supplies are carried out by a taxable person not established within that Member State.

Article 196 [Reverse charge – services rendered by non established person]

[see article 204]

VAT shall be payable by any taxable person, or non-taxable legal person **identified for VAT purposes**, to whom the **services** referred to in Article 44 [supply of services business-to-business general rule] are supplied, if the services are supplied by a taxable person not established within the territory of the Member State.

Article 197 [Reverse charge – Triangulation]

[see articles 43, 141 and 204]

1. VAT shall be payable by the **person to whom the goods are supplied** when the following conditions are met:

(a) the taxable transaction is a **supply of goods** carried out in accordance with the conditions laid down in Article 141 [Triangulation];

(b) the person **to whom** the goods are supplied is another **taxable person**, or a non-taxable legal person, **identified** for VAT purposes in the Member State in which the supply is carried out;

(c) the **invoice** issued by the taxable person not established in the Member State of the person to whom the goods are supplied is drawn up in accordance with Sections 3 to 5 of Chapter 3.

2. Where a tax representative is appointed as the person liable for payment of VAT pursuant to Article 204, Member States **may** provide for a derogation from paragraph 1 of this Article.

Article 198 [Reverse charge – Investment Gold]

1. Where specific transactions relating to **investment gold** between a taxable person who is a **member of a regulated gold bullion market** and **another taxable person who is not a member of that market** are taxed pursuant to Article 352, Member States shall designate the **customer as the person liable** for payment of VAT.

If the customer who is not a member of the regulated gold bullion market is a taxable person required to be identified for VAT purposes in the Member State in which the tax is due solely in respect of the transactions referred to in Article 352, the vendor shall fulfill the tax obligations on behalf of the customer, in accordance with the law of that Member State.

2. Where **gold material** or **semi-manufactured** products of a purity of 325 thousandths or greater, or investment gold as defined in Article 344(1) is supplied by a taxable person exercising one of

the options under Articles 348, 349 and 350, Member States may designate the customer as the person liable for payment of VAT.

3. Member States shall lay down the procedures and conditions for implementation of paragraphs 1 and 2.

Article 199 [Reverse charge – MS options]

1. Member States **may** provide that the person liable for payment of VAT is the taxable person to whom any of the following supplies are made:

   (a) the supply of **construction work**, including repair, cleaning, maintenance, alteration and demolition services in relation to immovable property, as well as the handing over of construction works regarded as a supply of goods pursuant to Article 14(3);

   (b) the **supply of staff** engaged in activities covered by point (a);

   (c) the **supply of immovable property**, as referred to in Article 135(1)(j) and (k), where the supplier has opted for taxation of the supply pursuant to Article 137;

   (d) the **supply of used material**, used material which cannot be re-used in the same state, scrap, industrial and non industrial waste, recyclable waste, part processed waste and certain goods and services, as listed in Annex VI;

   (e) the supply of goods provided as **security** by one taxable person to another in execution of that security;

   (f) the supply of goods following the **cession of a reservation of ownership** to an assignee and the exercising of this right by the assignee;

   (g) the supply of immovable property sold by a judgment debtor in a **compulsory sale procedure**.

2. When applying the option provided for in paragraph 1, Member States may specify the supplies of goods and services covered, and the categories of suppliers or recipients to whom these measures may apply.

3. For the purposes of paragraph 1, **Member States may** take the following measures:

   (a) provide that a taxable person who also carries out activities or transactions that are not considered to be taxable supplies of goods or services in accordance with Article 2 shall be regarded as a taxable person in respect of supplies received as referred to in paragraph 1 of this Article;

   (b) provide that a non-taxable body governed by public law, shall be regarded as a taxable person in respect of supplies received as referred to in points (e), (f) and (g) of paragraph 1.

4. Member States shall inform the VAT Committee of national legislative measures adopted pursuant to paragraph 1 in so far as these are not measures authorized by the Council prior to 13 August 2006 in accordance with Article 27(1) to (4) of Directive 77/388/EEC, and which are continued under paragraph 1 of this Article.

Article 199a

1. Member States may, until 31 December 2018 and for a minimum period of two years, provide that the person liable for payment of VAT is the taxable person to whom any of the following supplies are made

   (a) the **transfer of allowances to emit greenhouse gases** as defined in Article 3 of Directive 2003/87/EC of the European Parliament and of the Council of 13 October 2003 establishing a scheme for greenhouse gas emission allowance trading within the Community, transferable in accordance with Article 12 of that Directive;

(b) the transfer of **other units** that may be used by operators for compliance with the same Directive.

(c) supplies of **mobile telephones**, being devices made or adapted for use in connection with a licensed network and operated on specified frequencies, whether or not they have any other use;

(d) supplies of **integrated circuit** devices such as microprocessors and central processing units in a state prior to integration into end user products;

(e) supplies of **gas** and **electricity** to a taxable dealer as defined in Article 38(2);

(f) supplies of **gas** and **electricity certificates**;

(g) supplies of **telecommunication** services as defined in Article 24(2);

(h) supplies of **game consoles, tablet PC's** and **laptops**;

(i) supplies of **cereals** and **industrial crops** including oil seeds and sugar beet, that are not normally used in the unaltered state for final consumption;

(j) supplies of **raw** and **semi-finished metals**, including precious metals, where they are not otherwise covered by point (d) of Article 199(1), the special arrangements for second-hand goods, works of art, collector's items and antiques pursuant to Articles 311 to 343 or the special scheme for investment gold pursuant to Articles 344 to 356.

1a. Member States may lay down the conditions for the application of the mechanism provided for in paragraph 1.

1b. The application of the mechanism provided for in paragraph 1 to the supply of any of the goods or services listed in points (c) to (j) of that paragraph is **subject to the introduction of appropriate and effective reporting obligations** on taxable persons who supply the goods or services to which the mechanism provided for in paragraph 1 applies.

2. Member States shall inform the VAT Committee of the application of the mechanism provided for in paragraph 1 on the introduction of any such mechanism and shall provide the following information to the VAT Committee:

   (a) the scope of the measure applying the mechanism together with the type and the features of the fraud, and a detailed description of accompanying measures, including any reporting obligations on taxable persons and any control measures;

   (b) actions taken to inform the relevant taxable persons of the introduction of the application of the mechanism;

   (c) evaluation criteria to enable comparison between fraudulent activities in relation to the goods and services listed in paragraph 1 before and after the application of the mechanism, fraudulent activities in relation to other goods and services before and after the application of the mechanism, and any increase in other types of fraudulent activities before and after the application of the mechanism;

   (d) the date of commencement and the period to be covered by the measure applying the mechanism.

3. Member States applying the mechanism provided for in paragraph 1 shall, on the basis of the evaluation criteria provided for under point (c) of paragraph 2, submit a report to the Commission no later than 30 June 2017. The report shall clearly indicate the information to be treated as confidential and the information which may be published.

The report shall provide a detailed assessment of the measure's overall effectiveness and efficiency, in particular as regards:

(a) the impact on fraudulent activities in relation to supplies of goods or services covered by the measure;

(b) the possible shift of fraudulent activities to goods or other services;

(c) the compliance costs for taxable persons resulting from the measure.

4. Each Member State that has detected a shift in trends of fraudulent activities in its territory in relation to the goods or services listed in paragraph 1 from the date of entry into force of this Article with respect to such goods or services, shall submit a report to the Commission in that respect no later than 30 June 2017.

Article 199b [Quick reaction mechanism]

1. A Member State may, in cases of **imperative urgency** and in accordance with paragraphs 2 and 3, designate the recipient as the person liable to pay VAT on specific supplies of goods and services by derogation from Article 193 as a Quick Reaction Mechanism ("QRM") special measure to combat sudden and massive fraud liable to lead to considerable and irreparable financial losses.

The QRM special measure shall be subject to appropriate control measures by the Member State with respect to taxable persons who supply the goods or services to which that measure applies, and shall be for a period not exceeding nine months.

2. A Member State wishing to introduce a QRM special measure as provided for in paragraph 1 shall send a notification to the Commission using the standardized form established in accordance with paragraph 4 and at the same time send it to the other Member States. The Member State shall provide the Commission with the information indicating the sector concerned, the type and the features of the fraud, the existence of imperative grounds of urgency, the sudden and massive

character of the fraud and its consequences in terms of considerable and irreparable financial losses. If the Commission considers it does not have all the necessary information, it shall contact the Member State concerned within two weeks of receipt of the notification and specify what additional information is required. Any additional information provided by the Member State concerned to the Commission shall at the same time be sent to the other Member States. If the additional information provided is not sufficient, the Commission shall inform the Member State concerned thereof within one week.

The Member State wishing to introduce a QRM special measure as provided for in paragraph 1 shall at the same time also make an application to the Commission in accordance with the procedure laid down in Article 395(2) and (3).

3. Once the Commission has all the information it considers necessary for appraisal of the notification referred to in the first subparagraph of paragraph 2, it shall notify the Member States thereof. Where it objects to the QRM special measure, it shall produce a negative opinion within one month of that notification, and shall inform the Member State concerned and the VAT Committee thereof. Where the Commission does not object, it shall confirm this in writing to the Member State concerned and to the VAT Committee within the same time period. The Member State may adopt the QRM special measure from the date of receipt of that confirmation. In appraising the notification, the Commission shall take into account the views of any other Member State sent to it in writing.

4. The Commission shall adopt an implementing act establishing a standardized form for the submission of the notification for the QRM special measure referred to in paragraph 2 and of the information referred to in the first subparagraph of paragraph 2. That implementing act shall be adopted in accordance with the examination procedure referred to in paragraph 5.

5. Where reference is made to this paragraph, Article 5 of Regulation (EU) No 182/2011 of the European Parliament and of the Council shall apply and for this purpose the committee shall be the committee established by Article 58 of Council Regulation (EU) No 904/2010.

Article 200 [Reverse charge – intra-Community acquisitions]

VAT shall be payable by **any person making a taxable intra-Community acquisition** of goods.

Article 201 [Importation]

On **importation**, VAT shall be payable by any person or persons designated or recognized as **liable** by the Member State of **importation**.

Article 202

VAT shall be payable by any person who causes goods to cease to be covered by the arrangements or situations listed in Articles 156, 157, 158, 160 and 161.

Article 203

VAT shall be payable by any person who enters the VAT on an invoice.

Article 204 [Tax representative]

1. Where, pursuant to Articles 193 to 197 [see article 197(2)] and Articles 199 and 200, the person liable for payment of VAT is a taxable person who is not established in the Member State in which the VAT is due, Member States **may** allow that person to appoint a **tax representative** as the person liable for payment of the VAT.

Furthermore, where the taxable transaction is carried out by a taxable person who is not established in the Member State in which the VAT is due and no legal instrument exists, with the country in which that taxable person is established or has his seat, relating to mutual assistance similar in scope to that provided for in Directive 76/308/EEC and Regulation (EC) No 1798/2003, Member States may take measures to provide that the **person liable for payment of VAT is to be a tax representative** appointed by the non-established taxable person.

However, Member States **may not apply** the option referred to in the second subparagraph to a non-established taxable person, within the meaning of point (1) of Article 358 *[special scheme for electronically supplied services]*, who has opted for the special scheme for electronically supplied services.

2. The option under the first subparagraph of paragraph 1 shall be subject to the conditions and procedures laid down by each Member State.

Article 205

In the situations referred to in Articles 193 to 200 and Articles 202, 203 and 204, Member States may provide that a person other than the person liable for payment of VAT is to be held jointly and severally liable for payment of VAT.

Section 2: Payment arrangements

Article 206

Any taxable person liable for payment of VAT must pay the net amount of the VAT when submitting the VAT return provided for in Article 250. Member States may, however, set a different date for payment of that amount or may require interim payments to be made.

Article 207

Member States shall take the measures necessary to ensure that persons who are regarded as liable for payment of VAT in the stead of a taxable person not established in their respective territory, in accordance with Articles 194 to 197 and Articles 199 and 204, comply with the payment obligations set out in this Section.

Member States shall also take the measures necessary to ensure that those persons who, in accordance with Article 205, are held to be jointly and severally liable for payment of the VAT comply with these payment obligations.

Article 208

Where Member States designate the customer for investment gold as the person liable for payment of VAT pursuant to Article 198(1) or if, in the case of gold material, semi-manufactured products, or investment gold as defined in Article 344(1), they exercise the option provided for in Article 198(2) of designating the customer as the person liable for payment of VAT, they shall take the measures necessary to ensure that he complies with the payment obligations set out in this Section.

Article 209

Member States shall take the measures necessary to ensure that non-taxable legal persons who are liable for payment of VAT due in respect of intra-Community acquisitions of goods, as referred to in Article 2(1)(b)(i), comply with the payment obligations set out in this Section.

Article 210

Member States shall adopt arrangements for payment of VAT on intra-Community acquisitions of new means of transport, as referred to in Article 2(1)(b)(ii), and on intra-Community acquisitions of products subject to excise duty, as referred to in Article 2(1)(b)(iii).

Article 211

Member States shall lay down the detailed rules for payment in respect of the importation of goods.

In particular, Member States may provide that, in the case of the importation of goods by taxable persons or certain categories thereof, or by persons liable for payment of VAT or certain categories thereof, the VAT due by reason of the importation need not be paid at the time of importation, on condition that it is entered as such in the VAT return to be submitted in accordance with Article 250.

Article 212

Member States may release taxable persons from payment of the VAT due where the amount is insignificant.

Comments to Title XI RVD, Chapter 1: Obligations to Pay

A - Comments

A1. – General Considerations

The main question of the present Chapter is determining, for a given transaction, when the VAT is due, who is the person responsible for VAT collection, the person and what is the taxable basis of the VAT.

From a practical perspective, you reach this stage after determining who is the Taxable Person, that the transaction qualifies as a taxable transaction, where is the transaction located and that there is no exemption applicable. If all these previous elements check, then it is time to determine who needs to collect the VAT and what is its taxable basis.

Being liable to VAT implies the compliance with certain obligations (VAT registration, payment or deduction of the VAT, submission of VAT related returns, issuance of invoices, collecting the VAT, etc).

The VAT liability is built on one basic rule and a number of exceptions.

In this chapter we will tackle, first, the VAT liability (who is liable for the collection and remaining VAT obligations), then, what is the taxable basis (i.e. what is the amount that serves as a base to multiply by the VAT rate and compute the VAT to be added to the price) and the VAT rate that should be applicable to the taxable basis, and finally what is the moment when VAT should be charged and when is VAT due.

A2. – VAT Liability

A2.1 - Introduction

The first thing to understand about VAT liability is that, contrary to other taxes, the person who is liable for VAT is not necessarily the person who will bear its cost. Being liable in VAT means that the Taxable Person is responsible to charge the VAT to it's customer and deliver that VAT to the Tax Authorities (or offset it when applicable).

The general rule in what concerns VAT liability is that the taxable person carrying out the supply of goods and services (i.e. the supplier) is liable for the VAT. However, a number of exceptions do apply. Meaning that, in practice, the exceptions have to be checked first. In case they do not apply, then the general rule will take place.

When these exceptions take place, the liability will not be with the supplier but someone else, determined in the exception.

In terms of Methodology, our advice is then that when analyzing liability you go first through the exceptions. In case a given transaction is not listed as exception, then the general rule will apply.

A2.2 - General rule

As mentioned above, the general rule regarding VAT liability is that the taxable person responsible to collect and remit the VAT to the tax authorities is the taxable person carrying out a taxable supply of goods or services, unless an exception applies.

In other words, the person that needs to collect and remit is the supplier, unless an exception applies.

In practice, VAT will be a liability of any person who issues an invoice with VAT on it (even if the inclusion of VAT in the invoice was erroneous).

A2.3 - Exceptions

I - Supply of Gas, Electricity and Heat or Cooling

VAT is a liability of the taxable person who is identified for VAT purposes in the Member State in which the VAT is due and to whom goods are supplied under the conditions referred into the place of supply rules for gas, electricity, heat or cooling, as long as the supplies are carried out by a taxable person not established within that Member State.

II - Importation

VAT is a liability of the importer.

III - Supply of Services - B2B

In case of supply of services to which the B2B general rule (regarding place of supply) applies and the supplier is not established in the same Member State as of the recipient, the VAT shall be a liability of the recipient of the services.

In these cases the VAT should be self accounted making use of the reverse-charge mechanism.

IV - Intra-community transactions

In case of intra-community transactions of goods VAT shall be a liability of the taxable person making the Intra-community acquisition.

In these cases the VAT should be self accounted making use of the reverse-charge mechanism.

V - Domestic transactions

While the reverse charge was born as a mechanism to facilitate (and assure the neutrality) of intra-community transactions, it is worth pointing out that some member-States now also apply the concept for internal supplies (i.e., supplies within its territory) - doing what can be called an "internal or domestic reverse charge". This is forecasted in the RVD as a "may" clause and thus needs to be checked on a country-by-country basis. At the current stage only a minority of Countries apply the domestic reverse charge.

VI - Triangulation - simplification rules

An important exception to the general rule on VAT liability are the cases relating to the Triangulation that falls under the Simplification Rules. These are supplies involving a chain with 3 parties located in 3 different EU member-States and where the goods go directly from the first supplier to final destination.

Please be aware the simplification measure is quite strict. In order for it to apply, you need 3 different parties, 3 different member-States and the goods to go directly from the Member State of the first supplier to the Member State of final destination. If any of these conditions are not verified the triangulation simplification measure cannot apply and you are back in the general rule.

In order to understand the simplification measure regarding triangulation, let's take the following example:

- Company "A" (the first supplier), located in EU Member State 1 ("MS1") sells 10 containers of Dog Food to Company "B";
- Company "B" (the Middleman/Intermediate/second supplier) located in Member State 2 ("MS2"), resells the containers to Company "C" located in Member State 3 ("MS3");
- Company "B", instructs Company "A" to deliver the containers in Member State 3, at the warehouse of Company "C".

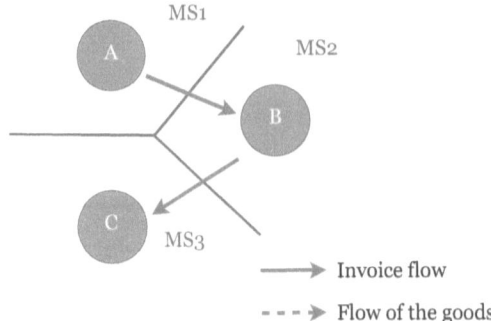

⟶ Invoice flow

- - -▸ Flow of the goods

If the simplification measure did not exist, the consequence of this transaction would be (depending on whether the transport would be connected with the sale from A to B or with the sale from B to C):

ALTERNATIVE 1 (Transport happens in sale from A to B)

Transaction from Company "A" to Company "B" could be qualified as an Intra-community transaction. Thus, company "A" would be exempt of VAT and Company "B" would need to declare this VAT in MS3 as a reverse charge.

Transaction between company "B" and company "C" would qualify as a supply of goods without transport (it would not be intra-community as the goods are not being transported). Thus the transaction would be situated in the place where the goods are located when the supply occurs which would be MS3.

This would mean that Company "B" would need to register in MS3, declare the reverse charge there (regarding the "A" to "B" transaction), charge MS3 VAT to Company "C" (regarding the "B" to "C" transaction) and perform all declarative obligations in MS3.

ALTERNATIVE 2 (transport happens in sale from B to C)

Transaction from Company "A" to Company "B" would be qualified as a supply of goods without transport (it would not be intra-community as the goods are not being transported). Thus the transaction would be situated in the place where the goods are located when the supply occurs which would be MS1. This would mean that Company "A" would need to charge MS1 VAT to Company "B".

Transaction between company "B" and company "C" would qualify as an Intra-community transaction from MS1, and, therefore, Company "B" would need to register in MS1 (even if the transaction would be exempted, there would still be the register and declarative obligations). Moreover, Company "C" would need to declare this VAT in MS3 as a reverse charge.

SIMPLIFICATION RULES

The RVD provides that in cases where a business established in one Member State sells goods to another business established in another Member State which in turn sells the goods to a third business established in a third Member State AND the goods are directly transported from the first Member State to the third Member State, then the third business is designated as the person liable for payment of the VAT, by use of the reverse charge mechanism.

The difference is that, contrary to what would happen if the simplification measures did not exist,"B" do not have to register in a different Member State and comply with the compliance burden derived from that.

DEROGATION TO THE SIMPLIFICATION RULES

Important to notice that the RVD foresees a "may" clause according to which that in case a tax representative is appointed as the person liable for payment of VAT, member-States may provide for a derogation from the simplification rule.

A2.4 - Reverse Charge Mechanism

The term "reverse charge" conveys that the recipient of the goods or services has to self account the VAT due in a given transaction.

Furthermore, please note that the definition of "reverse charge" is a "shall" clause in the RVD, meaning that it applies to all member-States (nevertheless the transactions where the reverse charge mechanism can be used vary, as we will see further ahead).

In practical terms, when the reverse charge applies, the recipient of the goods or services:

- Will receive invoice without VAT

- Will declare the VAT due for such transaction in its VAT return as both input VAT and output VAT.

Therefore the Reverse Charge mechanism has no impact in terms of VAT burden in case the taxable person has full deductibility right.

B – Implementation measures (see Regulation 282/2011)

SECTION 1

Persons liable to pay the VAT

(Articles 192a to 205 of Directive 2006/112/EC)

Article 53

1. For the application of Article 192a of Directive 2006/112/EC, a fixed establishment of the taxable person shall be taken into consideration only when it is characterized by a sufficient degree of permanence and a suitable structure in terms of human and technical resources to enable it to make the supply of goods or services in which it intervenes.

Guidance notes (arts 53 -1.): This paragraph provides that a fixed establishment shall only be taken into consideration when it has the resources available to enable it to make the supply of the goods or services in which it intervenes.

2. Where a taxable person has a fixed establishment within the territory of the Member

State where the VAT is due, that establishment shall be considered as not intervening in the supply of goods or services within the meaning of point (b) of Article 192a of Directive 2006/112/EC, unless the technical and human resources of that fixed establishment are used by him for transactions inherent in the fulfillment of the taxable supply of those goods or services made within that Member State, before or during this fulfillment.

Where the resources of the fixed establishment are only used for administrative support tasks such as accounting, invoicing and collection of debt-claims, they shall not be regarded as being used for the fulfillment of the supply of goods or services.

However, if an invoice is issued under the VAT identification number attributed by the Member State of the fixed establishment, that fixed establishment shall be regarded as having intervened in the supply of goods or services made in that Member State unless there is proof to the contrary.

Guidance notes (arts 53 -1.): This paragraph provides that a fixed establishment shall be considered as not intervening unless the technical and human resources of that fixed establishment are used for the fulfillment of that supply. Intervening may encompass installation, maintenance, technical support, but does not include administrative tasks such as accounting, invoicing, debt collection etc. However, if an invoice issues with the VAT number of the fixed establishment, then that fixed establishment is deemed to have intervened in the supply.

Guidance notes (arts 53 & 54): These articles relate to an intra-Community supply by a taxable person to a customer in a Member State where that supplier has a fixed establishment. Article 192a of the VAT Directive provides that where the fixed establishment in the Member State of the customer does not intervene in an intra-Community supply, and where the place of taxation is the Member State of that customer, then the customer will be liable to pay the tax on a reverse charge basis. If the fixed establishment does intervene in the supply, then the fixed establishment in the Member State of the customer will be required to invoice the customer and account for the VAT.

Article 54

Where a taxable person has established his place of business within the territory of the Member State where the VAT is due, Article 192a of Directive 2006/112/EC shall not apply whether or not that place of business intervenes in the supply of goods or services he makes within that Member State.

Guidance notes: This article provides that where a taxable person is established in a Member State, then Article 192a of the VAT Directive shall not apply. Therefore, all supplies within the Member State of establishment are deemed to be made by that establishment, even where the establishment does not intervene in the supply.

Example:

- TechnoCo UK provides an IT solution to a business customer in Cork. Techno Co has a fixed establishment in Ireland – TechnoCo Ireland.

- If TechnoCo Ireland do not provide any human or technical resources to enable the fulfillment of the supply, and are not envisaged as providing any subsequent support within the terms of the contract, then the supply is deemed to be made by TechnoCo UK, and the business customer in Cork is liable to account for the VAT to Revenue.

- If TechnoCo Ireland provide any services, including human or technical resources, or under the contract are required to provide maintenance or technical support, then TechnoCo Ireland are deemed to be the supplier, and will be required to raise the invoice and account for the VAT to Revenue.

- If TechnoCo Europe is established in Ireland, then irrespective of any intervention in the supply, TechnoCo is required to raise the invoice and account for the VAT.

C – Guidelines VAT Committee
Meeting 8, 9, 10, 52, 62, 86, 88, 91, 94

Chapter 2 Identification

Article 213

1. Every taxable person shall state when his activity as a taxable person commences, changes or ceases.

   Member States shall allow, and may require, the statement to be made by electronic means, in accordance with conditions which they lay down.

2. Without prejudice to the first subparagraph of paragraph 1, every taxable person or non-taxable legal person who makes intra-Community acquisitions of goods which are not subject to VAT pursuant to Article 3(1) must state that he makes such acquisitions if the conditions, laid down in that provision, for not making such transactions subject to VAT cease to be fulfilled.

Article 214

1. Member States shall take the measures necessary to ensure that the following persons are identified by means of an individual number:

   (a) every taxable person, with the exception of those referred to in Article 9(2), who within their respective territory carries out supplies of goods or services in respect of which VAT is deductible, other than supplies of goods or services in respect of which VAT is payable solely by the customer or the person for whom the goods or services are intended, in accordance with Articles 194 to 197 and Article 199;

   (b) every taxable person, or non-taxable legal person, who makes intra-Community acquisitions of goods subject to VAT pursuant to Article 2(1)(b) and every taxable person, or non-taxable legal person, who exercises the option under Article 3(3) of making their intra-Community acquisitions subject to VAT;

(c) every taxable person who, within their respective territory, makes intra-Community acquisitions of goods for the purposes of transactions which relate to the activities referred to in the second subparagraph of Article 9(1) and which are carried out outside that territory.

(d) every taxable person who within their respective territory receives services for which he is liable to pay VAT pursuant to Article 196;

(e) every taxable person, established within their respective territory, who supplies services within the territory of another Member State for which VAT is payable solely by the recipient pursuant to Article 196.

2. Member States **need not identify** certain taxable persons who carry out transactions on an occasional basis, as referred to in Article 12.

Article 215 [Prefix]

Each individual **VAT identification** number shall have a **prefix** in accordance with ISO code 3166 — alpha 2 — by which the Member State of issue may be identified.

Nevertheless, Greece may use the prefix "EL".

Article 216

Member States shall take the measures necessary to ensure that their identification systems enable the taxable persons referred to in Article 214 to be identified and to ensure the correct application of the transitional arrangements for the taxation of intra-Community transactions, as referred to in Article 402.

Chapter 3 Invoicing

Section 1: Definition

Article 217 [Definition of Electronic Invoice]

For the purposes of this Directive, "**electronic invoice**" means an invoice that contains the information required in this Directive, and which has been issued and received in any electronic format.

Comments to art 217

> **A - Explanatory notes to directive 2010/45/EU**
>
> The only purpose for the definition of an electronic invoice is to clarify the acceptance of the customer under Article 232 and to illustrate the use of the option given to Member States in Article 247(2), on the storage of invoices.
>
> An electronic invoice, exactly as it is with a paper invoice, must contain the elements as required by the VAT Directive.
>
> Additionally, for an invoice to be considered according to the VAT Directive to be an electronic invoice, it needs to be issued and also received in any electronic format. The choice of format is determined by the taxable persons. This would include invoices as structured messages (such as XML) or other types of electronic format (such as an email with a PDF attachment or a fax received in electronic not paper format).
>
> According to the definition, not all invoices created in an electronic format can be considered to be an "electronic invoice". Invoices created in an electronic format, through for instance accounting software or by word processing software, that are sent and received on paper are not electronic invoices.
>
> On the other hand invoices created in paper form, that are scanned, sent and received via e-mail can be considered as electronic invoices.
>
> The type of electronic format of the invoice should not be important but only the fact that the invoice is in an electronic format when it is issued and received. This would allow electronic invoices to be sent and received in one format, and then converted in to another format.
>
> An invoice should be regarded as issued when the supplier or a third party acting on behalf of the supplier, or the customer for self-billed invoices, makes the invoice available so that it can be received by the customer. This may mean the electronic invoice is transmitted directly to the customer through for instance email or a secure link, or indirectly through for instance one or several service providers, or that it is made available and accessible to the customer through a web portal or any other method. It is important to establish a date when the invoice is considered to be issued to fulfill the supplier's obligation to issue an invoice within the required period (Article 222) but also for the recipient's obligation in respect of the storage of invoices.

Section 2: Concept of invoice

Article 218 [Obligation to accept invoices paper and electronic]

For the purposes of this Directive, Member States **shall accept** documents or messages on paper or in electronic form as invoices if they meet the conditions laid down in this Chapter.

Article 219 [Documents amending invoices]

Any document or message that amends and refers specifically and unambiguously to the initial invoice shall be treated as an invoice.

Section 3: Issue of invoices

Article 219a

Without prejudice to Articles 244 to 248, the following shall apply:

1. **Invoicing** shall be **subject** to the **rules applying in the Member State in which the supply of goods or services is deemed to be made**, in accordance with the provisions of Title V.

2. By way of **derogation** from point (1), invoicing shall be subject to the rules applying in the Member State in which the supplier has established his business or has a fixed establishment from which the supply is made or, in the absence of such place of establishment or fixed establishment, the Member State where the supplier has his permanent address or usually resides, where:

(a) the supplier is not established in the Member State in which the supply of goods or services is deemed to be made, in accordance with the provisions of Title V, or his establishment in that Member State does not intervene in the supply within the meaning of Article 192a, and the person liable for the payment of the VAT is the person to whom the goods or services are supplied.

However where the customer issues the invoice (self-billing), point (1) shall apply.

(b) the supply of goods or services is deemed not to be made within the Community, in accordance with the provisions of Title V.

Comments to art 219a

A - Explanatory notes to directive 2010/45/EU
Where businesses make supplies to customers in other Member States it may be difficult to establish which Member State's invoicing rules apply. To clarify which rules apply and provide legal certainty for businesses Article 219a is introduced to the VAT Directive.
The objective of Article 219a is to provide clear rules on which Member State should establish the invoicing rules in relation to VAT supplies. These rules exclude those related to the storage of invoices but apply to other invoicing rules regarding the issue, content or simplification measures of invoices when there is an option for the Member State or the invoice requirement relates to a national matter.
For example the option to extend the time period for summary invoices or to require self-billed invoices to be issued in the name and on behalf of the taxable person is at the discretion of Member States. The Member State that applies these and other options is the Member State referred to in Article 219a, unless it is expressly stated elsewhere.
In terms of invoicing requirements such as the national reference for exempt supplies or the currency of the VAT amount, while not options for the Member State, these should still be clarified with reference to a particular Member State. In these and other cases where the appropriate national requirements are needed the relevant Member State should be that referred to in Article 219a.
The basic rule is that the Member State where the supply takes place sets the invoicing rules.
However, there are two exceptions to the basic rule which are contained in Article 219a(2)(a) and (2)(b). These are for cross-border supplies subject to the reverse charge and for supplies taxable outside the EU. In these cases the invoicing rules of the Member State where the supplier is established or has a fixed establishment from which the supply is made or has his permanent address or usually resides shall apply.

Although not exhaustive the tables in annex provide illustrative examples of which Member States' rules apply.

For suppliers not established in the EU making taxable supplies of goods or services in the EU, the exceptions do not apply and the basic invoicing rule always applies, that being the Member State where the supply takes place.

Equally the basic rule will always apply in the case of self-billed invoices where the customer issuing the invoice is also liable to pay the VAT under the reverse charge procedure. Thus the Member State where the supply takes place will set the invoicing rules.

In the case of a supply from a non-EU country to an EU Member State which results in an importation of goods, the place of the supply of the goods is outside the EU. As the supply does not take place within the EU and when the supplier is outside the EU no Member State's invoicing rules will apply. Additionally, there is no invoicing obligation relating to the importation of goods into the EU.

Where the customer is liable for payment of the VAT under the reverse charge procedure and he appoints a tax representative under Article 204 of the VAT Directive, Article 219a(2)(a) should be applied as if the customer was still liable for the payment of VAT. Where in this case the tax representative also issues the invoice it should be treated as if the customer had issued the invoice and so Article 219a(1) will apply.

See following tables:

A - Supply of Goods

Type of supply	Member State of country of supplier	Member State of country of customer	Movement of goods	Member State of country of taxation	Member State of application for Article 219a	Article 219a reference
Domestic supply of goods	A	A	A to A	A	A	Point (1)
Exempt intra-Community supply	A	B	A to B	A	A	Point (1)
Exempt intra-Community supply with self-billed invoice	A	B	A to B	A	A	Point (1)
Distance sales	A	B	A to B	B	B	Point (1)
Cross-border supply to private individual (below threshold for distance sales)	A	B	A to B	A	A	Point (1)
Second leg of an intra-Community triangular supply	B	C	A to C	C	B	Point (2) (a)
Customer liable to pay the VAT under Article 194	A	B	B to B	B	A	Point (2) (a)
Cross-border supply of gas or electricity	A	B	A to B	B	A	Point (2) (a)
Export	A	Third country	A to Third country	A	A	Point (1)
Supply outside the EU	A	Third country	In Third country	Outside EU	A	Point (2) (b)
Import	Third country	A	Third country to A	Outside EU	Outside EU	Point (1)

B - Supply of Services

Type of supply	Article	Member State of country of supplier	Member State of country of customer	Member State of country of taxation	Member State of application for Article 219a	Article 219a reference
General B2B supply of services	44	A	A	A	A	Point (1)
Cross-border B2B supply of services	44 and 196	A	B	B	A	Point (2) (a)
Cross-border B2B supply of services and customer issues the invoice	44, 196 and 224	A	B	B	B	Point (1)
General B2C supply of services	45	A	B	A	A	Point (1)
Services connected with immovable property (property in Member State C, no reverse charge)	47	A	B	C	C	Point (1)
B2B services for customer outside the EU	44	A	Third country	Third country	A	Point (2) (b)
Certain B2C services for customer outside the EU	59	A	Third country	Third country	A	Point (2) (b)

Article 220 [Cases where invoice needs to be issued]

1. Every taxable person shall ensure that, in respect of the following, an **invoice is issued**, either by himself or by his customer or, in his name and on his behalf, by a third party:

    (1) supplies of goods or services which he has made to another taxable person or to a non-taxable legal person;

    (2) supplies of goods as referred to in Article 33;

    (3) supplies of goods carried out in accordance with the conditions specified in Article 138;

    (4) any payment on account made to him before one of the supplies of goods referred to in points (1) and (2) was carried out;

    (5) any payment on account made to him by another taxable person or non-taxable legal person before the provision of services was completed.

2. By way of derogation from paragraph 1, and without prejudice to Article 221(2), the **issue of an invoice shall not be required** in respect of supplies of services exempted under points (a) to (g) of Article 135(1).

Article 220a [Simplified invoice]

1. Member States shall allow taxable persons to issue a simplified invoice in any of the following cases:

    (a) where the amount of the invoice is **not higher than EUR 100** or the equivalent in national currency;

    (b) where the invoice issued is a document or message treated as an invoice pursuant to Article 219 *[documents amending invoices]*.

2. Member States shall **not allow** taxable persons to issue a **simplified invoice** where invoices are required to be issued pursuant to points (2) and (3) of Article 220(1) or where the taxable supply of goods or services is carried out by a taxable person who is not established in the Member State in which the VAT is due, or whose establishment in that Member State does not intervene in the supply within the meaning of Article 192a, and the person liable for the payment of VAT is the person to whom the goods or services are supplied.

Article 221 [Option to impose/release obligation to issuance of invoice]

1. Member States **may impose** on taxable persons an **obligation to issue an invoice** in accordance with the details required under Article 226 or 226b in respect of supplies of goods or services other than those referred to in Article 220(1).

2. Member States **may impose** on taxable persons who have established their business in their territory or who have a fixed establishment in their territory from which the supply is made, an **obligation to issue an invoice** in accordance with the details required in Article 226 or 226b in respect of supplies of services exempted under points (a) to (g) of Article 135(1) which those taxable persons have made in their territory or outside the Community.

3. Member States **may release** taxable persons from the obligation laid down in Article 220(1) or in Article 220a to **issue an invoice** in respect of [i] supplies of goods or services which they have made in their territory and [ii] which are exempt, with or without deductibility of the VAT paid in the preceding stage, pursuant to Articles 110 and 111, Article 125(1), Article 127, Article 128(1), Article 132, points (h) to (l) of Article 135(1), Articles 136, 371, 375, 376 and 377, Articles 378(2) and 379(2) and Articles 380 to 390c

Comments to arts 220 and 221

A - Explanatory notes to directive 2010/45/EU

Article 220 (2) and 221 (2)

Background:

In general invoices are required for taxable supplies between taxable persons, with the option for Member States to allow certain exempt supplies to be released from this invoicing obligation.

Directive 2010/45/EU for supplies of services exempt under points (a) to (g) of Article 135(1) changes the rules so that these supplies no longer require an invoice (Article 220(2)) but Member States may, if they choose, impose an invoicing obligation.

The invoice can be required only where the supplier is established in that Member State and the place of taxation is there, or it is supplied outside the EU.

Comments:

Member States may not require an invoice for supplies exempt under points (a) to (g) of Article 135(1) when the supplier – established in their territory or who has a fixed establishment in their territory from which the supply is made – makes such a supply taxable in another Member State.

When the place of taxation and the establishment of the supplier making the supply are in the same Member Sate then for B2B and B2C supplies that Member State may require an invoice.

In conclusion the option in Article 221(2) can be used for domestic supplies and supplies outside the EU but not in respect of B2B transactions with other Member States.

Article 221 (3)

Background:

Article 219a establishes which Member State's invoicing rules apply. However, Article 221(3) provides invoicing options for Member States when the supply takes place in that Member State. This raises an issue where two rules combine, such as that between Article 219a which sets which Member State's invoicing rules apply and Article 221(3) which allows other Member States to apply options.

Comments:

For a cross-border exempt supply mentioned in Article 221(3) for which the supplier is not established in the Member State where the supply takes place (A) and the customer is liable for payment of the VAT (reverse charge) the Member State where the supplier is established (B) sets the invoicing rules (Article 219a(2)(a)). However, the Member State where the supply is made (A) may release the taxable person from issuing an invoice (Article 221(3)). Since in this case that Member State (A) is not the Member State that sets the invoicing rules (B), there will always be a requirement to issue an invoice for these supplies.

In the above case the mention "reverse charge" according to Article 226(11a) should be mentioned on the invoice (see also document reference C3).

> Only when the exempt supply mentioned in Article 221(3) is made in the same Member State that sets the invoicing rules in Article 219a, may that Member State release the taxable person from issuing an invoice.
>
> In conclusion these cross-border B2B exempt supplies will always require an invoice.

Article 222 [timing to issue invoice]

For supplies of goods carried out in accordance with the conditions specified in Article 138 [*intra-Community supplies*] or for supplies of **services** for which VAT is payable by the customer pursuant to Article 196, an invoice shall be issued no later than on the **fifteenth day** of the month following that in which the chargeable event occurs.

For **other supplies** of goods or services Member States may impose **time limits** on taxable persons for the issue of invoices.

Article 223 [Summary invoices]

Member States shall allow taxable persons to issue **summary invoices** which detail several separate supplies of goods or services provided that VAT on the supplies mentioned in the summary invoice becomes chargeable during the same calendar month.

Without prejudice to Article 222, Member States may allow summary invoices to include supplies for which VAT has become chargeable during a period of time longer than one calendar month.

Article 224 [Self-billing]

Invoices may be **drawn up by the customer** in respect of the supply to him, by a taxable person, of goods or services, where there is a prior agreement between the two parties and provided that a procedure exists for the acceptance of each invoice by the taxable person supplying the goods or services. Member State may require that such invoices be issued in the name and on behalf of the taxable person.

Comments to art 224

A - Explanatory notes to directive 2010/45/EU

Background:

The rules on self-billed invoices should have a more uniform application with the removal of many of the options and conditions that Member States can apply. Although the condition for a prior agreement between the buyer and seller as well as a procedure for acceptance of each invoice remains, the reference to the Member State determining those terms and conditions is deleted. Thus clarification on what is meant by prior agreement and acceptance of each invoice is now required.

Comments:

The terms and conditions of the prior agreement and the acceptance procedures for each invoice between the supplier and the customer as laid down in Article 224 shall be determined by the two parties.

Member States cannot prescribe the type of agreement between the two parties.

Nevertheless, a "prior" agreement means that the agreement is made before the commencement of issuing self-billed invoices. Also, on request from the tax authorities the two parties must be able to show that a prior agreement existed. With this in mind, it is recommended that for the legal certainty of the trading parties evidence of the prior agreement is kept.

The acceptance procedure of each invoice can be explicit or implicit. It can be agreed and described through the prior agreement or it can be evidenced through the processing of the invoice or the receipt of payment by the supplier of the goods or services.

Article 225

Member States may impose specific conditions on taxable persons in cases where the **third party**, or the **customer**, who issues invoices is established in a country with which no legal instrument exists relating to mutual assistance similar in scope to that provided for in Directive 2010/24/EU and Regulation (EC) No 1798/2003.

Section 4: Content of invoices

Article 226 [Content of the invoice]

Without prejudice to the particular provisions laid down in this Directive, only the **following details are required** for VAT purposes on invoices issued pursuant to Articles 220 and 221:

(1) the **date** of issue;

(2) a **sequential number**, based on one or more series, which uniquely identifies the invoice;

(3) the **VAT identification** number referred to in Article 214 under which the taxable person supplied the goods or services;

(4) the **customer's VAT identification** number, as referred to in Article 214, under which the customer received a supply of goods or services in respect of which he is liable for payment of VAT, or received a supply of goods as referred to in Article 138;

(5) the **full name** and **address** of the **taxable person** and of the **customer**;

(6) the **quantity** and **nature** of the **goods** supplied or the **extent** and **nature** of the **services** rendered;

(7) the **date** on which the **supply** of goods or services **was made** or **completed** or the date on which the **payment on account** referred to in points (4) and (5) of Article 220 **was made**, in so far as that date can be determined and differs from the date of issue of the invoice;

(7a) where the VAT becomes chargeable at the time when the payment is received in accordance with Article 66(b) and the right of deduction arises at the time the deductible tax becomes chargeable, **the mention "Cash accounting"**;

(8) the **taxable amount** per rate or exemption, the **unit price** exclusive of VAT and any **discounts** or **rebates** if they are not included in the unit price;

(9) the **VAT rate** applied;

(10) the **VAT amount payable**, except where a **special arrangement** is applied under which, in accordance with this Directive, such a detail is excluded;

(10a) where the customer receiving a supply issues the invoice instead of the supplier, the mention **"Self-billing"**;

(11) in the case of an **exemption, reference** to the **applicable provision of this Directive, or** to the corresponding **national provision**, or any other reference indicating that the supply of goods or services is exempt;

(11a) where the **customer is liable** for the payment of the VAT, the mention "**Reverse charge**";

(12) in the case of the **supply of a new means of transport** made in accordance with the conditions specified in Article 138(1) and (2)(a), the **characteristics** as identified in point (b) of Article 2(2);

(13) where the margin scheme for travel agents is applied, the mention "**Margin scheme — Travel agents**";

(14) where one of the special arrangements applicable to second-hand goods, works of art, collectors' items and antiques is applied, the mention "**Margin scheme — Second-hand goods**"; "**Margin scheme — Works of art**" or "**Margin scheme — Collector's items and antiques**" respectively";

(15) where the person liable for payment of VAT is a **tax representative** for the purposes of Article 204, the **VAT identification number**, referred to in Article 214, **of that tax representative**, together with his full name and address.

Comments to arts 226

A - Explanatory notes to directive 2010/45/EU

226 (2) - Sequential numbering

The sequential number required in Article 226(2) to uniquely identify the invoice may be based on one or more series of numbers, which may include as well alphanumeric characters. The choice of using a different series of numbers lies with the business and it may be used for instance for each branch, or for each type of supply or for each customer, and covers as well self-billed invoices or invoices issued by third parties.

Where Member States choose to require sequential numbers for simplified invoices the basis for a different series of numbers remains the same as with a full VAT invoice.

226 (7a) - Cash accounting

The cash accounting scheme allows the supplier to declare the VAT in the tax period in which the payment for the supplies of goods or services is received or made. In order for the customer to know when his VAT becomes deductible the supplier should mention on the invoice that he is using the "Cash accounting" scheme.

There are two conditions to be fulfilled for the supplier to mention "Cash accounting" on the invoice.

1. The supplier meets the conditions and is applying the cash accounting scheme.

2. For the customer of a taxable person applying such a cash accounting scheme, the right

to deduct VAT arises at the moment the tax is due by the supplier.

226 (11) - Cash accounting

The taxable person has the choice for exempt supplies (Note: exempt supplies are also in some cases referred to as "zero-rated" when there is a right to deduct VAT) to mention a reference to the appropriate article in the VAT Directive or national law, but may also choose to provide any other reference that shows the supply is exempt. In the case where the taxable person chooses to provide any other reference, the word "Exempt" shall be sufficient as the reference that a supply of goods or services is exempt. Other wording as appropriate may also be used.

When the supply is subject to the reverse charge, and that supply is also an exempt supply in the Member State of taxation, it is sufficient to only mention the wording "Reverse charge" as contained in Article 226(11a).

Article 226a [Invoice issued by non established person]

Where the invoice is **issued by a taxable person, who is not established in the Member State** where the tax is due or whose establishment in that Member State **does not intervene** in the supply within the meaning of Article 192a, and who is making a supply of goods or services to a customer who is liable for payment of VAT, the taxable person **may omit the details referred to** in points (8), (9) and (10) of Article 226 and instead **indicate**, by reference to the **quantity** or **extent** of the goods or services supplied and their **nature**, the **taxable amount** of those goods or services.

Article 226b [Content of simplified invoices]

As regards **simplified invoices** issued pursuant to Article 220a and Article 221(1) and (2), Member States shall require at least the following details:

(a) the **date** of issue;

(b) **identification** of the taxable **person supplying** the goods or services;

(c) **identification** of the **type of goods** or **services** supplied;

(d) the **VAT amount** payable or the information needed to calculate it;

(e) where the invoice issued is a document or message treated as an invoice pursuant to Article 219, **specific** and **unambiguous reference** to that **initial invoice** and the **specific details** which are **being amended**.

They may not require details on invoices other than those referred to in Articles 226, 227 and 230.

Comments to arts 226b

A - **Explanatory notes to directive 2010/45/EU**

The contents of simplified invoices that taxable persons may issue should contain at least the details in Article 226b but not all the details in Article 226, otherwise the objective of reducing burdens on business is not met. More details on a simplified invoice than those required in Article 226 is not allowed.

This will apply in the case of simplified invoices allowed under Article 220a for amounts lower than EUR 100 or for credit notes, under Article 238 after Member States have consulted the VAT Committee and under Articles 221(1) and (2) for B2C supplies or exempt insurance and financial supplies.

However, simplified invoices cannot be allowed for distance sales, exempt intra-Community supplies of goods or for cross-border reverse charge supplies (Articles 220a(2) and 238(3)).

Article 227

Member States may require taxable persons established in their territory and supplying goods or services there to indicate the VAT identification number, referred to in Article 214, of the customer in cases other than those referred to in point (4) of Article 226.

Article 228

[Deleted]

Article 229 [Signature not required]

Member States shall not require invoices to be signed.

Article 230 [Currency on invoice]

The amounts which appear on the invoice may be expressed in **any currency**, provided that the **amount of VAT payable** or to be adjusted is **expressed in the national currency** of the Member State, using the conversion rate mechanism provided for in Article 91.

Comments to arts 230

A - Explanatory notes to directive 2010/45/EU
Where the VAT amount on the invoice is converted into the national currency as required by Article 230 and this is done using the exchange rate published by the European Central Bank (ECB), a Member State that requires this notification may only require one notification before the taxable person begins to use the rate of the ECB.
A taxable person is not required to apply the conversion rate of the ECB to all invoices even where the Member State requires notification for use of the ECB rate.

> Article 230 does not allow any requirement for a reference on the invoice, such as the exchange rate used or the method of conversion, as these would be details above those required in Article 226.

Article 231

[Deleted]

Section 5: Paper invoices and electronic invoices

Article 232 [Requirement for use of electronic invoice]

The use of an electronic invoice shall be subject to acceptance by the recipient.

Article 233 [Ensuring authenticity, integrity and legibility of invoice]

1. The **authenticity of the origin**, the **integrity of the content** and the **legibility** of an invoice, whether on paper or in electronic form, **shall be ensured** from the point in time of issue until the end of the period for storage of the invoice.

Each **taxable person** shall **determine the way** to ensure the authenticity of the origin, the integrity of the content and the legibility of the invoice. This may be achieved by any **business controls** which create a reliable audit trail between an invoice and a supply of goods or services.

"**Authenticity of the origin**" means the assurance of the identity of the supplier or the issuer of the invoice.

"**Integrity of the content**" means that the content required according to this Directive has not been altered.

2. Other than by way of the type of business controls described in paragraph 1, the following are **examples** of technologies that ensure the authenticity of the origin and the integrity of the content of an electronic invoice:

   (a) an **advanced electronic signature** within the meaning of point (2) of Article 2 of Directive 1999/93/EC of the European Parliament and of the Council of 13 December 1999 on a Community framework for electronic signatures, based on a qualified certificate and created by a secure signature creation device, within the meaning of points (6) and (10) of Article 2 of Directive 1999/93/EC;

   (b) **electronic data interchange** (EDI), as defined in Article 2 of Annex 1 to Commission Recommendation 1994/820/EC of 19 October 1994 relating to the legal aspects of electronic data interchange, where the agreement relating to the exchange provides for the use of procedures guaranteeing the authenticity of the origin and integrity of the data.

Comments to art 233

A - Explanatory notes to directive 2010/45/EU

A1. 233(1) first and second subparagraphs - Legibility

Legibility of an invoice means that the invoice is human readable. It must remain so until the end of the storage period. The invoice should be presentable in a style where all the VAT contents of the invoice are clearly readable, on paper or on screen, without the need for excessive scrutiny or interpretation, e.g. EDI messages, XML messages and other structured messages in the original format are not considered human readable (after a conversion process they may be considered human readable – see below).

For electronic invoices, this condition will be considered as being fulfilled if the invoice can be presented on request within a reasonable time in the same manner as is required without delay in Article 245(1) – including after a conversion process – in a human readable form on screen or through printing. It should be possible to check the information between the original electronic file and the readable document presented has not changed.

In order to ensure legibility, a suitable and reliable viewer for the e-invoice format should be available throughout the entire storage period.

The legibility of an electronic invoice from the point of issue until the end of the period of storage can be ensured by any means, but advanced electronic signatures and EDI, as mentioned in Article 233(2) are not sufficient by themselves to ensure legibility.

A1. 233(1) first subparagraph - Point in time of issue and end of storage period

The period for which the authenticity of the origin, the integrity of the content and the legibility of the invoice must be ensured is from the time of issue until the end of the storage period. The storage period is that determined by the Member State according to the VAT Directive (Article 247). The deadline for the time of issue of an invoice is also that determined by the VAT Directive (Article 222).

At all moments between the time of issue and the end of the storage period the taxable person must be able to ensure the authenticity of the origin, the integrity of the content and the legibility of the invoice. However, as business practices change over time, the means by which the authenticity of the origin, the integrity of the content and the legibility of the invoice are ensured can also change.

A2. 233(1) Second paragraph - Choice of means of ensuring the authenticity of origin, integrity of content and legibility

Both the supplier and customer are free to choose how to ensure the authenticity of the origin, the integrity of the content and the legibility of the invoice. The choice should not be restricted by Member States.

Where Member States provide guidance it should be made clear that this only represents guidance and it does not restrict the choice of the taxable person.

The three examples of procedures or technologies listed in Directive 2010/45/EU (business controls creating a reliable audit trail, advanced electronic signatures and EDI), should not prevent other technologies or procedures from being used if they meet the conditions of ensuring the authenticity of the origin, the integrity of the content and the legibility of the invoice.

A3. 233(1) Second paragraph - Business controls

Business control is a wide concept. It is the process created, implemented and kept up to date by those responsible (management, personnel and owners) for providing reasonable assurance on financial, accounting and regulatory reporting and that legal requirements are complied with.

Specifically, in the context of Article 233, it should be taken to mean the process by which a taxable person has created, implemented and kept up to date a reasonable level of assurance on the identity of the supplier or issuer of the invoice (authenticity of the origin), that the VAT content has not been altered (integrity of the content) and the legibility of the invoice from the moment of issue until the end of the storage period.

The business controls should be appropriate to the size, activity and type of taxable person and should take account of the number and value of transactions as well as the number and type of suppliers and customers. Where relevant other factors should also be taken into consideration.

An example of a business control is the matching of supporting documents. The importance attached to supporting documents should reflect factors such as the degree of independence of the issuer of the supporting documents from the taxable person and the weight attached to those documents in the accounting process. An important aspect of this type of business control is that the invoice is checked as a document within the business and accounting process and is not treated as an independent stand alone document.

It is important to keep in mind that invoices, whether paper or electronic, are generally only one document in a set of documents (e.g. purchase order, contract, transport document, payment notice etc.) related to and documenting a transaction.

For the supplier, the invoice could be matched with a purchase order, transport documents and receipt of payment. For the customer, the invoice could be matched with the approved purchase order (purchase confirmation note), the delivery note, the payment and remittance advice. However, these are only examples of typical documents that may be available and many other documents could be matched with the invoice.

A4. 233(1) Second paragraph - Reliable audit trail

Within accounting, an audit trail can be described as a documented flow of a transaction from initiation, the source document such as a purchase order, to completion, such as the final recording in the annual accounts, and vice versa, that provides links between the various documents in the process. An audit trail includes source documents, processed transactions and references to the link between the two.

An audit trail can be described as reliable when the link between supporting documents and processed transactions is easy to follow (through having sufficient detail to link the documents), compliant with stated procedures and reflects the processes that have actually occurred. This can be achieved with for example third party documents e.g.

bank statements, documents from the customer or supplier (second party documents) and internal controls e.g. segregation of duties.

For VAT purposes an audit trail should, as stipulated in the second subparagraph of Article 233(1), provide an auditable link between an invoice and a supply of goods or services to enable the checking of whether an invoice reflects that a supply of goods or services has taken place.

The means by which a taxable person can demonstrate the link between an invoice and a supply of goods or services is left to the discretion of the taxable person. The Member State may issue guidance to help the taxable person establish a reliable audit trail but this guidance must not include any mandatory requirements. An example could be a set of different documents such a purchase order, transport documents and the invoice itself with the trace of the matching of those documents or even the mere fact that the three documents actually match.

As with business controls, a reliable audit trail should be appropriate to the size, activity and type of taxable person and should take account of the number and value of transactions as well as the number and type of suppliers and customers. Where relevant other factors should also be taken into consideration, such as requirements for financial reporting and auditing.

A5. 233(1) Third paragraph - Authenticity of origin

The authenticity of the origin of an invoice is an obligation for the taxable person receiving the supply of goods or services as well as for the taxable person making the supply. Both can independently of each other ensure the authenticity of the origin.

There are four elements to be considered.

1. Assurance by the supplier

The supplier must be able to provide assurance that the invoice was indeed issued by him or in his name and on his behalf. This can be achieved by having a record of the invoice in the accounting documents. Where there is self-billing or a third party issues the invoice this may be evidenced through supporting documents.

2. Assurance by the customer

The taxable person receiving the supply must be able to ensure that the invoice received is from the supplier or the issuer of the invoice.

This gives two alternatives to the taxable person to choose from. The first alternative concerns verifying the correctness of the information concerning the supplier's identity mentioned on an invoice. The second alternative concerns ensuring the identity of the issuer of the invoice.

a) Assurance of the identity of the supplier

The identity of the supplier is a detail that is always required on the invoice. This, though, is not sufficient in itself to assure the authenticity of the origin. The customer should in this case ensure that the supplier mentioned on the invoice has in reality carried out the supply of the goods or services to which the invoice refers. The taxable person can apply any business controls creating a reliable audit trail between an invoice and a supply of goods or services to fulfill this obligation.

b) Assurance of the identity of the issuer of the invoice

The taxable person can choose to ensure the identity of the issuer of an invoice by for example an advanced electronic signature or EDI. Nevertheless, this is without prejudice to recital 10 of Directive 2010/45/EU which states, first and foremost, that invoices should reflect actual supplies.

Assuring the identity of the issuer of the invoice can apply equally to cases where the supplier has issued the invoice as well as to those where a third party has issued the invoice or in the case of self-billing

A6. 233(1) Fourth paragraph - Integrity of content

The invoice content for which integrity must be ensured is that defined in the VAT Directive.

The integrity of the content of an invoice is an obligation for both the taxable person making the supply as well as for the taxable person receiving the supply. They can both independently of each other choose the way in which they fulfill this obligation, or they can agree together through for instance a certain technology like EDI or advanced electronic signatures, to ensure the content is unchanged. The taxable person can choose whether he applies, for example, business controls which create a reliable audit trail between an invoice and a supply or specific technologies in fulfilling the obligation.

That the content of the invoice has not been altered (integrity of the content) does not relate to the format of an electronic invoice. Providing that the invoice content as required by the VAT Directive is not changed, the format in which such content is held may be converted to other formats. This allows the customer or a service provider acting on his behalf, to convert or present in a different way the electronic data in order to fit with his own IT system or because of technological changes over time.

In the case where the taxable person has chosen to fulfill the requirement of integrity of the content by using an advanced electronic signature, when converting from one format to another, the change must be recorded in an audit trail.

Even if Member States use the option in Article 247(2) to require that the invoice is kept in the original form, either paper or electronic, the format of an invoice can in any case still be changed.

Form is taken to mean the type of invoice (paper or electronic) and format relates to the presentation of the electronic invoice. A format change can for instance be a change to the way the date is presented e.g. dd/mm/yy to yyyy/mm/dd, or of the file type itself e.g. XML

A6. 233(2) - Advanced electronic signature and EDI

The two options, an advanced electronic signature and EDI, are only examples of electronic invoicing technologies to ensure the authenticity of the origin and the integrity of the content and cannot be mandatory requirements. Where electronic invoices do not meet the conditions of Article 233(2)(a) or (b) they may still meet the requirements of business controls in the second subparagraph of Article 233(1) or may fulfill the condition of authenticity of the origin and integrity of the content through an alternative technology (including for instance advanced electronic signatures which are not based on a qualified certificate) or procedure.

EDI is based on an agreement to exchange structured data in accordance with

Commission Recommendation 1994/820/EC and can refer to any standardized format. It does not refer only to EDIFACT, which is just one example of such formats.

Article 234

[Deleted]

Article 235 [MS specific conditions for Electronic invoices]

Member States may lay down **specific conditions** for electronic invoices issued in respect of goods or services supplied in their territory **from a country with which no legal instrument exists** relating to mutual assistance similar in scope to that provided for in Directive 2010/24/EU and Regulation (EC) No 1798/2003.

Article 236 [Rule for batches of invoices]

Where batches containing several electronic invoices are sent or made available to the same recipient, the details common to the individual invoices may be mentioned only once where, for each invoice, all the information is accessible.

Article 237

By 31 December 2016 at the latest, the Commission shall present to the European Parliament and the Council an overall assessment report, based on an independent economic study, on the impact of the invoicing rules applicable from 1 January 2013 and notably on the extent to which they have effectively led to a decrease in administrative burdens for businesses, accompanied where necessary by an appropriate proposal to amend the relevant rules.

Section 6: Simplification measures

Article 238

1. After consulting the VAT Committee, Member States may, in accordance with conditions which they may lay down, provide that in the following cases only the information required pursuant to Article 226b shall be entered on invoices in respect of supplies of goods or services:

    (a) where the amount of the invoice is higher than EUR 100 but not higher than EUR 400, or the equivalent in national currency;

    (b) where commercial or administrative practice in the business sector concerned or the technical conditions under which the invoices are issued make it particularly difficult to comply with all the obligations referred to in Article 226 or 230.

2. [Deleted]

3. The simplified arrangements provided for in paragraph 1 shall not be applied where invoices are required to be issued pursuant to points (2) and (3) of Article 220(1) or where the taxable supply of goods or services is carried out by a taxable person who is not established in the Member State in which the VAT is due or whose establishment in that Member State does not intervene in the supply within the meaning of Article 192a and the person liable for the payment of VAT is the person to whom the goods or services are supplied.

Article 239

In cases where Member States make use of the option under point (b) of the first subparagraph of Article 272(1) of not allocating a VAT identification number to taxable persons who do not carry out any of the transactions referred to in Articles 20, 21, 22, 33, 36, 138 and 141, and where the supplier or the customer has not been allocated an identification number of that type, another number called the tax reference number, as defined by the Member States concerned, shall be entered on the invoice instead.

Article 240

Where the taxable person has been allocated a VAT identification number, the Member States exercising the option under point (b) of the first subparagraph of Article 272(1) may also require the invoice to show the following:

>   (1) in respect of the supply of services, as referred to in Articles 44, 47, 50, 53, 54 and 55, and the supply of goods, as referred to in Articles 138 and 141, the VAT identification number and the tax reference number of the supplier;

>   (2) in respect of other supplies of goods or services, only the tax reference number of the supplier or only the VAT identification number.

Comments to Title XI RVD, Chapter 3: Invoicing

A - Explanatory notes to directive 2010/45/EU

Invoices must reflect actual supply (Reference: Recital 10 of Directive 2010/45/EU)

Invoices must reflect actual supplies and their authenticity, integrity and legibility should therefore be ensured. Business controls can be used to establish reliable audit trails linking invoices and supplies, thereby ensuring that any invoice (whether on paper or in electronic form) complies with those requirements.

Comments:

Recital 10 mentions that an invoice must reflect an actual supply and, therefore, the authenticity of the origin, integrity of content and legibility should be ensured. It is up to each taxable person to ensure that the invoice information being exchanged accurately reflects an actual supply. How this is done is the choice of the taxable person.

Business controls creating a reliable audit trail between an invoice and a supply can be one way by establishing a reliable audit trail linking invoices and supplies. As well, the text of Article 233(2) states that the taxable person can fulfill his obligation to ensure the authenticity of the origin and integrity of the content, for example, by using those technologies mentioned in that paragraph: an advanced electronic signature or electronic data interchange (EDI). These technologies cannot, though, of themselves show a supply took place. The choice of methods to fulfill these obligations lies according to Article 233 on the taxable person.

Chapter 4 Accounting

Section 1: Definition

Article 241 [Definition of storage of an invoice by electronic means]

For the purposes of this Chapter, "**storage of an invoice by electronic means**" shall mean storage of data using electronic equipment for processing (including digital compression) and storage, and employing wire, radio, optical or other electromagnetic means.

Section 2: General obligations

Article 242 [Keep accounts]

Every taxable person shall keep accounts in sufficient detail for VAT to be applied and its application checked by the tax authorities.

Article 243 [Register and accounts regarding goods transported or dispatched]

1. Every taxable person shall keep a **register of the goods dispatched** or **transported** by him, or on his behalf, to a destination outside the territory of the Member State of departure but within the Community **for the purposes of** transactions consisting in **valuations** of those goods or **work on them** or their **temporary use** as referred to in points (f), (g) and (h) of Article 17(2).

2. Every taxable person shall **keep accounts** in sufficient detail to enable the **identification of goods dispatched** to him from another Member State, by or on behalf of a taxable person identified for VAT purposes in that other Member State, and used for services consisting in **valuations of those goods** or **work on those goods**.

Section 3: Specific obligations relating to the storage of all invoices

Article 244 [Obligation to Store]

Every taxable person shall ensure that **copies** of the invoices issued by himself, or by his customer or, in his name and on his behalf, by a third party, and all the invoices which he has received, **are stored**.

Article 245 [Place of storage]

1. For the purposes of this Directive, the taxable person may decide the **place of storage** of all invoices provided that he makes the invoices or information stored in accordance with Article 244 available to the competent authorities without undue delay whenever they so request.

2. Member States may require taxable persons established in their territory to notify them of the place of storage, if it is outside their territory.

Member States may also require taxable persons established in their territory to store within that territory invoices issued by themselves or by their customers or, in their name and on their behalf, by a third party, as well as all the invoices that they have received, when the storage is not by electronic means guaranteeing full on-line access to the data concerned.

Article 246

[Deleted]

Article 247 [Storage Period]

1. Each Member State shall determine the **period** throughout which taxable persons must ensure the storage of invoices relating to the supply of goods or services in its territory and invoices received by taxable persons established in its territory.

2. In order to ensure that the requirements laid down in Article 233 are met, the Member State referred to in paragraph 1 **may require that invoices be stored in the original form** in which they were sent or made available, whether paper or electronic. Additionally, in the case of invoices stored by electronic means, the Member State may require that the **data guaranteeing the authenticity** of the origin of the invoices and the **integrity** of their **content**, as provided for in Article 233, also **be stored by electronic means**.

3. The Member State referred to in paragraph 1 may lay down **specific conditions** prohibiting or restricting the storage of invoices in a country with which no legal instrument exists relating to mutual assistance similar in scope to that provided for in Directive 2010/24/EU and Regulation (EC) No 1798/2003 or to the right referred to in Article 249 to access by electronic means, to download and to use.

Comments to art. 247

A - Explanatory notes to directive 2010/45/EU
247 (1) - Storage period
The period of storage of invoices is set by Member States according to Article 247(1). Article 219a does not apply as regards the storage of invoices.
The Member State may only set the storage period for the supplier of goods or services when the place of supply is in that Member State. A supplier making supplies taxable in another Member State, such as under the reverse charge procedure, should comply with the storage rules in the Member State where the supply takes place.

> In addition, for a taxable person receiving supplies, the invoice storage period is set by the Member State where that business is established.
>
> 247 (2) – Medium of Storage
>
> Article 247(2) allows Member States to require that the storage of invoices is kept in the original form in which they were sent. This means paper invoices can be required to be stored in paper form and electronic invoices in electronic form.
>
> For electronic invoices it does not prevent the format being changed, which may often be required due to the evolution of storage technologies. Any format change must meet the requirements referred to in Article 233(1).
>
> Where invoices are stored by electronic means, Article 247(2) allows Member States to require that the data guaranteeing the authenticity of the origin, the integrity of the content and legibility of the invoice is also stored by electronic means. Where the taxable person uses an advanced electronic signature or EDI the data guaranteeing the authenticity of origin and integrity of content will be that associated with those particular technologies.
>
> Where the taxable person uses business controls which create a reliable audit trail between the invoice and the supply of goods or services, the data referred to is that of the supporting documents. However, under Article 233 it is the choice of business how to guarantee the authenticity of origin and integrity of content.
>
> Where invoices are kept in paper form the taxable person may choose to keep supporting documents electronically but the tax authorities cannot oblige him to do so. Equally, supporting documents kept in electronic form cannot be required to be held in paper form.
>
> Taxable persons may as a part of their business control keep the checks they perform between the supporting documents and invoice but this is not a requirement for VAT purposes.

Article 248

Member States **may**, subject to conditions which they lay down, require the storage of invoices received by non-taxable persons.

Article 248a [Language and translation of invoices]

For control purposes, and as regards invoices in respect of supplies of goods or services supplied in their territory and invoices received by taxable persons established in their territory, Member States **may**, for certain taxable persons or certain cases, **require translation into their official languages**. **Member States may, however, not impose a general requirement that invoices be** translated.

Comments to art. 248a

A - Explanatory notes to directive 2010/45/EU
Language used on invoices
The VAT legislation does not prescribe the use of any language. Where a language is used other than a national language the Member State must not restrict the right of deduction only because of the language used on the invoice. Translations can however be requested in certain cases during an audit.
Translation of invoices Regarding the option in Article 248a for Member States to require the translation of invoices, this should relate only to the specific invoices or to invoices of specific taxable persons that need to be checked for control purposes. Member States cannot implement in advance any general obligation that all invoices, for instance of a certain type or by a certain taxable person, are translated in to a national language.

Section 4: Right of access to invoices stored by electronic means in another Member State

Article 249 [Right of access]

For control purposes, where a taxable person stores, by electronic means guaranteeing online access to the data concerned, invoices which he issues or receives, the competent authorities of the Member State in which he is established and, where the VAT is due in another Member State, the competent authorities of that Member State, shall have the **right to access, download and use those invoices.**

Chapter 5 Returns

Article 250 [*VAT Return*]

1. Every taxable person shall submit a **VAT return** setting out all the information needed to calculate the tax that has become chargeable and the deductions to be made including, in so far as is necessary for the establishment of the basis of assessment, the total value of the transactions relating to such tax and deductions and the value of any exempt transactions.

2. Member States shall **allow**, and **may require**, the VAT return referred to in paragraph 1 to be submitted by **electronic means**, in accordance with conditions which they lay down.

Article 251 [Content of VAT return]

In addition to the information referred to in Article 250, the VAT return covering a given tax period shall show the following:

   (a) the **total value**, exclusive of VAT, of the **supplies** of goods referred to in Article 138 in respect of which VAT has become chargeable during this tax period;

   (b) the **total value**, exclusive of VAT, of the **supplies** of goods referred to in Articles 33 and 36 carried out within the territory of another Member State, in respect of which VAT has become chargeable during this tax period, where the place where dispatch or transport of the goods began is situated in the Member State in which the return must be submitted;

   (c) the **total value**, exclusive of VAT, of the **intra-Community acquisitions** of goods, or transactions treated as such, pursuant to Articles 21 or 22, made in the Member State in which the return must be submitted and in respect of which VAT has become chargeable during this tax period;

(d) the **total value**, exclusive of VAT, of the supplies of goods referred to in Articles 33 and 36 carried out in the Member State in which the return must be submitted and in respect of which VAT has become chargeable during this tax period, where the place where dispatch or transport of the goods began is situated within the territory of another Member State;

(e) the **total value**, exclusive of VAT, of the supplies of goods carried out in the Member State in which the return must be submitted and in respect of which the taxable person has been designated, in accordance with Article 197, **as liable for payment** of VAT and in respect of which VAT has become chargeable during this tax period.

Article 252 [Deadline VAT return & tax period]

1. The VAT return shall be submitted by a **deadline** to be determined by Member States. That deadline **may not be more** than **two months after the end of each tax period.**

2. The **tax period** shall be set by each Member State at **one month, two months** or **three months.**

Member States may, however, set **different tax periods** provided that those periods do **not exceed one year**.

Article 253

Sweden may apply a simplified procedure for small and medium-sized enterprises, whereby taxable persons carrying out only transactions taxable at national level may submit VAT returns **three months after the end of the annual direct tax period.**

Article 254 [Obligations of vendor in supply of new means of transport]

In the case of supplies of **new means of transport** carried out in accordance with the conditions specified in Article 138(2)(a) by a taxable person identified for VAT purposes for a customer not identified for VAT purposes, or by a taxable person as defined in Article 9(2), Member States shall take the measures necessary to ensure that the **vendor communicates all the information needed for VAT** to be applied and its application checked by the tax authorities.

Article 255 [Obligations on Specific cases of self billing]

Where Member States designate the customer of **investment gold** as the person liable for payment of VAT pursuant to Article 198(1) or if, in the case of **gold material, semi-manufactured products** or **investment gold** as defined in Article 344(1), they exercise the option provided for in Article 198(2) of designating the customer as the person liable for payment of VAT, they shall **take the measures necessary to ensure that he complies with the obligations** relating to submission of a VAT return set out in this Chapter.

Article 256

Member States shall take the measures necessary to ensure that persons who are regarded as liable for payment of VAT in the stead of a taxable person not established within their territory, in accordance with Articles 194 to 197 and Article 204, comply with the obligations relating to submission of a VAT return, as laid down in this Chapter.

Article 257

Member States shall take the measures necessary to ensure that non-taxable legal persons who are liable for payment of VAT due in respect of intra-Community acquisitions of goods, as referred to in Article 2(1)(b)(i), comply with the obligations relating to submission of a VAT return, as laid down in this Chapter.

Article 258

Member States **shall** lay down detailed rules for the submission of VAT returns in respect of intra-Community acquisitions of new means of transport, as referred to in Article 2(1)(b)(ii), and intra-Community acquisitions of products subject to excise duty, as referred to in Article 2(1)(b)(iii).

Article 259

Member States **may** require persons who make intra-Community acquisitions of new means of transport as referred to in Article 2(1)(b)(ii), to provide, when submitting the VAT return, all the information needed for VAT to be applied and its application checked by the tax authorities.

Article 260

Member States **shall** lay down detailed rules for the submission of VAT returns in respect of the importation of goods.

Article 261 [*Annual return*]

1. Member States **may** require the taxable person to submit a return showing all the particulars specified in Articles 250 and 251 in respect of **all transactions** carried out in the preceding year. That return shall provide all the information necessary for any adjustments.

2. Member States shall allow, and may require, the return referred to in paragraph 1 to be submitted by electronic means, in accordance with conditions which they lay down.

Chapter 6 Recapitulative Statements

Article 262 [Cases where recapitulative statement is submitted]

Every taxable person identified for VAT purposes shall submit a **recapitulative statement** of the following:

(a) the acquirers identified for VAT purposes to whom he has supplied goods in accordance with the conditions specified in Article 138(1) and (2)(c) [i.e. intra-community transactions];

(b) the persons identified for VAT purposes to whom he has supplied goods which were supplied to him by way of intra-Community acquisitions referred to in Article 42 [i.e., triangulation transactions];

(c) the taxable persons, and the non-taxable legal persons identified for VAT purposes, to whom he has supplied **services, other than services that are exempted** from VAT in the Member State where the transaction is taxable, and for which the recipient is liable to pay the tax pursuant to Article 196.

Article 263 [*Periodicity*]

1. The recapitulative statement shall be drawn up for **each** calendar **month** within a period not exceeding one month and in accordance with procedures to be determined by the Member States.

1a. However, Member States, in accordance with the conditions and limits which they may lay down, may allow taxable persons to submit the recapitulative statement for each calendar **quarter** within a time limit not exceeding one month from the end of the quarter, where the total quarterly amount, excluding VAT, of the supplies of goods as referred to in

Articles 264(1)(d) and 265(1)(c) does not exceed either in respect of the quarter concerned or in respect of any of the previous four quarters the sum of EUR 50 000 or its equivalent in national currency.

The option provided for in the first subparagraph shall cease to be applicable after the end of the month during which the total value, excluding VAT, of the supplies of goods as referred to in Article 264(1)(d) and 265(1)(c) exceeds, in respect of the current quarter, the sum of EUR 50,000 or its equivalent in national currency. In this case, a recapitulative statement shall be drawn up for the month(s) which has (have) elapsed since the beginning of the quarter, within a time limit not exceeding one month.

1b. Until 31 December 2011, Member States are allowed to set the sum mentioned in paragraph 1a at EUR 100,000 or its equivalent in national currency.

1c. In the case of supplies of services as referred to in Article 264(1)(d), Member States, in accordance with the conditions and limits which they may lay down, may allow taxable persons to submit the recapitulative statement for each calendar quarter within a time limit not exceeding one month from the end of the quarter.

Member States may, in particular, require the taxable persons who carry out supplies of both goods and services as referred to in Article 264(1)(d) to submit the recapitulative statement in accordance with the deadline resulting from paragraphs 1 to 1b.

2. Member States shall allow, and may require, the recapitulative statement referred to in paragraph 1 to be submitted by electronic file transfer, in accordance with conditions which they lay down.

Article 264 [Content of recapitulative statement]

1. The recapitulative statement shall set out the following **information**:

   (a) the VAT **identification number** of the **taxable person** in the Member State in which the recapitulative statement must be submitted and under which he has carried out the **supply of goods** in accordance with the conditions specified in Article 138(1) and under which he effected taxable **supplies of services** in accordance with the conditions laid down in Article 44;

   (b) the VAT **identification number** of the **person acquiring** the goods or **receiving** the services in a Member State other than that in which the recapitulative statement must be submitted and under which the goods or services were supplied to him;

   (c) the VAT **identification number** of the **taxable person** in the Member State in which the recapitulative statement must be submitted and under which he has carried out a **transfer to another Member State**, as referred to in Article 138(2)(c), and the number by means of which he is identified in the Member State in which the dispatch or transport ended;

   (d) **for each person** who acquired goods or received services, the **total value of the supplies** of goods **and** the **total** value of the supplies of services carried out by the taxable person;

   (e) in respect of supplies of goods consisting in **transfers** to another Member State, as referred to in Article 138(2)(c), the **total value** of the supplies, determined in accordance with Article 76;

   (f) the amounts of **adjustments** made pursuant to Article 90.

2. The value referred to in paragraph 1(d) shall be declared for the **period of submission** established in accordance with Article 263(1) to (1c) during which VAT became chargeable.

The amounts referred to in paragraph 1(f) shall be declared for the period of submission established in accordance with Article 263(1) to (1c) during which the person acquiring the goods was **notified** of the **adjustment**.

Article 265

1. In the case of intra-Community acquisitions of goods, as referred to in Article 42, the taxable person identified for VAT purposes in the Member State which issued him with the VAT identification number under which he made such acquisitions shall set the following information out clearly on the recapitulative statement:

    (a) his VAT identification number in that Member State and under which he made the acquisition and subsequent supply of goods;

    (b) the VAT identification number, in the Member State in which dispatch or transport of the goods ended, of the person to whom the subsequent supply was made by the taxable person;

    (c) for each person to whom the subsequent supply was made, the total value, exclusive of VAT, of the supplies made by the taxable person in the Member State in which dispatch or transport of the goods ended.

2. The value referred to in paragraph 1(c) shall be declared for the period of submission established in accordance with Article 263(1) to (1b) during which VAT became chargeable.

Article 266 [Additional info on recapitulative statements]

By way of derogation from Articles 264 and 265, Member States **may** provide that additional information is to be given in recapitulative statements.

Article 267

Member States shall take the measures necessary to ensure that those persons who, in accordance with Articles 194 and 204, are regarded as liable for payment of VAT, in the stead of a taxable person who is not established in their territory, comply with the obligation to submit a recapitulative statement as provided for in this Chapter.

Article 268

Member States may require that taxable persons who, in their territory, make intra-Community acquisitions of goods, or transactions treated as such, pursuant to Articles 21 or 22, submit statements giving details of such acquisitions, provided, however, that such statements are not required in respect of a period of less than one month.

Article 269

Acting unanimously on a proposal from the Commission, the Council may authorize any Member State to introduce the special measures provided for in Articles 270 and 271 to simplify the obligation, laid down in this Chapter, to submit a recapitulative statement. Such measures may not jeopardize the proper monitoring of intra-Community transactions.

Article 270

By virtue of the authorization referred to in Article 269, Member States may permit taxable persons to submit annual recapitulative statements indicating the VAT identification numbers, in another Member State, of the persons to whom those taxable persons have supplied goods in accordance with the conditions specified in Article 138(1) and (2)(c), where the taxable persons meet the following three conditions:

(a) the total annual value, exclusive of VAT, of their supplies of goods and services does not exceed by more than EUR 35,000, or the equivalent in national currency, the amount of the annual turnover which is used as a reference for application of the exemption for small enterprises provided for in Articles 282 to 292;

(b) the total annual value, exclusive of VAT, of supplies of goods carried out by them in accordance with the conditions specified in Article 138 does not exceed EUR 15,000 or the equivalent in national currency;

(c) none of the supplies of goods carried out by them in accordance with the conditions specified in Article 138 is a supply of new means of transport.

Article 271

By virtue of the authorization referred to in Article 269, Member States which set at over three months the tax period in respect of which taxable persons must submit the VAT return provided for in Article 250 may permit such persons to submit recapitulative statements in respect of the same period where those taxable persons meet the following three conditions:

(a) the total annual value, exclusive of VAT, of their supplies of goods and services does not exceed EUR 200,000 or the equivalent in national currency;

(b) the total annual value, exclusive of VAT, of supplies of goods carried out by them in accordance with the conditions specified in Article 138 does not exceed EUR 15,000 or the equivalent in national currency;

(c) none of the supplies of goods carried out by them in accordance with the conditions specified in Article 138 is a supply of new means of transport.

Chapter 7 Miscellaneous Provisions

Article 272 [*Release from all obligations* except payment]

1. Member States may **release** the following taxable persons from certain or **all obligations** referred to in Chapters 2 to 6:

    (a) taxable persons whose intra-Community acquisitions of goods are not subject to VAT pursuant to Article 3(1);

    (b) taxable persons carrying out none of the transactions referred to in Articles 20, 21, 22, 33, 36, 138 and 141;

    (c) taxable persons carrying out only supplies of goods or of services which are exempt pursuant to Articles 132, 135 and 136, Articles 146 to 149 and Articles 151, 152 or 153;

    (d) taxable persons covered by the exemption for small enterprises provided for in Articles 282 to 292;

    (e) taxable persons covered by the common flat-rate scheme for farmers.

    Member States may not release the taxable persons referred to in point (b) of the first subparagraph from the invoicing obligations laid down in Sections 3 to 6 of Chapter 3 and Section 3 of Chapter 4.

2. If Member States exercise the option under point (e) of the first subparagraph of paragraph 1, they shall take the measures necessary to ensure the correct application of the transitional arrangements for the taxation of intra-Community transactions.

3. Member States may release taxable persons other than those referred to in paragraph 1 from certain of the accounting obligations referred to in Article 242.

Article 273

Member States **may** impose other obligations which they deem necessary to ensure **the correct collection of VAT** and to prevent **evasion**, subject to the requirement of equal treatment as between domestic transactions and transactions carried out between Member States by taxable persons and provided that such obligations do not, in trade between Member States, give rise to formalities connected with the crossing of frontiers.

The option under the first paragraph may not be relied upon in order to **impose additional invoicing obligations** over and above those laid down in Chapter 3.

Comments to Title XI, Chapter 7 – Miscellaneous provisions

Article 55
For the transactions referred to in Article 262 of Directive 2006/112/EC, taxable persons to whom a VAT identification number has been attributed in accordance with Article 214 of that Directive and non-taxable legal persons identified for VAT purposes shall be required, when acting as such, to communicate their VAT identification number forthwith to those supplying goods and services to them.
The taxable persons referred to in point (b) of Article 3(1) of Directive 2006/112/EC, who are entitled to non-taxation of their intra-Community acquisitions of goods in accordance with the first paragraph of Article 4 of this Regulation, shall not be required to communicate their VAT identification number to those supplying goods to them when a VAT identification number has been attributed to them in accordance with Article 214(1)(d) or (e) of that Directive.
<u>Guidance notes</u>: Taxable persons to whom a VAT identification number has been attributed and non-taxable legal persons identified for VAT purposes shall be required, when acting as such, to communicate their VAT identification number to those supplying goods and services to them. This enables suppliers to fulfill their obligations to submit recapitulative statements of intra-Community transactions of goods and services

Chapter 8 Obligations Relating to Certain Importations and Exportations

Section 1: Importation

Article 274

Articles 275, 276 and 277 shall apply to the importation of goods in free circulation which enter the Community from a third territory forming part of the customs territory of the Community.

Article 275

The formalities relating to the **importation of the goods** referred to in Article 274 shall be the same as those laid down by the **Community customs provisions** in force for the importation of goods into the customs territory of the Community.

Article 276

Where **dispatch** or **transport** of the goods referred to in Article 274 **ends at a place situated outside the Member State of their entry** into the Community, they shall circulate in the Community under the **internal Community transit procedure** laid down by the Community customs provisions in force, in so far as they have been the subject of a declaration placing them under that procedure on their entry into the Community.

Article 277

Where, on their entry into the Community, the goods referred to in Article 274 are in one of the situations which would entitle them, if they were imported within the meaning of the first paragraph of Article 30, to be covered by one of the arrangements or situations referred to in Article 156, or by a temporary importation arrangement with full exemption from import duties, Member States **shall** take the measures necessary to ensure that the goods may **remain in the Community under the same conditions** as those laid down for the application of those arrangements or situations.

Section 2: Exportation

Article 278

Articles 279 and 280 shall apply to the **exportation** of goods in free circulation which are dispatched or transported from a Member State to a third territory forming part of the customs territory of the Community.

Article 279

The formalities relating to the exportation of the goods referred to in Article 278 from the territory of the Community shall be the same as those laid down by the **Community customs** provisions in force for the exportation of goods from the customs territory of the Community.

Article 280 [Goods temporarily exported in order to be re-imported]

In the case of goods which **are temporarily exported** from the Community, **in order to be reimported**, Member States shall take the measures necessary to ensure that, on re-importation into the Community, such goods may be covered by the same provisions as would have applied if they had been temporarily exported from the customs territory of the Community.

Title XII - Special Schemes

Chapter 1 Special Scheme for Small Enterprises

Section 1: Simplified procedures for charging and collection

Article 281

Member States which might encounter difficulties in applying the normal VAT arrangements to small enterprises, by reason of the activities or structure of such enterprises, may, subject to such conditions and limits as they may set, and after consulting the VAT Committee, apply simplified procedures, such as flat-rate schemes, for charging and collecting VAT provided that they do not lead to a reduction thereof.

Section 2: Exemptions or graduated relief

Article 282

The exemptions and graduated tax relief provided for in this Section shall apply to the supply of goods and services by small enterprises.

Article 283

1. The arrangements provided for in this Section shall not apply to the following transactions:

    (a) transactions carried out on an occasional basis, as referred to in Article 12;

(b) supplies of new means of transport carried out in accordance with the conditions specified in Article 138(1) and (2)(a);

(c) supplies of goods or services carried out by a taxable person who is not established in the Member State in which the VAT is due.

2. Member States may exclude transactions other than those referred to in paragraph 1 from the arrangements provided for in this Section.

Article 284

1. Member States which have exercised the option under Article 14 of Council Directive 67/228/EEC of 11 April 1967 on the harmonization of legislation of Member States concerning turnover taxes — Structure and procedures for application of the common system of value added tax of introducing exemptions or graduated tax relief may retain them, and the arrangements for applying them, if they comply with the VAT rules.

2. Member States which, at 17 May 1977, exempted taxable persons whose annual turnover was less than the equivalent in national currency of 5000 European units of account at the conversion rate on that date, may raise that ceiling up to EUR 5000.

Member States which applied graduated tax relief may neither raise the ceiling for graduated tax relief nor render the conditions for the granting of it more favorable.

Article 285

Member States which have not exercised the option under Article 14 of Directive 67/228/EEC may exempt taxable persons whose annual turnover is no higher than EUR 5000 or the equivalent in national currency.

The Member States referred to in the first paragraph may grant graduated tax relief to taxable persons whose annual turnover exceeds the ceiling fixed by them for its application.

Article 286

Member States which, at 17 May 1977, exempted taxable persons whose annual turnover was equal to or higher than the equivalent in national currency of 5,000 European units of account at the conversion rate on that date, may raise that ceiling in order to maintain the value of the exemption in real terms.

Article 287

Member States which acceded after 1 January 1978 may exempt taxable persons whose annual turnover is no higher than the equivalent in national currency of the following amounts at the conversion rate on the day of their accession:

(1) Greece: 10,000 European units of account;

(2) Spain: ECU 10,000;

(3) Portugal: ECU 10,000;

(4) Austria: ECU 35,000;

(5) Finland: ECU 10,000;

(6) Sweden: ECU 10,000;

(7) Czech Republic: EUR 35,000;

(8) Estonia: EUR 16,000;

(9) Cyprus: EUR 15,600;

(10) Latvia: EUR 17,200;

(11) Lithuania: EUR 29,000;

(12) Hungary: EUR 35,000;

(13) Malta: EUR 37,000 if the economic activity consists principally in the supply of goods, EUR 24,300 if the economic activity consists principally in the supply of services with a low value added (high inputs), and EUR 14,600 in other cases, namely supplies of services with a high value added (low inputs);

(14) Poland: EUR 10,000;

(15) Slovenia: EUR 25,000;

(16) Slovakia: EUR 35,000.

(17) Bulgaria: EUR 25,600;

(18) Romania: EUR 35,000.

(19) Croatia: EUR 35,000.

Article 288

The turnover serving as a reference for the purposes of applying the arrangements provided for in this Section shall consist of the following amounts, exclusive of VAT:

(1) the value of supplies of goods and services, in so far as they are taxed;

(2) the value of transactions which are exempt, with deductibility of the VAT paid at the preceding stage, pursuant to Articles 110 or 111, Article 125(1), Article 127 or Article 128(1);

(3) the value of transactions which are exempt pursuant to Articles 146 to 149 and Articles 151, 152 or 153;

(4) the value of real estate transactions, financial transactions as referred to in points (b) to (g) of Article 135(1), and insurance services, unless those transactions are ancillary transactions.

However, disposals of the tangible or intangible capital assets of an enterprise shall not be taken into account for the purposes of calculating turnover.

Article 289

Taxable persons exempt from VAT shall not be entitled to deduct VAT in accordance with Articles 167 to 171 and Articles 173 to 177, and may not show the VAT on their invoices.

Article 290

Taxable persons who are entitled to exemption from VAT may opt either for the normal VAT arrangements or for the simplified procedures provided for in Article 281. In this case, they shall be entitled to any graduated tax relief provided for under national legislation.

Article 291

Subject to the application of Article 281, taxable persons enjoying graduated relief shall be regarded as taxable persons subject to the normal VAT arrangements.

Article 292

The arrangements provided for in this Section shall apply until a date to be fixed by the Council in accordance with Article 93 of the Treaty, which may not be later than that on which the definitive arrangements referred to in Article 402 enter into force.

Section 3: Reporting and review

Article 293

Every four years starting from the adoption of this Directive, the Commission shall present to the Council, on the basis of information obtained from the Member States, a report on the application of this Chapter, together, where appropriate and taking into account the need to ensure the long-term convergence of national regulations, with proposals on the following subjects:

(1) improvements to the special scheme for small enterprises;

(2) the adaptation of national systems as regards exemptions and graduated tax relief;

(3) the adaptation of the ceilings provided for in Section 2.

Article 294

The Council shall decide, in accordance with Article 93 of the Treaty, whether a special scheme for small enterprises is necessary under the definitive arrangements and, if appropriate, shall lay down the common limits and conditions for the implementation of that scheme.

Chapter 2 Common Flat-Rate Scheme for Farmers

Article 295

1. For the purposes of this Chapter, the following definitions shall apply:

    (1) "**farmer**" means any taxable person whose activity is carried out in an agricultural, forestry or fisheries undertaking;

    (2) "**agricultural, forestry or fisheries undertaking**" means an undertaking regarded as such by each Member State within the framework of the production activities listed in Annex VII;

    (3) "**flat-rate farmer**" means any farmer covered by the flat-rate scheme provided for in this Chapter;

    (4) "**agricultural products**" means goods produced by an agricultural, forestry or fisheries undertaking in each Member State as a result of the activities listed in Annex VII;

    (5) "**agricultural services**" means services, and in particular those listed in Annex VIII, supplied by a farmer using his labor force or the equipment normally employed in the agricultural, forestry or fisheries undertaking operated by him and normally playing a part in agricultural production;

    (6) "**input VAT charged**" means the amount of the total VAT attaching to the goods and services purchased by all agricultural, forestry and fisheries undertakings of each Member State subject to the flat-rate scheme where such tax would be deductible in accordance with Articles 167, 168 and 169 and Articles 173 to 177 by a farmer subject to the normal VAT arrangements;

(7) "**flat-rate compensation percentages**" means the percentages fixed by Member States in accordance with Articles 297, 298 and 299 and applied by them in the cases specified in Article 300 in order to enable flat-rate farmers to offset at a fixed rate the input VAT charged;

(8) "**flat-rate compensation**" means the amount arrived at by applying the flat-rate compensation percentage to the turnover of the flat-rate farmer in the cases specified in Article 300.

2. Where a farmer processes, using means normally employed in an agricultural, forestry or fisheries undertaking, products deriving essentially from his agricultural production, such processing activities shall be treated as agricultural production activities, as listed in Annex VII.

Article 296

1. Where the application to farmers of the normal VAT arrangements, or the special scheme provided for in Chapter 1, is likely to give rise to difficulties, Member States may apply to farmers, in accordance with this Chapter, a flat-rate scheme designed to offset the VAT charged on purchases of goods and services made by the flat-rate farmers.

2. Each Member State may exclude from the flat-rate scheme certain categories of farmers, as well as farmers for whom application of the normal VAT arrangements, or of the simplified procedures provided for in Article 281, is not likely to give rise to administrative difficulties.

3. Every flat-rate farmer may opt, subject to the rules and conditions to be laid down by each Member State, for application of the normal VAT arrangements or, as the case may be, the simplified procedures provided for in Article 281.

Article 297

Member States shall, where necessary, fix the flat-rate compensation percentages. They may fix varying percentages for forestry, for the different sub-divisions of agriculture and for fisheries.

Member States shall notify the Commission of the flat-rate compensation percentages fixed in accordance with the first paragraph before applying them.

Article 298

The flat-rate compensation percentages shall be calculated on the basis of macro-economic statistics for flat-rate farmers alone for the preceding three years.

The percentages may be rounded up or down to the nearest half-point. Member States may also reduce such percentages to a nil rate.

Article 299

The flat-rate compensation percentages may not have the effect of obtaining for flat-rate farmers refunds greater than the input VAT charged.

Article 300

The flat-rate compensation percentages shall be applied to the prices, exclusive of VAT, of the following goods and services:

> (1) agricultural products supplied by flat-rate farmers to taxable persons other than those covered, in the Member State in which these products were supplied, by this flat-rate scheme;

(2) agricultural products supplied by flat-rate farmers, in accordance with the conditions specified in Article 138, to non-taxable legal persons whose intra-Community acquisitions of goods are subject to VAT, pursuant to Article 2(1)(b), in the Member State in which dispatch or transport of those agricultural products ends;

(3) agricultural services supplied by flat-rate farmers to taxable persons other than those covered, in the Member State in which these services were supplied, by this flat-rate scheme.

Article 301

1. In the case of the supply of agricultural products or agricultural services specified in Article 300, Member States shall provide that the flat-rate compensation is to be paid either by the customer or by the public authorities.

2. In respect of any supply of agricultural products or agricultural services other than those specified in Article 300, the flat-rate compensation shall be deemed to be paid by the customer.

Article 302

If a flat-rate farmer is entitled to flat-rate compensation, he shall not be entitled to deduction of VAT in respect of activities covered by this flat-rate scheme.

Article 303

1. Where the taxable customer pays flat-rate compensation pursuant to Article 301(1), he shall be entitled, in accordance with the conditions laid down in Articles 167, 168 and 169 and Articles 173 to 177 and the procedures laid down by the Member States, to deduct the compensation amount from the

VAT for which he is liable in the Member State in which his taxed transactions are carried out.

2. Member States shall refund to the customer the amount of the flat-rate compensation he has paid in respect of any of the following transactions:

   (a) the supply of agricultural products, carried out in accordance with the conditions specified in Article 138, to taxable persons, or to non-taxable legal persons, acting as such in another Member State within the territory of which their intra-Community acquisitions of goods are subject to VAT pursuant to Article 2(1)(b);

   (b) the supply of agricultural products, carried out in accordance with the conditions specified in Articles 146, 147, 148 and 156, Article 157(1)(b) and Articles 158, 160 and 161, to a taxable customer established outside the Community, in so far as the products are used by that customer for the purposes of the transactions referred to in Article 169(a) and (b) or for the purposes of supplies of services which are deemed to take place within the territory of the Member State in which the customer is established and in respect of which VAT is payable solely by the customer pursuant to Article 196;

   (c) the supply of agricultural services to a taxable customer established within the Community but in another Member State or to a taxable customer established outside the Community, in so far as the services are used by the customer for the purposes of the transactions referred to in Article 169(a) and (b) or for the purposes of supplies of services which are deemed to take place within the territory of the Member State in which the customer is established and in respect of which VAT is payable solely by the customer pursuant to Article 196.

3. Member States shall determine the method by which the refunds provided for in paragraph 2 are to be made. In

particular, they may apply the provisions of Directives 79/1072/EEC and 86/560/EEC.

Article 304

Member States shall take all measures necessary to verify payments of flat-rate compensation to flat-rate farmers.

Article 305

Whenever Member States apply this flat-rate scheme, they shall take all measures necessary to ensure that the supply of agricultural products between Member States, carried out in accordance with the conditions specified in Article 33, is always taxed in the same way, whether the supply is effected by a flat-rate farmer or by another taxable person.

Chapter 3 Special Scheme for Travel Agents

Article 306

1. Member States shall apply a special VAT scheme, in accordance with this Chapter, to transactions carried out by travel agents who deal with customers in their own name and use supplies of goods or services provided by other taxable persons, in the provision of travel facilities.

This special scheme shall not apply to travel agents where they act solely as intermediaries and to whom point (c) of the first paragraph of Article 79 applies for the purposes of calculating the taxable amount.

2. For the purposes of this Chapter, tour operators shall be regarded as travel agents.

Article 307

Transactions made, in accordance with the conditions laid down in Article 306, by the travel agent in respect of a journey shall be regarded as a single service supplied by the travel agent to the traveler.

The single service shall be taxable in the Member State in which the travel agent has established his business or has a fixed establishment from which the travel agent has carried out the supply of services.

Article 308

The taxable amount and the price exclusive of VAT, within the meaning of point (8) of Article 226, in respect of the single service provided by the travel agent shall be the travel agent's margin, that is to say, the difference between the total amount, exclusive of VAT, to be paid by the traveler and the actual cost to the travel agent of supplies of goods or services provided by other taxable persons, where those transactions are for the direct benefit of the traveler.

Article 309

If transactions entrusted by the travel agent to other taxable persons are performed by such persons outside the Community, the supply of services carried out by the travel agent shall be treated as an intermediary activity exempted pursuant to Article 153.

If the transactions are performed both inside and outside the Community, only that part of the travel agent's service relating to transactions outside the Community may be exempted.

Article 310

VAT charged to the travel agent by other taxable persons in respect of transactions which are referred to in Article 307 and which are for the direct benefit of the traveler shall not be deductible or refundable in any Member State.

Chapter 4 Special Arrangements for Second-Hand Goods, Works of Art, Collectors' Items and Antiques

Section 1: Definitions

Article 311

1. For the purposes of this Chapter, and without prejudice to other Community provisions, the following definitions shall apply:

    (1) "**second-hand goods**" means movable tangible property that is suitable for further use as it is or after repair, other than works of art, collectors' items or antiques and other than precious metals or precious stones as defined by the Member States;

    (2) "**works of art**" means the objects listed in Annex IX, Part A;

    (3) "**collectors' items**" means the objects listed in Annex IX, Part B;

    (4) "**antiques**" means the objects listed in Annex IX, Part C;

    (5) "**taxable dealer**" means any taxable person who, in the course of his economic activity and with a view to resale, purchases, or applies for the purposes of his business, or imports, second-hand goods, works of art, collectors' items or antiques, whether that taxable person is acting for himself or on behalf of another person pursuant to a contract under which commission is payable on purchase or sale;

    (6) "**organizer of a sale by public auction**" means any taxable person who, in the course of his economic activity, offers goods for sale by public auction

with a view to handing them over to the highest bidder;

(7) "**principal of an organizer of a sale by public auction**" means any person who transmits goods to an organizer of a sale by public auction pursuant to a contract under which commission is payable on a sale.

2. Member States need not regard as works of art the objects listed in points (5), (6) or (7) of Annex IX, Part A.

3. The contract under which commission is payable on a sale, referred to in point (7) of paragraph 1, must provide that the organizer of the sale is to put up the goods for public auction in his own name but on behalf of his principal and that he is to hand over the goods, in his own name but on behalf of his principal, to the highest bidder at the public auction.

Section 2: Special arrangements for taxable dealers

Subsection 1: Margin scheme

Article 312

For the purposes of this Subsection, the following definitions shall apply:

(1) "**selling price**" means everything which constitutes the consideration obtained or to be obtained by the taxable dealer from the customer or from a third party, including subsidies directly linked to the transaction, taxes, duties, levies and charges and incidental expenses such as commission, packaging, transport and insurance costs charged by the taxable dealer to the customer, but excluding the amounts referred to in Article 79;

(2) "**purchase price**" means everything which constitutes the consideration, for the purposes of point (1), obtained or to be obtained from the taxable dealer by his supplier.

Article 313

1. In respect of the supply of second-hand goods, works of art, collectors' items or antiques carried out by taxable dealers, Member States shall apply a special scheme for taxing the profit margin made by the taxable dealer, in accordance with the provisions of this Subsection.

2. Pending introduction of the definitive arrangements referred to in Article 402, the scheme referred to in paragraph 1 of this Article shall not apply to the supply of new means of transport, carried out in accordance with the conditions specified in Article 138(1) and (2)(a).

Article 314

The margin scheme shall apply to the supply by a taxable dealer of second-hand goods, works of art, collectors' items or antiques where those goods have been supplied to him within the Community by one of the following persons:

(a) a non-taxable person;

(b) another taxable person, in so far as the supply of goods by that other taxable person is exempt pursuant to Article 136;

(c) another taxable person, in so far as the supply of goods by that other taxable person is covered by the exemption for small enterprises provided for in Articles 282 to 292 and involves capital goods;

(d) another taxable dealer, in so far as VAT has been applied to the supply of goods by that other taxable dealer in accordance with this margin scheme.

Article 315

The taxable amount in respect of the supply of goods as referred to in Article 314 shall be the profit margin made by the taxable dealer, less the amount of VAT relating to the profit margin.

The profit margin of the taxable dealer shall be equal to the difference between the selling price charged by the taxable dealer for the goods and the purchase price.

Article 316

1. Member States shall grant taxable dealers the right to opt for application of the margin scheme to the following transactions:

    (a) the supply of works of art, collectors' items or antiques, which the taxable dealer has imported himself;

    (b) the supply of works of art supplied to the taxable dealer by their creators or their successors in title;

    (c) the supply of works of art supplied to the taxable dealer by a taxable person other than a taxable dealer where the reduced rate has been applied to that supply pursuant to Article 103.

2. Member States shall lay down the detailed rules for exercise of the option provided for in paragraph 1, which shall in any event cover a period of at least two calendar years.

Article 317

If a taxable dealer exercises the option under Article 316, the taxable amount shall be determined in accordance with Article

315.

In respect of the supply of works of art, collectors' items or antiques which the taxable dealer has imported himself, the purchase price to be taken into account in calculating the profit margin shall be equal to the taxable amount on importation, determined in accordance with Articles 85 to 89, plus the VAT due or paid on importation.

Article 318

1. In order to simplify the procedure for collecting the tax and after consulting the VAT Committee, Member States may provide that, for certain transactions or for certain categories of taxable dealers, the taxable amount in respect of supplies of goods subject to the margin scheme is to be determined for each tax period during which the taxable dealer must submit the VAT return referred to in Article 250.

In the event that such provision is made in accordance with the first subparagraph, the taxable amount in respect of supplies of goods to which the same rate of VAT is applied shall be the total profit margin made by the taxable dealer less the amount of VAT relating to that margin.

2. The total profit margin shall be equal to the difference between the following two amounts:

   (a) the total value of supplies of goods subject to the margin scheme and carried out by the taxable dealer during the tax period covered by the return, that is to say, the total of the selling prices;

   (b) the total value of purchases of goods, as referred to in Article 314, effected by the taxable dealer during the tax period covered by the return, that is to say, the total of the purchase prices.

3. Member States shall take the measures necessary to ensure that the taxable dealers referred to in paragraph 1 do not enjoy unjustified advantage or sustain unjustified harm.

Article 319

The taxable dealer may apply the normal VAT arrangements to any supply covered by the margin scheme.

Article 320

1. Where the taxable dealer applies the normal VAT arrangements to the supply of a work of art, a collectors' item or an antique which he has imported himself, he shall be entitled to deduct from the VAT for which he is liable the VAT due or paid on the import.

Where the taxable dealer applies the normal VAT arrangements to the supply of a work of art supplied to him by its creator, or the creator's successors in title, or by a taxable person other than a taxable dealer, he shall be entitled to deduct from the VAT for which he is liable the VAT due or paid in respect of the work of art supplied to him.

2. A right of deduction shall arise at the time when the VAT due on the supply in respect of which the taxable dealer opts for application of the normal VAT arrangements becomes chargeable.

Article 321

If carried out in accordance with the conditions specified in Articles 146, 147, 148 or 151, the supply of second-hand goods, works of art, collectors' items or antiques subject to the margin scheme shall be exempt.

Article 322

In so far as goods are used for the purpose of supplies carried out by him and subject to the margin scheme, the taxable dealer may not deduct the following from the VAT for which he is liable:

- (a) the VAT due or paid in respect of works of art, collectors' items or antiques which he has imported himself;
- (b) the VAT due or paid in respect of works of art which have been, or are to be, supplied to him by their creator or by the creator's successors in title;
- (c) the VAT due or paid in respect of works of art which have been, or are to be, supplied to him by a taxable person other than a taxable dealer.

Article 323

Taxable persons may not deduct from the VAT for which they are liable the VAT due or paid in respect of goods which have been, or are to be, supplied to them by a taxable dealer, in so far as the supply of those goods by the taxable dealer is subject to the margin scheme.

Article 324

Where the taxable dealer applies both the normal VAT arrangements and the margin scheme, he must show separately in his accounts the transactions falling under each of those arrangements, in accordance with the rules laid down by the Member States.

Article 325

The taxable dealer may not enter separately on the invoices which he issues the VAT relating to supplies of goods to which he applies the margin scheme.

Subsection 2: Transitional arrangements for second-hand means of transport

Article 326

Member States which, at 31 December 1992, were applying special tax arrangements other than the margin scheme to the supply by taxable dealers of second-hand means of transport may, pending introduction of the definitive arrangements referred to in Article 402, continue to apply those arrangements in so far as they comply with, or are adjusted to comply with, the conditions laid down in this Subsection.

Denmark is authorized to introduce tax arrangements as referred to in the first paragraph.

Article 327

1. These transitional arrangements shall apply to supplies of second-hand means of transport carried out by taxable dealers, and subject to the margin scheme.

2. These transitional arrangements shall not apply to the supply of new means of transport carried out in accordance with the conditions specified in Article 138(1) and (2)(a).

3. For the purposes of paragraph 1, the land vehicles, vessels and aircraft referred to in point (a) of Article 2(2) shall be regarded as "second-hand means of transport" where they are second-hand goods which do not meet the conditions necessary to be regarded as new means of transport.

Article 328

The VAT due in respect of each supply referred to in Article 327 shall be equal to the amount of VAT that would have been due if that supply had been subject to the normal VAT arrangements, less the amount of VAT regarded as being incorporated by the taxable dealer in the purchase price of the means of transport.

Article 329

The VAT regarded as being incorporated by the taxable dealer in the purchase price of the means of transport shall be calculated in accordance with the following method:

(a) the purchase price to be taken into account shall be the purchase price within the meaning of point (2) of Article 312;

(b) that purchase price paid by the taxable dealer shall be deemed to include the VAT that would have been due if the taxable dealer's supplier had applied the normal VAT arrangements to the supply;

(c) the rate to be taken into account shall be the rate applicable, pursuant to Article 93, in the Member State in the territory of which the place of the supply to the taxable dealer, as determined in accordance with Articles 31 and 32, is deemed to be situated.

Article 330

The VAT due in respect of each supply of means of transport as referred to in Article 327(1), determined in accordance with Article 328, may not be less than the amount of VAT that would be due if that supply were subject to the margin scheme.

Member States may provide that, if the supply is subject to the margin scheme, the margin may not be less than 10 % of the selling price within the meaning of point (1) of Article 312.

Article 331

Taxable persons may not deduct from the VAT for which they are liable the VAT due or paid in respect of second-hand means of transport supplied to them by a taxable dealer, in so far as the supply of those goods by the taxable dealer is subject to VAT in accordance with these transitional arrangements.

Article 332

The taxable dealer may not enter separately on the invoices he issues the VAT relating to supplies to which he applies these transitional arrangements.

Section 3: Special arrangements for sales by public auction

Article 333

1. Member States may, in accordance with the provisions of this Section, apply special arrangements for taxation of the profit margin made by an organizer of a sale by public auction in respect of the supply of second-hand goods, works of art, collectors' items or antiques by that organizer, acting in his own name and on behalf of the persons referred to in Article 334, pursuant to a contract under which commission is payable on the sale of those goods by public auction.

2. The arrangements referred to in paragraph 1 shall not apply to the supply of new means of transport, carried out in accordance with the conditions specified in Article 138(1) and (2)(a).

Article 334

These special arrangements shall apply to supplies carried out by an organizer of a sale by public auction, acting in his own name, on behalf of one of the following persons:

(a) a non-taxable person;

(b) another taxable person, in so far as the supply of goods, carried out by that taxable person in accordance with a contract under which commission is payable on a sale, is exempt pursuant to Article 136;

(c) another taxable person, in so far as the supply of goods, carried out by that taxable person in accordance with a contract under which commission is payable on a sale, is covered by the exemption for small enterprises provided for in Articles 282 to 292 and involves capital goods;

(d) a taxable dealer, in so far as the supply of goods, carried out by that taxable dealer in accordance with a contract under which commission is payable on a sale, is subject to VAT in accordance with the margin scheme.

Article 335

The supply of goods to a taxable person who is an organizer of sales by public auction shall be regarded as taking place when the sale of those goods by public auction takes place.

Article 336

The taxable amount in respect of each supply of goods referred to in this Section shall be the total amount invoiced in accordance with Article 339 to the purchaser by the organizer of the sale by public auction, less the following:

(a) the net amount paid or to be paid by the organizer of the sale by public auction to his principal, as determined in accordance with Article 337;

(b) the amount of the VAT payable by the organizer of the sale by public auction in respect of his supply.

Article 337

The net amount paid or to be paid by the organizer of the sale by public auction to his principal shall be equal to the difference between the auction price of the goods and the amount of the commission obtained or to be obtained by the organizer of the sale by public auction from his principal pursuant to the contract under which commission is payable on the sale.

Article 338

Organizers of sales by public auction who supply goods in accordance with the conditions laid down in Articles 333 and 334 must indicate the following in their accounts, in suspense accounts:

(a) the amounts obtained or to be obtained from the purchaser of the goods;

(b) the amounts reimbursed or to be reimbursed to the vendor of the goods.

The amounts referred to in the first paragraph must be duly substantiated.

Article 339

The organizer of the sale by public auction must issue to the purchaser an invoice itemizing the following:

(a) the auction price of the goods;

(b) taxes, duties, levies and charges;

(c) incidental expenses, such as commission, packing, transport and insurance costs, charged by the organizer to the purchaser of the goods.

The invoice issued by the organizer of the sale by public auction must not indicate any VAT separately.

Article 340

1. The organizer of the sale by public auction to whom the goods have been transmitted pursuant to a contract under which commission is payable on a public auction sale must issue a statement to his principal.

The statement issued by the organizer of the sale by public auction must specify separately the amount of the transaction, that is to say, the auction price of the goods less the amount of the commission obtained or to be obtained from the principal.

2. The statement drawn up in accordance with paragraph 1 shall serve as the invoice which the principal, where he is a taxable person, must issue to the organizer of the sale by public auction in accordance with Article 220.

Article 341

Member States which apply the arrangements provided for in this Section shall also apply these arrangements to supplies of second-hand means of transport, as defined in Article 327(3), carried out by an organizer of sales by public auction, acting in his own name, pursuant to a contract under which commission is payable on the sale of those goods by public auction, on behalf of a taxable dealer, in so far as those supplies by that taxable dealer would be subject to VAT in accordance with the transitional arrangements for second-hand means of transport.

Section 4: Measures to prevent distortion of competition and tax evasion

Article 342

Member States may take measures concerning the right of deduction in order to ensure that the taxable dealers covered by special arrangements as provided for in Section 2 do not enjoy unjustified advantage or sustain unjustified harm.

Article 343

Acting unanimously on a proposal from the Commission, the Council may authorize any Member State to introduce special measures to combat tax evasion, pursuant to which the VAT due under the margin scheme may not be less than the amount of VAT which would be due if the profit margin were equal to a certain percentage of the selling price.

The percentage of the selling price shall be fixed in the light of the normal profit margins made by economic operators in the sector concerned.

Chapter 5 Special Scheme for Investment Gold

Section 1: General provisions

Article 344

1. For the purposes of this Directive, and without prejudice to other Community provisions, "investment gold" shall mean:

    (1) gold, in the form of a bar or a wafer of weights accepted by the bullion markets, of a purity equal to or greater than 995 thousandths, whether or not represented by securities;

    (2) gold coins of a purity equal to or greater than 900 thousandths and minted after 1800, which are or have been legal tender in the country of origin, and are normally sold at a price which does not exceed the open market value of the gold contained in the coins by more than 80 %.

2. Member States may exclude from this special scheme small bars or wafers of a weight of 1 g or less.

3. For the purposes of this Directive, the coins referred to in point (2) of paragraph 1 shall not be regarded as sold for numismatic interest.

Article 345

Starting in 1999, each Member State shall inform the Commission by 1 July each year of the coins meeting the criteria laid down in point (2) of Article 344(1) which are traded in that Member State. The Commission shall, before 1 December each year, publish a comprehensive list of those coins in the "C" series of the Official Journal of the European Union. Coins included in the published list shall be deemed to fulfill those criteria throughout the year for which the list is published.

Section 2: Exemption from VAT

Article 346

Member States shall exempt from VAT the supply, the intra-Community acquisition and the importation of investment gold, including investment gold represented by certificates for allocated or unallocated gold or traded on gold accounts and including, in particular, gold loans and swaps, involving a right of ownership or claim in respect of investment gold, as well as transactions concerning investment gold involving futures and forward contracts leading to a transfer of right of ownership or claim in respect of investment gold.

Article 347

Member States shall exempt the services of agents who act in the name and on behalf of another person, when they take part in the supply of investment gold for their principal.

Section 3: Taxation option

Article 348

Member States shall allow taxable persons who produce investment gold or transform gold into investment gold the right to opt for the taxation of supplies of investment gold to another taxable person which would otherwise be exempt pursuant to Article 346.

Article 349

1. Member States may allow taxable persons who, in the course of their economic activity, normally supply gold for industrial purposes, the right to opt for the taxation of supplies of gold bars or wafers, as referred to in point (1) of Article 344(1), to another taxable person, which would otherwise be exempt pursuant to Article 346.

2. Member States may restrict the scope of the option provided for in paragraph 1.

Article 350

Where the supplier has exercised the right under Articles 348 and 349 to opt for taxation, Member States shall allow the agent to opt for taxation of the services referred to in Article 347.

Article 351

Member States shall lay down detailed rules for the exercise of the options provided for in this Section, and shall inform the Commission accordingly.

Section 4: Transactions on a regulated gold bullion market

Article 352

Each Member State may, after consulting the VAT Committee, apply VAT to specific transactions relating to investment gold which take place in that Member State between taxable persons who are members of a gold bullion market regulated by the Member State concerned or between such a taxable person and another taxable person who is not a member of that market.

However, the Member State may not apply VAT to supplies carried out in accordance with the conditions specified in Article 138 or to exports of investment gold.

Article 353

Member States which, pursuant to Article 352, tax transactions between taxable persons who are members of a regulated gold bullion market shall, for the purposes of simplification, authorize suspension of the tax to be collected and relieve taxable persons of the accounting requirements in respect of VAT.

Section 5: Special rights and obligations for traders in investment gold

Article 354

Where his subsequent supply of investment gold is exempt pursuant to this Chapter, the taxable person shall be entitled to deduct the following:

(a) the VAT due or paid in respect of investment gold supplied to him by a person who has exercised the right of option under Articles 348 and 349 or supplied to him in accordance with Section 4;

(b) the VAT due or paid in respect of a supply to him, or in respect of an intra-Community acquisition or importation carried out by him, of gold other than investment gold which is subsequently transformed by him or on his behalf into investment gold;

(c) the VAT due or paid in respect of services supplied to him consisting in a change of form, weight or purity of gold including investment gold.

Article 355

Taxable persons who produce investment gold or transform gold into investment gold shall be entitled to deduct the VAT due or paid by them in respect of the supply, intra-Community acquisition or importation of goods or services linked to the production or transformation of that gold, as if the subsequent supply of the gold exempted pursuant to Article 346 were taxed.

Article 356

1. Member States shall ensure that traders in investment gold keep, as a minimum, accounts of all substantial transactions in investment gold and keep the documents which enable the customers in such transactions to be identified.

Traders shall keep the information referred to in the first subparagraph for a period of at least five years.

2. Member States may accept equivalent obligations under measures adopted pursuant to other Community legislation, such as Directive 2005/60/EC of the European Parliament and of the Council of 26 October 2005 on the prevention of the use of the financial system for the purpose of money laundering and terrorist financing, to comply with the requirements under paragraph 1.

3. Member States may lay down obligations which are more stringent, in particular as regards the keeping of special records or special accounting requirements.

Chapter 6 Special Scheme for Non-Established Taxable Persons supplying Electronic Services to Non-Taxable Persons

Section 1: General provisions

Article 357

This Chapter shall apply until 31 December 2014.

Article 358

[see article 204(1) subparagraph 3]

For the purposes of this Chapter, and without prejudice to other provisions, the following definitions shall apply:

(1) "**non-established taxable person**" means a taxable person who has not established his business in the territory of the Community and who has no fixed establishment there and who is not otherwise required to be identified pursuant to Article 214;

(2) "**electronic services**" and "electronically supplied services" mean the services referred to in point (k) of the first paragraph of Article 59;

(3) "**Member State of identification**" means the Member State which the non-established taxable person chooses to contact to state when his activity as a taxable person within the territory of the Community commences in accordance with the provisions of this Chapter;

(4) "**Member State of consumption**" means the Member State in which, pursuant to Article 58, the

supply of the electronic services is deemed to take place;

(5) "**VAT return**" means the statement containing the information necessary to establish the amount of VAT due in each Member State.

Section 2: Special scheme for electronically supplied services

Article 359

Member States shall permit any non-established taxable person supplying electronic services to a non-taxable person who is established in a Member State or who has his permanent address or usually resides in a Member State, to use this special scheme. This scheme applies to all electronic services supplied in the Community.

Article 360

The non-established taxable person shall state to the Member State of identification when he commences or ceases his activity as a taxable person, or changes that activity in such a way that he no longer meets the conditions necessary for use of this special scheme. He shall communicate that information electronically.

Article 361

1. The information which the non-established taxable person must provide to the Member State of identification when he commences a taxable activity shall contain the following details:

    (a) name;

(b) postal address;

(c) electronic addresses, including websites;

(d) national tax number, if any;

(e) a statement that the person is not identified for VAT purposes within the Community.

2. The non-established taxable person shall notify the Member State of identification of any changes in the information provided.

Article 362

The Member State of identification shall allocate to the non-established taxable person an individual VAT identification number and shall notify him of that number by electronic means. On the basis of the information used for that identification, Member States of consumption may have recourse to their own identification systems.

Article 363

The Member State of identification shall strike the non-established taxable person from the identification register in the following cases:

(a) if he notifies that Member State that he no longer supplies electronic services;

(b) if it may otherwise be assumed that his taxable activities have ceased;

(c) if he no longer meets the conditions necessary for use of this special scheme;

(d) if he persistently fails to comply with the rules relating to this special scheme.

Article 364

The non-established taxable person shall submit by electronic means to the Member State of identification a VAT return for each calendar quarter, whether or not electronic services have been supplied. The VAT return shall be submitted within 20 days following the end of the tax period covered by the return.

Article 365

The VAT return shall show the identification number and, for each Member State of consumption in which VAT is due, the total value, exclusive of VAT, of supplies of electronic services carried out during the tax period and the total amount of the corresponding VAT. The applicable rates of VAT and the total VAT due must also be indicated on the return.

Article 366

1. The VAT return shall be made out in euro.

Member States which have not adopted the euro may require the VAT return to be made out in their national currency. If the supplies have been made in other currencies, the non-established taxable person shall, for the purposes of completing the VAT return, use the exchange rate applying on the last day of the tax period.

2. The conversion shall be made by applying the exchange rates published by the European Central Bank for that day, or, if there is no publication on that day, on the next day of publication.

Article 367

The non-established taxable person shall pay the VAT when submitting the VAT return.

Payment shall be made to a bank account denominated in euro, designated by the Member State of identification. Member States which have not adopted the euro may require payment to be made to a bank account denominated in their own currency.

Article 368

The non-established taxable person making use of this special scheme may not deduct VAT pursuant to Article 168 of this Directive. Notwithstanding Article 1(1) of Directive 86/560/EEC, the taxable person in question shall be refunded in accordance with the said Directive. Articles 2(2) and (3) and Article 4(2) of Directive 86/560/EEC shall not apply to refunds relating to electronic services covered by this special scheme.

Article 369

1. The non-established taxable person shall keep records of the transactions covered by this special scheme. Those records must be sufficiently detailed to enable the tax authorities of the Member State of consumption to verify that the VAT return is correct.

2. The records referred to in paragraph 1 must be made available electronically on request to the Member State of identification and to the Member State of consumption.

Those records must be kept for a period of ten years from the end of the year during which the transaction was carried out.

Comments to Title XII RVD: Special schemes

A – Implementation measures (see Regulation 282/2011)

SECTION 1

Special scheme for investment gold

(Articles 344 to 356 of Directive 2006/112/EC)

Article 56

'Weights accepted by the bullion markets' as referred to in point (l) of Article 344(1) of Directive 2006/112/EC shall at least cover the units and the weights traded as set out in Annex III to this Regulation.

Guidance notes: 'Weights accepted by the bullion markets' shall at least cover the units and the weights traded as set out in Annex III to this Regulation.

Article 57

For the purposes of establishing the list of gold coins referred to in Article 345 of Directive 2006/112/EC, 'price' and 'open market value' as referred to in point (2) of Article 344(1) of that Directive shall be the price and open market value on 1 April of each year. If 1 April does not fall on a day on which those values are fixed, the values of the next day on which they are fixed shall be used.

Guidance notes: For the purposes of establishing the list of gold coins traded in a Member State 'price' and 'open market value' shall be the price and open market value on 1 April of each year. If 1 April does not fall on a day on which those values are fixed, the values of the next day on which they are fixed shall be used.

Guidance notes (art. 56 & 57): These articles concern the special scheme for investment gold.

SECTION 2

Special scheme for non-established taxable persons supplying electronic services to non-taxable persons

(Articles 357 to 369 of Directive 2006/112/EC)

Article 58

Where, in the course of a calendar quarter, a non-established taxable person using the special scheme for electronically supplied services provided for in Articles 357 to 369 of Directive 2006/112/EC meets at least one of the criteria for exclusion laid down in Article 363 of that Directive, the Member State of identification shall exclude that non-established taxable person from the special scheme. In such cases the non-established taxable person may subsequently be excluded from the special scheme at any time during that quarter.

In respect of services supplied electronically prior to exclusion but during the calendar quarter in which exclusion occurs, the non-established taxable person shall submit a VAT return for the entire quarter in accordance with Article 364 of Directive 2006/112/EC. The requirement to submit this return shall have no effect on the requirement, if any, to be identified for VAT purposes in a Member State under the normal rules.

Guidance notes: Where, in the course of a calendar quarter, a non-established taxable person using the special scheme for electronically supplied services does not comply with the rules laid down, the Member State of identification shall exclude that non-established taxable person from the special scheme. In such cases the non-established taxable person may subsequently be excluded from the special scheme at any time during that quarter.

In respect of services supplied electronically prior to exclusion but during the calendar quarter in which exclusion occurs, the non-established taxable person shall submit a VAT return for the entire quarter. The requirement to submit this return shall have no effect on the requirement, if any, to be identified for VAT purposes in a Member State under the normal rules.

Article 59

Any return period (calendar quarter) within the meaning of Article 364 of Directive 2006/112/EC shall be a separate return period.

Guidance notes: Any return period (calendar quarter) shall be a separate return period.

Article 60

Once a VAT return has been submitted as provided for under Article 364 of Directive 2006/112/EC, any subsequent changes to the figures contained therein may be made only by means of an amendment to that return and not by an adjustment to a subsequent return.

Guidance notes: Once a VAT return has been submitted, any subsequent changes to the figures contained therein may be made only by means of an amendment to that return and not by an adjustment to a subsequent return.

Article 61

Amounts on VAT returns made under the special scheme for electronically supplied services provided for in Articles 357 to 369 of Directive 2006/112/EC shall not be rounded up or down to the nearest whole monetary unit. The exact amount of VAT shall be reported and remitted.

Guidance notes: Amounts on VAT returns shall be the exact amount of VAT reported and remitted.

Article 62

A Member State of identification which receives a payment in excess of that resulting from the VAT return submitted for electronically supplied services under Article 364 of Directive 2006/112/EC shall reimburse the overpaid amount directly to the taxable person concerned.

Where the Member State of identification has received an amount pursuant to a VAT return subsequently found to be incorrect, and that Member State has already distributed that amount among the Member States of consumption, those Member States shall directly reimburse the overpayment to the non-established taxable person and inform the Member State of identification of the adjustment to be made.

Guidance notes: A Member State of identification which receives a payment in excess of that resulting from the VAT return submitted shall reimburse the overpaid amount directly to the taxable person concerned

Article 63

Amounts of VAT paid under Article 367 of Directive 2006/112/EC shall be specific to the VAT return submitted pursuant to Article 364 of that Directive. Any subsequent amendments to the amounts paid may be effected only by reference to that return and may not be allocated to another return, or adjusted on a subsequent return.

Guidance notes: Amounts of VAT paid shall be specific to the VAT return submitted. Any subsequent amendments to the amounts paid may be effected only by reference to that return and may not be allocated to another return, or adjusted on a subsequent return.

Guidance notes (arts. 58 to 63)5: These articles concern the special scheme for non-EU providers of e-services to non-taxable persons.

Title XIII Derogations

Chapter 1 Derogations Applying Until the Adoption of Definitive Arrangements

Section 1: Derogations for States which were members of the Community on 1 January 1978

Article 370

Member States which, at 1 January 1978, taxed the transactions listed in Annex X, Part A, may continue to tax those transactions.

Article 371

[also refer to article 13(2)]

Member States which, at 1 January 1978, exempted the transactions listed in Annex X, Part B, may continue to exempt those transactions, in accordance with the conditions applying in the Member State concerned on that date.

Article 372

Member States which, at 1 January 1978, applied provisions derogating from the principle of immediate deduction laid down in the first paragraph of Article 179 may continue to apply those provisions.

Article 373

Member States which, at 1 January 1978, applied provisions derogating from Article 28 or from point (c) of the first paragraph of Article 79 may continue to apply those provisions.

Article 374

[also refer to article 13(2)]

By way of derogation from Articles 169 and 309, Member States which, at 1 January 1978, exempted, without deductibility of the VAT paid at the preceding stage, the services of travel agents, as referred to in Article 309, may continue to exempt those services. That derogation shall apply also in respect of travel agents acting in the name and on behalf of the traveler.

Section 2: Derogations for States which acceded to the Community after 1 January 1978

Article 375

[also refer to article 13(2)]

Greece may continue to exempt the transactions listed in points (2), (8), (9), (11) and (12) of Annex X, Part B, in accordance with the conditions applying in that Member State on 1 January 1987.

Article 376

[also refer to article 13(2)]

Spain may continue to exempt the supply of services performed by authors, listed in point (2) of Annex X, Part B, and the transactions listed in points (11) and (12) of Annex X, Part B, in accordance with the conditions applying in that Member State on 1 January 1993.

Article 377

[also refer to article 13(2)]

Portugal may continue to exempt the transactions listed in points (2), (4), (7), (9), (10) and (13) of Annex X, Part B, in accordance with the conditions applying in that Member State on 1 January 1989.

Article 378

1. Austria may continue to tax the transactions listed in point (2) of Annex X, Part A.

2. For as long as the same exemptions are applied in any of the Member States which were members of the Community on 31 December 1994, Austria may, in accordance with the conditions applying in that Member State on the date of its accession, continue to exempt the following transactions [also refer to article 13(2)]:

    (a) the transactions listed in points (5) and (9) of Annex X, Part B;

    (b) with deductibility of the VAT paid at the preceding stage, all parts of international passenger transport operations, carried out by air, sea or inland waterway, other than passenger transport operations on Lake Constance.

Article 379

1. Finland may continue to tax the transactions listed in point (2) of Annex X, Part A, for as long as the same transactions are taxed in any of the Member States which were members of the Community on 31 December 1994.

2. Finland may, in accordance with the conditions applying in that Member State on the date of its accession, continue to exempt the supply of services by authors, artists and performers, listed in point (2) of Annex X, Part B, and the transactions listed in points (5), (9) and (10) of Annex X, Part

B, for as long as the same exemptions are applied in any of the Member States which were members of the Community on 31 December 1994 [also refer to article 13(2)].

Article 380

[also refer to article 13(2)]

Sweden may, in accordance with the conditions applying in that Member State on the date of its accession, continue to exempt the supply of services by authors, artists and performers, listed in point (2) of Annex X, Part B, and the transactions listed in points (1), (9) and (10) of Annex X, Part B, for as long as the same exemptions are applied in any of the Member States which were members of the Community on 31 December 1994.

Article 381

[also refer to article 13(2)]

The Czech Republic may, in accordance with the conditions applying in that Member State on the date of its accession, continue to exempt the international transport of passengers, as referred to in point (10) of Annex X, Part B, for as long as the same exemption is applied in any of the Member States which were members of the Community on 30 April 2004.

Article 382

[also refer to article 13(2)]

Estonia may, in accordance with the conditions applying in that Member State on the date of its accession, continue to exempt the international transport of passengers, as referred to in point (10) of Annex X, Part B, for as long as the same exemption is applied in any of the Member States which were members of the Community on 30 April 2004.

Article 383

[also refer to article 13(2)]

Cyprus may, in accordance with the conditions applying in that Member State on the date of its accession, continue to exempt the following transactions:

(a) the supply of building land referred to in point (9) of Annex X, Part B, until 31 December 2007;

(b) the international transport of passengers, as referred to in point (10) of Annex X, Part B, for as long as the same exemption is applied in any of the Member States which were members of the Community on 30 April 2004.

Article 384

[also refer to article 13(2)]

For as long as the same exemptions are applied in any of the Member States which were members of the Community on 30 April 2004, Latvia may, in accordance with the conditions applying in that Member State on the date of its accession, continue to exempt the following transactions:

(a) the supply of services by authors, artists and performers, as referred to in point (2) of Annex X, Part B;

(b) the international transport of passengers, as referred to in point (10) of Annex X, Part B.

Article 385

[also refer to article 13(2)]

Lithuania may, in accordance with the conditions applying in that Member State on the date of its accession, continue to exempt the international transport of passengers, as referred to in point (10) of Annex X, Part B, for as long as the same exemption is applied in any of the Member States which were members of the Community on 30 April 2004.

Article 386

[also refer to article 13(2)]

Hungary may, in accordance with the conditions applying in that Member State on the date of its accession, continue to exempt the international transport of passengers, as referred to in point (10) of Annex X, Part B, for as long as the same exemption is applied in any of the Member States which were members of the Community on 30 April 2004.

Article 387

[also refer to article 13(2)]

For as long as the same exemptions are applied in any of the Member States which were members of the Community on 30 April 2004, Malta may, in accordance with the conditions applying in that Member State on the date of its accession, continue to exempt the following transactions:

(a) without deductibility of the VAT paid at the preceding stage, the supply of water by a body governed by public law, as referred to in point (8) of Annex X, Part B;

(b) without deductibility of the VAT paid at the preceding stage, the supply of buildings and building land, as referred to in point (9) of Annex X, Part B;

(c) with deductibility of the VAT paid at the preceding stage, inland passenger transport, international passenger transport and domestic inter-island sea passenger transport, as referred to in point (10) of Annex X, Part B.

Article 388

[also refer to article 13(2)]

Poland may, in accordance with the conditions applying in that Member State on the date of its accession, continue to exempt the international transport of passengers, as referred to in point (10) of Annex X, Part B, for as long as the same exemption is applied in any of the Member States which were members of the Community on 30 April 2004.

Article 389

[also refer to article 13(2)]

Slovenia may, in accordance with the conditions applying in that Member State on the date of its accession, continue to exempt the international transport of passengers, as referred to in point (10) of Annex X, Part B, for as long as the same exemption is applied in any of the Member States which were members of the Community on 30 April 2004.

Article 390

[also refer to article 13(2)]

Slovakia may, in accordance with the conditions applying in that Member State on the date of its accession, continue to exempt the international transport of passengers, as referred to in point (10) of Annex X, Part B, for as long as the same exemption is applied in any of the Member States which were members of the Community on 30 April 2004.

Article 390a

[also refer to article 13(2)]

Bulgaria may, in accordance with the conditions applying in that Member State on the date of its accession, continue to exempt the international transport of passengers as referred to in point 10 of Annex X, Part B, for as long as the same exemption is applied in any of the Member States which were members of the Community on 31 December 2006.

Article 390b

[also refer to article 13(2)]

Romania may, in accordance with the conditions applying in that Member State on the date of its accession, continue to exempt the international transport of passengers, as referred to in point 10 of Annex X, Part B, for as long as the same exemption is applied in any of the Member States which were members of the Community on 31 December 2006.

Article 390c

[also refer to article 13(2)]

Croatia may, in accordance with the conditions applying in that Member State on the date of its accession, continue to exempt the following transactions:

(a) the supply of building land, with or without buildings built on it, as referred to in point (j) of Article 135(1) and in point (9) of Annex X, Part B, non-renewable, until 31 December 2014;

(b) the international transport of passengers, as referred to in point (10) of Annex X, Part B, for as long as the same exemption is applied in any of the Member States which were members of the Union before the accession of Croatia.

Section 3: Provisions common to Sections 1 and 2

Article 391

Member States which exempt the transactions referred to in Articles 371, 375, 376 or 377, Article 378(2), Article 379(2) or Articles 380 to 390c may grant taxable persons the right to opt for taxation of those transactions.

Article 392

Member States may provide that, in respect of the supply of buildings and building land purchased for the purpose of resale by a taxable person for whom the VAT on the purchase was not deductible, the taxable amount shall be the difference between the selling price and the purchase price.

Article 393

1. With a view to facilitating the transition to the definitive arrangements referred to in Article 402, the Council shall, on the basis of a report from the Commission, review the situation with regard to the derogations provided for in Sections 1 and 2 and shall, acting in accordance with Article 93 of the Treaty decide whether any or all of those derogations is to be abolished.

2. By way of definitive arrangements, passenger transport shall be taxed in the Member State of departure for that part of the journey taking place within the Community, in accordance with the detailed rules to be laid down by the Council, acting in accordance with Article 93 of the Treaty.

Chapter 2 Derogations Subject to Authorization

Section 1: Simplification measures and measures to prevent tax evasion or avoidance

Article 394

Member States which, at 1 January 1977, applied special measures to simplify the procedure for collecting VAT or to prevent certain forms of tax evasion or avoidance may retain them provided that they have notified the Commission accordingly before 1 January 1978 and that such simplification measures comply with the criterion laid down in the second subparagraph of Article 395(1).

Article 395

1. The Council, acting unanimously on a proposal from the Commission, may authorize any Member State to introduce special measures for derogation from the provisions of this Directive, in order to simplify the procedure for collecting VAT or to prevent certain forms of tax evasion or avoidance.

Measures intended to simplify the procedure for collecting VAT may not, except to a negligible extent, affect the overall amount of the tax revenue of the Member State collected at the stage of final consumption.

2. A Member State wishing to introduce the measure referred to in paragraph 1 shall send an application to the Commission and provide it with all the necessary information. If the Commission considers that it does not have all the necessary information, it shall contact the Member State concerned within two months of receipt of the application and specify what additional information is required.

Once the Commission has all the information it considers

necessary for appraisal of the request it shall within one month notify the requesting Member State accordingly and it shall transmit the request, in its original language, to the other Member States.

3. Within three months of giving the notification referred to in the second subparagraph of paragraph 2, the Commission shall present to the Council either an appropriate proposal or, should it object to the derogation requested, a communication setting out its objections.

4. The procedure laid down in paragraphs 2 and 3 shall, in any event, be completed within eight months of receipt of the application by the Commission.

5. In cases of imperative urgency as set out in Article 199b(1), the procedure laid down in paragraphs 2 and 3 shall be completed within six months of receipt of the application by the Commission.

Section 2: International Agreements

Article 396

1. The Council, acting unanimously on a proposal from the Commission, may authorize any Member State to conclude with a third country or an international body an agreement which may contain derogations from this Directive.

2. A Member State wishing to conclude an agreement as referred to in paragraph 1 shall send an application to the Commission and provide it with all the necessary information. If the Commission considers that it does not have all the necessary information, it shall contact the Member State concerned within two months of receipt of the application and specify what additional information is required.

Once the Commission has all the information it considers

necessary for appraisal of the request it shall within one month notify the requesting Member State accordingly and it shall transmit the request, in its original language, to the other Member States.

3. Within three months of giving the notification referred to in the second subparagraph of paragraph 2, the Commission shall present to the Council either an appropriate proposal or, should it object to the derogation requested, a communication setting out its objections.

3. The procedure laid down in paragraphs 2 and 3 shall, in any event, be completed within eight months of receipt of the application by the Commission.

Title XIV - Miscellaneous

Chapter 1 Implementing Measures

Article 397

The Council, acting unanimously on a proposal from the Commission, shall adopt the measures necessary to implement this Directive.

Chapter 2 VAT Committee

Article 398

1. An advisory committee on value added tax, called "the VAT Committee", is set up.

2. The VAT Committee shall consist of representatives of the Member States and of the Commission.

The chairman of the Committee shall be a representative of the Commission.

Secretarial services for the Committee shall be provided by the Commission.

3. The VAT Committee shall adopt its own rules of procedure.

4. In addition to the points forming the subject of consultation pursuant to this Directive, the VAT Committee shall examine questions raised by its chairman, on his own initiative or at the request of the representative of a Member State, which concern the application of Community provisions on VAT.

Chapter 3 Conversion Rates

Article 399

Without prejudice to any other particular provisions, the equivalents in national currency of the amounts in euro specified in this Directive shall be determined on the basis of the euro conversion rate applicable on 1 January 1999. Member States having acceded to the European Union after that date, which have not adopted the euro as single currency, shall use the euro conversion rate applicable on the date of their accession.

Article 400

When converting the amounts referred to in Article 399 into national currencies, Member States may adjust the amounts resulting from that conversion either upwards or downwards by up to 10 %.

Chapter 4 Other Taxes, Duties and Charges

Article 401

Without prejudice to other provisions of Community law, this Directive shall not prevent a Member State from maintaining or introducing taxes on insurance contracts, taxes on betting and gambling, excise duties, stamp duties or, more generally, any taxes, duties or charges which cannot be characterized as turnover taxes, provided that the collecting of those taxes, duties or charges does not give rise, in trade between Member States, to formalities connected with the crossing of frontiers.

Title XV - Final Provisions

Chapter 1 Transitional Arrangements for the Taxation of Trade between Member States

Article 402

1. The arrangements provided for in this Directive for the taxation of trade between Member States are transitional and shall be replaced by definitive arrangements based in principle on the taxation in the Member State of origin of the supply of goods or services.

2. Having concluded, upon examination of the report referred to in Article 404, that the conditions for transition to the definitive arrangements are met, the Council shall, acting in accordance with Article 93 of the Treaty, adopt the provisions necessary for the entry into force and for the operation of the definitive arrangements.

Article 403

The Council shall, acting in accordance with Article 93 of the Treaty, adopt Directives appropriate for the purpose of supplementing the common system of VAT and, in particular, for the progressive restriction or the abolition of derogations from that system.

Article 404

Every four years starting from the adoption of this Directive, the Commission shall, on the basis of information obtained from the Member States, present a report to the European Parliament and to the Council on the operation of the common system of VAT in the Member States and, in particular, on the operation of the transitional arrangements for taxing trade between Member States.

That report shall be accompanied, where appropriate, by proposals concerning the definitive arrangements.

Chapter 2 Transitional Measures applicable in the Context of Accession to the European Union

Article 405

For the purposes of this Chapter, the following definitions shall apply:

1. "**Community**" means the territory of the Community as defined in point (1) of Article 5 before the accession of new Member States;

2. "**new Member States**" means the territory of the Member States which acceded to the European Union after 1 January 1995, as defined for each of those Member States in point (2) of Article 5;

3. "**enlarged Community**" means the territory of the Community as defined in point (1) of Article 5 after the accession of new Member States.

Article 406

The provisions in force at the time the goods were placed under temporary importation arrangements with total exemption from import duty or under one of the arrangements or situations referred to in Article 156, or under similar arrangements or situations in one of the new Member States, shall continue to apply until the goods cease to be covered by these arrangements or situations after the date of accession, where the following conditions are met:

(a) the goods entered the Community or one of the new Member States before the date of accession;

(b) the goods were placed, on entry into the Community or one of the new Member States, under these arrangements or situations;

(c) the goods have not ceased to be covered by these arrangements or situations before the date of accession.

Article 407

The provisions in force at the time the goods were placed under customs transit arrangements shall continue to apply until the goods cease to be covered by these arrangements after the date of accession, where the following conditions are met:

(a) the goods were placed, before the date of accession, under customs transit arrangements;

(b) the goods have not ceased to be covered by these arrangements before the date of accession.

Article 408

1. The following shall be treated as an importation of goods where it is shown that the goods were in free circulation in one of the new Member States or in the Community:

    (a) the removal, including irregular removal, of goods from temporary importation arrangements under which they were placed before the date of accession under the conditions provided for in Article 406;

    (b) the removal, including irregular removal, of goods either from one of the arrangements or situations referred to in Article 156 or from similar arrangements or situations under which they were placed before the date of accession under the conditions provided for in Article 406;

    (c) the cessation of one of the arrangements referred to in Article 407, started before the date of accession in the territory of one of the new Member States, for the purposes of a supply of goods for consideration effected before that date in the territory of that Member State by a taxable person acting as such;

    (d) any irregularity or offence committed during customs transit arrangements started under the conditions referred to in point (c).

2. In addition to the case referred to in paragraph 1, the use after the date of accession within the territory of a Member State, by a taxable or non-taxable person, of goods supplied to him before the date of accession within the territory of the Community or one of the new Member States shall be treated as an importation of goods where the following conditions are met:

    (a) the supply of those goods has been exempted, or was likely to be exempted, either under points (a) and (b) of

Article 146(1) or under a similar provision in the new Member States;

(b) the goods were not imported into one of the new Member States or into the Community before the date of accession.

Article 409

In the cases referred to in Article 408(1), the place of import within the meaning of Article 61 shall be the Member State within whose territory the goods cease to be covered by the arrangements or situations under which they were placed before the date of accession.

Article 410

1. By way of derogation from Article 71, the importation of goods within the meaning of Article 408 shall terminate without the occurrence of a chargeable event if one of the following conditions is met:

    (a) the imported goods are dispatched or transported outside the enlarged Community;

    (b) the imported goods within the meaning of Article 408(1)(a) are other than means of transport and are re-dispatched or transported to the Member State from which they were exported and to the person who exported them;

    (c) the imported goods within the meaning of Article 408(1)(a) are means of transport which were acquired or imported before the date of accession in accordance with the general conditions of taxation in force on the domestic market of one of the new Member States or of one of the Member States of the Community or which have not been subject, by reason of their exportation, to any exemption from, or refund of, VAT.

2. The condition referred to in paragraph 1(c) shall be deemed to be fulfilled in the following cases:

    (a) when the date of first entry into service of the means of transport was more than eight years before the accession to the European Union.

    (b) when the amount of tax due by reason of the importation is insignificant.

Chapter 3 Transposition and Entry Into Force

Article 411

1. Directive 67/227/EEC and Directive 77/388/EEC are repealed, without prejudice to the obligations of the Member States concerning the time-limits, listed in Annex XI, Part B, for the transposition into national law and the implementation of those Directives.

2. References to the repealed Directives shall be construed as references to this Directive and shall be read in accordance with the correlation table in Annex XII.

Article 412

1. Member States shall bring into force the laws, regulations and administrative provisions necessary to comply with Article 2(3), Article 44, Article 59(1), Article 399 and Annex III, point (18) with effect from 1 January 2008. They shall forthwith communicate to the Commission the text of those provisions and a correlation table between those provisions and this Directive.

When Member States adopt those provisions, they shall contain a reference to this Directive or be accompanied by such a reference on the occasion of their official publication. Member States shall determine how such reference is to be made.

2. Member States shall communicate to the Commission the text of the main provisions of national law which they adopt in the field covered by this Directive.

Article 413

This Directive shall enter into force on 1 January 2007.

Article 414

This Directive is addressed to the Member States.

Annex I

List of the Activities referred to in the Third subparagraph of article 13(1)

(1) Telecommunications services;

(2) supply of water, gas, electricity and thermal energy;

(3) transport of goods;

(4) port and airport services;

(5) passenger transport;

(6) supply of new goods manufactured for sale;

(7) transactions in respect of agricultural products, carried out by agricultural intervention agencies pursuant to Regulations on the common organization of the market in those products;

(8) organization of trade fairs and exhibitions;

(9) warehousing;

(10) activities of commercial publicity bodies;

(11) activities of travel agents;

(12) running of staff shops, cooperatives and industrial canteens and similar institutions;

(13) activities carried out by radio and television bodies in so far as these are not exempt pursuant to Article 132(1)(q).

Annex II

Indicative List of the Electronically Supplied Services referred to in article 58 and point (k) of the first paragraph of article 59

(1) Website supply, web-hosting, distance maintenance of programs and equipment;

(2) supply of software and updating thereof;

(3) supply of images, text and information and making available of databases;

(4) supply of music, films and games, including games of chance and gambling games, and of political, cultural, artistic, sporting, scientific and entertainment broadcasts and events;

(5) supply of distance teaching.

Annex III

List of Supplies of Goods and Services to which the Reduced Rates referred to in article 98 may be applied

(1) Foodstuffs (including beverages but excluding alcoholic beverages) for human and animal consumption; live animals, seeds, plants and ingredients normally intended for use in the preparation of foodstuffs; products normally used to supplement foodstuffs or as a substitute for foodstuffs;

(2) supply of water;

(3) pharmaceutical products of a kind normally used for health care, prevention of illnesses and as treatment for medical and veterinary purposes, including products used for contraception and sanitary protection;

(4) medical equipment, aids and other appliances normally intended to alleviate or treat disability, for the exclusive personal use of the disabled, including the repair of such goods, and supply of children's car seats;

(5) transport of passengers and their accompanying luggage;

(6) supply, including on loan by libraries, of books on all physical means of support (including brochures, leaflets and similar printed matter, children's picture, drawing or coloring books, music printed or in manuscript form, maps and hydrographic or similar charts), newspapers and periodicals, other than material wholly or predominantly devoted to advertising;

(7) admission to shows, theatres, circuses, fairs, amusement parks, concerts, museums, zoos, cinemas, exhibitions and similar cultural events and facilities;

(8) reception of radio and television broadcasting services;

(9) supply of services by writers, composers and performing artists, or of the royalties due to them;

(10) provision, construction, renovation and alteration of housing, as part of a social policy;

(10a) renovation and repairing of private dwellings, excluding materials which account for a significant part of the value of the service supplied;

(10b) window-cleaning and cleaning in private households;

(11) supply of goods and services of a kind normally intended for use in agricultural production but excluding capital goods such as machinery or buildings;

(12) accommodation provided in hotels and similar establishments, including the provision of holiday accommodation and the letting of places on camping or caravan sites;

(12a) restaurant and catering services, it being possible to exclude the supply of (alcoholic and/or non-alcoholic) beverages;

(13) admission to sporting events;

(14) use of sporting facilities;

(15) supply of goods and services by organizations recognized as being devoted to social wellbeing by Member States and engaged in welfare or social security work, in so far as those transactions are not exempt pursuant to Articles 132, 135 and 136;

(16) supply of services by undertakers and cremation services, and the supply of goods related thereto;

(17) provision of medical and dental care and thermal treatment in so far as those services are not exempt pursuant to points (b) to (e) of Article 132(1);

(18) supply of services provided in connection with street cleaning, refuse collection and waste treatment, other than the supply of such services by bodies referred to in Article 13.

(19) minor repairing of bicycles, shoes and leather goods, clothing and household linen (including mending and alteration);

(20) domestic care services such as home help and care of young, elderly, sick or disabled;

(21) hairdressing.

Annex IV

[Deleted]

Annex V

Categories of Goods covered by Warehousing Arrangements other than Customs Warehousing as provided for under article 160(2)

	CN-code	Description of goods
(1)	0701	Potatoes
(2)	071120	Olives
(3)	0801	Coconuts, Brazil nuts and cashew nuts
(4)	0802	Other nuts
(5)	09011100 09011200	Coffee, not roasted
(6)	0902	Tea
(7)	1001 to 1005 1007 to 1008	Cereals
(9)	1006	Husked rice
(8)	1201 to 1207	Grains and oil seeds (including soya beans) and oleaginous fruits
(10)	1507 to 1515	Vegetable oils and fats and their fractions, whether or not refined, but not chemically modified
(11)	170111 170112	Raw sugar
(12)	1801	Cocoa beans, whole or broken, raw or roasted
(13)	2709 2710 271112 271113	Mineral oils (including propane and butane; also including crude petroleum oils)
(14)	Chapters 28 and 29	Chemicals in bulk
(15)	4001 4002	Rubber, in primary forms or in plates, sheets or strip
(16)	5101	Wool
(17)	7106	Silver
(18)	71101100 71102100 71103100	Platinum (palladium, rhodium)
(19)	7402 7403 7405 7408	Copper
(20)	7502	Nickel
(21)	7601	Aluminium
(22)	7801	Lead
(23)	7901	Zinc
(24)	8001	Tin
(25)	ex811292 326 ex811299	Indium

Annex VI

List of Supplies of Goods and Services as referred to in point (d) of article 199(1)

(1) Supply of ferrous and non ferrous waste, scrap, and used materials including that of semi-finished products resulting from the processing, manufacturing or melting down of ferrous and non-ferrous metals and their alloys;

(2) supply of ferrous and non-ferrous semi-processed products and certain associated processing services;

(3) supply of residues and other recyclable materials consisting of ferrous and non-ferrous metals, their alloys, slag, ash, scale and industrial residues containing metals or their alloys and supply of selection, cutting, fragmenting and pressing services of these products;

(4) supply of, and certain processing services relating to, ferrous and non-ferrous waste as well as parings, scrap, waste and used and recyclable material consisting of cullet, glass, paper, paperboard and board, rags, bone, leather, imitation leather, parchment, raw hides and skins, tendons and sinews, twine, cordage, rope, cables, rubber and plastic;

(5) supply of the materials referred to in this annex after processing in the form of cleaning, polishing, selection, cutting, fragmenting, pressing or casting into ingots;

(6) supply of scrap and waste from the working of base materials.

Annex VII

List of the Agricultural Production Activities referred to in point (4) of article 295(1)

(1) Crop production:

    (a) general agriculture, including viticulture;

    (b) growing of fruit (including olives) and of vegetables, flowers and ornamental plants, both in the open and under glass;

    (c) production of mushrooms, spices, seeds and propagating materials;

    (d) running of nurseries;

(2) stock farming together with cultivation:

    (a) general stock farming;

    (b) poultry farming;

    (c) rabbit farming;

    (d) beekeeping;

    (e) silkworm farming;

    (f) snail farming;

(3) forestry;

(4) fisheries:

    (a) freshwater fishing;

    (b) fish farming;

    (c) breeding of mussels, oysters and other mollusks and crustaceans;

    (d) frog farming.

Annex VIII

Indicative List of the Agricultural Services referred to in point (5) of article 295(1)

(1) Field work, reaping and mowing, threshing, baling, collecting, harvesting, sowing and planting;

(2) packing and preparation for market, such as drying, cleaning, grinding, disinfecting and ensilage of agricultural products;

(3) storage of agricultural products;

(4) stock minding, rearing and fattening;

(5) hiring out, for agricultural purposes, of equipment normally used in agricultural, forestry or fisheries undertakings;

(6) technical assistance;

(7) destruction of weeds and pests, dusting and spraying of crops and land;

(8) operation of irrigation and drainage equipment;

(9) lopping, tree felling and other forestry services.

Annex IX

Works of Art, Collectors' Items and Antiques, as referred to in points (2), (3) and (4) of article 311(1)

PART A: Works of art

(1) Pictures, collages and similar decorative plaques, paintings and drawings, executed entirely by hand by the artist, other than plans and drawings for architectural, engineering, industrial, commercial, topographical or similar purposes, hand-decorated manufactured articles, theatrical scenery, studio back cloths or the like of painted canvas (CN code 9701);

(2) original engravings, prints and lithographs, being impressions produced in limited numbers directly in black and white or in color of one or of several plates executed entirely by hand by the artist, irrespective of the process or of the material employed, but not including any mechanical or photomechanical process (CN code 97020000);

(3) original sculptures and statuary, in any material, provided that they are executed entirely by the artist; sculpture casts the production of which is limited to eight copies and supervised by the artist or his successors in title (CN code 97030000); on an exceptional basis, in cases determined by the Member States, the limit of eight copies may be exceeded for statuary casts produced before 1 January 1989;

(4) tapestries (CN code 58050000) and wall textiles (CN code 63040000) made by hand from original designs provided by artists, provided that there are not more than eight copies of each;

(5) individual pieces of ceramics executed entirely by the artist and signed by him;

(6) enamels on copper, executed entirely by hand, limited to eight numbered copies bearing the signature of the artist or the studio, excluding articles of jewellery and goldsmiths' and silversmiths' wares;

(7) photographs taken by the artist, printed by him or under his supervision, signed and numbered and limited to 30 copies, all sizes and mounts included.

PART B: Collectors' items

(1) Postage or revenue stamps, postmarks, first-day covers, pre-stamped stationery and the like, used, or if unused not current and not intended to be current (CN code 97040000);

(2) collections and collectors' pieces of zoological, botanical, mineralogical, anatomical, historical, archaeological, paleontological, ethnographic or numismatic interest (CN code 97050000).

PART C: Antiques

Goods, other than works of art or collectors' items, which are more than 100 years old (CN code 97060000).

Annex X

List of transactions covered by the derogations referred to in Articles 370 and 371 and Articles 375 to 390c

PART A: Transactions which Member States may continue to tax

(1) The supply of services by dental technicians in their professional capacity and the supply of dental prostheses by dentists and dental technicians;

(2) the activities of public radio and television bodies other than those of a commercial nature;

(3) the supply of a building, or parts thereof, or of the land on which it stands, other than as referred to in point (a) of Article 12(1), where carried out by taxable persons who were entitled to deduction of the VAT paid at the preceding stage in respect of the building concerned;

(4) the supply of the services of travel agents, as referred to in Article 306, and those of travel agents acting in the name and on behalf of the traveler, in relation to journeys outside the Community.

PART B: Transactions which Member States may continue to exempt

(1) Admission to sporting events;

(2) the supply of services by authors, artists, performers, lawyers and other members of the liberal professions, other than the medical and paramedical professions, with the exception of the following:

   (a) assignments of patents, trade marks and other similar rights, and the granting of licenses in respect of such rights;

   (b) work, other than the supply of contract work, on movable tangible property, carried out for a taxable person;

   (c) services to prepare or coordinate the carrying out of construction work, such as services provided by architects and by firms providing on-site supervision of works;

   (d) commercial advertising services;

   (e) transport and storage of goods, and ancillary services;

   (f) hiring out of movable tangible property to a taxable person;

   (g) provision of staff to a taxable person;

   (h) provision of services by consultants, engineers, planning offices and similar services in scientific, economic or technical fields;

   (i) compliance with an obligation to refrain from exercising, in whole or in part, a business activity or a right covered by points (a) to (h) or point (j);

- (j) the services of forwarding agents, brokers, business agents and other independent intermediaries, in so far as they relate to the supply or importation of goods or the supply of services covered by points (a) to (i);

(3) the supply of telecommunications services, and of goods related thereto, by public postal services;

(4) the supply of services by undertakers and cremation services and the supply of goods related thereto;

(5) transactions carried out by blind persons or by workshops for the blind, provided that those exemptions do not cause significant distortion of competition;

(6) the supply of goods and services to official bodies responsible for the construction, setting out and maintenance of cemeteries, graves and monuments commemorating the war dead;

(7) transactions carried out by hospitals not covered by point (b) of Article 132(1);

(8) the supply of water by a body governed by public law;

(9) the supply before first occupation of a building, or parts thereof, or of the land on which it stands and the supply of building land, as referred to in Article 12;

(10) the transport of passengers and, in so far as the transport of the passengers is exempt, the transport of goods accompanying them, such as luggage or motor vehicles, or the supply of services relating to the transport of passengers;

(11) the supply, modification, repair, maintenance, chartering and hiring of aircraft used by State institutions, including equipment incorporated or used in such aircraft;

(12) the supply, modification, repair, maintenance, chartering and hiring of fighting ships;

(13) the supply of the services of travel agents, as referred to in Article 306, and those of travel agents acting in the name and on behalf of the traveler, in relation to journeys within the Community.

Annex XI

Repealed directives and time limits for transposition

Part A Repealed Directives with their successive amendments

(1)	Directive 67/227/EEC (OJ71, 14.4.1967, p.1301
(2)	Directive 77/388/EEC (Sixth Directive) (OJ L 145 of 13.6.1977, p. 1) Directive 78/583/EEC (OJ L 194 of 19.7.1978, p. 16) Directive 80/368/EEC (OJ L 90 of 3.4.1980, p. 41) Directive 84/386/EEC (OJ L 208 of 3.8.1984, p. 58) Directive 89/465/EEC (OJ L 226 of 3.8.1989, p. 21) Directive 91/680/EEC (OJ L 376 of 31.12.1991, p. 1) - (except for Article 2) Directive 92/77/EEC (OJ L 316 of 31.10.1992, p. 1) Directive 92/111/EEC (OJ L 384 of 30.12.1992, p. 47) Directive 94/4/EC (OJ L 60 of 3.3.1994, p. 14) - (only Article 2) Directive 94/5/EC (OJ L 60 of 3.3.1994, p. 16) Directive 94/76/EC (OJ L 365 of 31.12.1994, p. 53) Directive 95/7/EC (OJ L 102 of 5.5.1995, p. 18) Directive 96/42/EC (OJ L 170 of 9.7.1996, p. 34) Directive 96/95/EC (OJ L 338 of 28.12.1996, p. 89) Directive 98/80/EC (OJ L 281 of 17.10.1998, p. 31) Directive 1999/49/EC (OJ L 139 of 2.6.1999, p. 27) Directive 1999/59/EC (OJ L 162 of 26.6.1999, p. 63) Directive 1999/85/EC (OJ L 277 of 28.10.1999, p. 34) Directive 2000/17/EC (OJ L 84 of 5.4.2000, p. 24) Directive 2000/65/EC (OJ L 269 of 21.10.2000, p. 44) Directive 2001/4/EC (OJ L 22 of 24.1.2001, p. 17) Directive 2001/115/EC (OJ L 15 of 17.1.2001, p. 24) Directive 2002/38/EC (OJ L 128 of 15.5.2002, p. 41) Directive 2002/93/EC (OJ L 331 of 7.12.2002, p. 27) Directive 2003/92/EC (OJ L 260 of 11.10.2003, p. 8) Directive 2004/7/EC (OJ L 27 of 30.1.2004, p. 44) Directive 2004/15/EC (OJ L 52 of 21.2.2004, p. 61) Directive 2004/66/EC (OJ L 168 of 1.5.2004, p. 35) - (only Point V of the Annex) Directive 2005/92/EC (OJ L 345 of 28.12.2005, p. 19) Directive 2006/18/EC (OJ L 51 of 22.2.2006, p. 12) Directive 2006/58/EC (OJ L 174 of 28.6.2006, p. 5) Directive 2006/69/EC (OJ L 221 of 12.8.2006, p. 9) - (only Article 1) Directive 2006/98/EC (OJ L 363 of 20.12.2006, p. 129) - (only Point 2 of the Annex)

Part B Time limits for transposition into national law (referred to in Article 411)

Directive	Deadline for transposition
Directive 67/227/EEC	1 January 1970
Directive 77/388/EEC	1 January 1978
Directive 78/583/EEC	1 January 1979
Directive 80/368/EEC	1 January 1979
Directive 84/386/EEC	1 July 1985
Directive 89/465/EEC	1 January 1990 1 January 1991 1 January 1992 1 January 1993 1 January 1994 for Portugal
Directive 91/680/EEC	1 January 1993
Directive 92/77/EEC	31 December 1992
Directive 92/111/EEC	1 January 1993 1 January 1994 1 October 1993 for Germany
Directive 94/4/EC	1 April 1994
Directive 94/5/EC	1 January 1995
Directive 94/76/EC	1 January 1995
Directive 95/7/EC	1 January 1996 1 January 1997 for Germany and Luxembourg
Directive 96/42/EC	1 January 1995
Directive 96/95/EC	1 January 1997
Directive 98/80/EC	1 January 2000
Directive 1999/49/EC	1 January 1999
Directive 1999/59/EC	1 January 2000
Directive 1999/85/CE	—
Directive 2000/17/EC	—
Directive 2000/65/EC	31 December 2001
Directive 2001/4/EC	1 January 2001
Directive 2001/115/EC	1 January 2004
Directive 2002/38/EC	1 July 2003
Directive 2002/93/EC	—
Directive 2003/92/EC	1 January 2005
Directive 2004/7/EC	30 January 2004
Directive 2004/15/EC	—
Directive 2004/66/EC	1 May 2004
Directive 2005/92/EC	1 January 2006
Directive 2006/18/EC	—
Directive 2006/58/EC	1 July 2006
Directive 2006/69/EC	1 January 2008
Directive 2006/98/EC	1 January 2007

Annex XII

Correlation Table

Directive 67/227/EEC	Directive 77/388/EEC	Amending Directives	Other acts	This Directive
Article 1, first paragraph				Article 1(1)
Article 1, second and third paragraphs				—
Article 2, first, second and third paragraphs				Article 1(2), first, second and third subparagraphs
Articles 3, 4 and 6				—
	Article 1			—
	Article 2, point (1)			Article 2(1)(a) and (c)
	Article 2, point (2)			Article 2(1)(d)
	Article 3(1), first indent			Article 5, point (2)
	Article 3(1), second indent			Article 5, point (1)
	Article 3(1), third indent			Article 5, points (3) and (4)
	Article 3(2)			—
	Article 3(3), first subparagraph, first indent			Article 6(2)(a) and (b)
	Article 3(3), first subparagraph, second indent			Article 6(2)(c) and (d)
	Article 3(3), first subparagraph, third indent			Article 6(2)(e), (f) and (g)

Directive 67/227/EEC	Directive 77/388/EEC	Amending Directives	Other acts	This Directive
	Article 3(3) second subparagraph, first indent			Article 6(1)(b)
	Article 3(3) second subparagraph, second indent			Article 6(1)(c)
	Article 3(3), second subparagraph, third indent			Article 6(1)(a)
	Article 3(4) first subparagraph, first and second indents			Article 7(1)
	Article 3(4), second subparagraph, first, second and third indents			Article 7(2)
	Article 3(5)			Article 8
	Article 4(1) and (2)			Article 9(1), first and second subparagraphs
	Article 4(3)(a), first subparagraph, first sentence			Article 12(1)(a)
	Article 4(3)(a), first subparagraph, second sentence			Article 12(2), second subparagraph
	Article 4(3)(a), second subparagraph			Article 12(2), third subparagraph
	Article 4(3)(a), third subparagraph			Article 12(2), first subparagraph
	Article 4(3)(b), first subparagraph			Article 12(1)(b)
	Article 4(3)(b), second subparagraph			Article 12(3)

Directive 67/227/EEC	Directive 77/388/EEC	Amending Directives	Other acts	This Directive
	Article 6(2), first subparagraph, points (a) and (b)			Article 26(1)(a) and (b)
	Article 6(2), second subparagraph			Article 26(2)
	Article 6(3)			Article 27
	Article 6(4)			Article 28
	Article 6(5)			Article 29
	Article 7(1)(a) and (b)			Article 30, first and second paragraphs
	Article 7(2)			Article 60
	Article 7(3), first and second subparagraphs			Article 61, first and second paragraphs
	Article 8(1)(a), first sentence			Article 32, first paragraph
	Article 8(1)(a), second and third sentences			Article 36, first and second paragraphs
	Article 8(1)(b)			Article 31
	Article 8(1)(c), first subparagraph			Article 37(1)
	Article 8(1)(c), second subparagraph, first indent			Article 37(2), first subparagraph
	Article 8(1)(c), second subparagraph, second and third indents			Article 37(2), second and third subparagraphs
	Article 8(1)(c), third subparagraph			Article 37(2), fourth subparagraph

Directive 67/227/EEC	Directive 77/388/EEC	Amending Directives	Other acts	This Directive
	Article 8(1)(c), fourth subparagraph			Article 37(3), first subparagraph
	Article 8(1)(c), fifth subparagraph			—
	Article 8(1)(c), sixth subparagraph			Article 37(3), second subparagraph
	Article 8(1)(d), first and second subparagraphs			Article 38(1) and (2)
	Article 8(1)(e), first sentence			Article 39, first paragraph
	Article 8(1)(e), second and third sentences			Article 39, second paragraph
	Article 8(2)			Article 32, second paragraph
	Article 9(1)			Article 43
	Article 9(2) introductory sentence			—
	Article 9(2)(a)			Article 45
	Article 9(2)(b)			Article 46
	Article 9(2)(c), first and second indents			Article 52(a) and (b)
	Article 9(2)(c), third and fourth indents			Article 52(c)
	Article 9(2)(e), first to sixth indents			Article 56(1)(a) to (f)

Directive 67/227/EEC	Directive 77/388/EEC	Amending Directives	Other acts	This Directive
	Article 9(2)(e), seventh indent			Article 56(1)(f)
	Article 9(2)(e), eighth indent			Article 56(1)(g)
	Article 9(2)(e), ninth indent			Article 56(1)(h)
	Article 9(2)(e), tenth indent, first sentence			Article 56(1)(i)
	Article 9(2)(e), tenth indent, second sentence			Article 24(2)
	Article 9(2)(e), tenth indent, third sentence			Article 56(1)(i)
	Article 9(2)(e), eleventh and twelfth indents			Article 56(1)(j) and (k)
	Article 9(2)(f)			Article 57(1)
	Article 9(3)			Article 58, first and second paragraphs
	Article 9(3)(a) and (b)			Article 58, first paragraph, points (a) and (b)
	Article 9(4)			Article 59(1) and (2)
	Article 10(1)(a) and (b)			Article 62, points (1) and (2)
	Article 10(2), first subparagraph, first sentence			Article 63

Directive 67/227/EEC	Directive 77/388/EEC	Amending Directives	Other acts	This Directive
	Article 10(2), first subparagraph, second and third sentences			Article 64(1) and (2)
	Article 10(2), second subparagraph			Article 65
	Article 10(2), third subparagraph, first, second and third indents			Article 66(a), (b) and (c)
	Article 10(3), first subparagraph, first sentence			Article 70
	Article 10(3), first subparagraph, second sentence			Article 71(1), first subparagraph
	Article 10(3), second subparagraph			Article 71(1), second subparagraph
	Article 10(3), third subparagraph			Article 71(2)
	Article 11(A)(1)(a)			Article 73
	Article 11(A)(1)(b)			Article 74
	Article 11(A)(1)(c)			Article 75
	Article 11(A)(1)(d)			Article 77
	Article 11(A)(2)(a)			Article 78, first paragraph, point (a)
	Article 11(A)(2)(b), first sentence			Article 78, first paragraph, point (b)
	Article 11(A)(2)(b), second sentence			Article 78, second paragraph
	Article 11(A)(3)(a) and (b)			Article 79, first paragraph, points (a) and (b) Article 87(a) and (b)
	Article 11(A)(3)(c), first sentence			Article 79, first paragraph, point (c)

Directive 67/227/EEC	Directive 77/388/EEC	Amending Directives	Other acts	This Directive
	Article 11(A)(3)(c), second sentence			Article 79, second paragraph
	Article 11(A)(4), first and second subparagraphs			Article 81, first and second paragraphs
	Article 11(A)(5)			Article 82
	Article 11(A)(6), first subparagraph, first and second sentences			Article 80(1), first subparagraph
	Article 11(A)(6), first subparagraph, third sentence			Article 80(1), second subparagraph
	Article 11(A)(6), second subparagraph			Article 80(1), first subparagraph
	Article 11(A)(6), third subparagraph			–Article 80(2)
	Article 11(A)(6), fourth subparagraph			Article 80(3)
	Article 11(A)(7), first and second subparagraphs			Article 72, first and second paragraphs
	Article 11(B)(1)			Article 85
	Article 11(B)(3)(a)			Article 86(1)(a)
	Article 11(B)(3)(b), first subparagraph			Article 86(1)(b)
	Article 11(B)(3)(b), second subparagraph			Article 86(2)

Directive 67/227/EEC	Directive 77/388/EEC	Amending Directives	Other acts	This Directive
	Article 11(B)(3)(b), third subparagraph			Article 86(1)(b)
	Article 11(B)(4)			Article 87
	Article 11(B)(5)			Article 88
	Article 11(B)(6), first and second subparagraphs			Article 89, first and second paragraphs
	Article 11(C)(1), first and second subparagraphs			Article 90(1) and (2)
	Article 11(C)(2), first subparagraph			Article 91(1)
	Article 11(C)(2), second subparagraph, first and second sentences			Article 91(2), first and second subparagraphs
	Article 11(C)(3), first and second indents			Article 92(a) and (b)
	Article 12(1)			Article 93, first paragraph
	Article 12(1)(a)			Article 93, second paragraph, point (a)
	Article 12(1)(b)			Article 93, second paragraph, point (c)
	Article 12(2), first and second indents			Article 95, first and second paragraphs
	Article 12(3)(a), first subparagraph, first sentence			Article 96

Directive 67/227/EEC	Directive 77/388/EEC	Amending Directives	Other acts	This Directive
	Article 12(3)(a), first subparagraph, second sentence			Article 97(1)
	Article 12(3)(a), second subparagraph			Article 97(2)
	Article 12(3)(a), third subparagraph, first sentence			Article 98(1)
	Article 12(3)(a), third subparagraph, second sentence			Article 98(2), first subparagraph Article 99(1)
	Article 12(3)(a), fourth subparagraph			Article 98(2), second subparagraph
	Article 12(3)(b), first sentence			Article 102, first paragraph
	Article 12(3)(b), second, third and fourth sentences			Article 102, second paragraph
	Article 12(3)(c), first subparagraph			Article 103(1)
	Article 12(3)(c), second subparagraph, first and second indents			Article 103(2)(a) and (b)
	Article 12(4), first subparagraph			Article 99(2)
	Article 12(4), second subparagraph, first and second sentences			Article 100, first and second paragraphs
	Article 12(4), third subparagraph			Article 101
	Article 12(5)			Article 94(2)
	Article 12(6)			Article 105

Directive 67/227/EEC	Directive 77/388/EEC	Amending Directives	Other acts	This Directive
	Article 13(A)(1), introductory sentence			Article 131
	Article 13(A)(1)(a) to (n)			Article 132(1)(a) to (n)
	Article 13(A)(1)(o), first sentence			Article 132(1)(o)
	Article 13(A)(1)(o), second sentence			Article 132(2)
	Article 13(A)(1)(p) and (q)			Article 132(1)(p) and (q)
	Article 13(A)(2)(a), first to fourth indents			►C1 Article 133, first paragraph, points (a) to (d) ◄
	Article 13(A)(2)(b), first and second indents			Article 134(a) and (b)
	Article 13(B), introductory sentence			Article 131
	Article 13(B)(a)			Article 135(1)(a)
	Article 13(B)(b), first subparagraph			Article 135(1)(l)
	Article 13(B)(b), first subparagraph, points (1) to (4)			Article 135(2), first subparagraph, points (a) to (d)
	Article 13(B)(b), second subparagraph			Article 135(2), second subparagraph
	Article 13(B)(c)			Article 136(a) and (b)
	Article 13(B)(d)			—
	Article 13(B)(d), points (1) to (5)			Article 135(1)(b) to (f)

Directive 67/227/EEC	Directive 77/388/EEC	Amending Directives	Other acts	This Directive
	Article 13(B)(d), point (5), first and second indents			Article 135(1)(f)
	Article 13(B)(d), point (6)			Article 135(1)(g)
	Article 13(B)(e) to (h)			Article 135(1)(h) to (k)
	Article 13(C), first subparagraph, point (a)			Article 137(1)(d)
	Article 13(C), first subparagraph, point (b)			Article 137(1)(a), (b) and (c)
	Article 13(C), second subparagraph			Article 137(2), first and second subparagraphs
	Article 14(1), introductory sentence			Article 131
	Article 14(1)(a)			►C1 Article 143 (a) ◄
	Article 14(1)(d), first and second subparagraphs			Article 143(b) and (c)
	Article 14(1)(e)			Article 143(e)
	Article 14(1)(g), first to fourth indents			Article 143(f) to (i)
	Article 14(1)(h)			Article 143(j)
	Article 14(1)(i)			Article 144
	Article 14(1)(j)			Article 143(k)
	Article 14(1)(k)			Article 143(l)
	Article 14(2), first subparagraph			Article 145(1)

Directive 67/227/EEC	Directive 77/388/EEC	Amending Directives	Other acts	This Directive
	Article 14(2), second subparagraph, first, second and third indents			Article 145(2), first, second and third subparagraphs
	Article 14(2), third subparagraph			Article 145(3)
	Article 15, introductory sentence			Article 131
	Article 15, point (1)			Article 146(1)(a)
	Article 15, point (2), first subparagraph			Article 146(1)(b)
	Article 15, point (2), second subparagraph, first and second indents			Article 147(1), first subparagraph, points (a) and (b)
	Article 15, point (2), second subparagraph, third indent, first part of the sentence			Article 147(1), first subparagraph, point (c)
	Article 15, point (2), second subparagraph, third indent, second part of the sentence			Article 147(1), second subparagraph
	Article 15, point (2), third subparagraph, first and second indents			Article 147(2), first and second subparagraphs
	Article 15, point (2), fourth subparagraph			Article 147(2), third subparagraph
	Article 15, point (3)			Article 146(1)(d)
	Article 15, point (4), first subparagraph, points (a) and (b)			Article 148(a)
	Article 15, point (4), first subparagraph, point (c)			Article 148(b)
	Article 15, point (4), second subparagraph, first and second sentences			Article 150(1) and (2)
	Article 15, point (5)			Article 148(c)

Directive 67/227/EEC	Directive 77/388/EEC	Amending Directives	Other acts	This Directive
	Article 15, point (6)			Article 148(f)
	Article 15, point (7)			Article 148(e)
	Article 15, point (8)			Article 148(d)
	Article 15, point (9)			Article 148(g)
	Article 15, point (10), first subparagraph, first to fourth indents			Article 151(1), first subparagraph, points (a) to (d)
	Article 15, point (10), second subparagraph			Article 151(1), second subparagraph
	Article 15, point (10), third subparagraph			Article 151(2)
	Article 15, point (11)			Article 152
	Article 15, point (12), first sentence			Article 146(1)(c)
	Article 15, point (12), second sentence			Article 146(2)
	Article 15, point (13)			Article 146(1)(e)
	Article 15, point (14), first and second subparagraphs			Article 153, first and second paragraphs
	Article 15, point (15)			Article 149
	Article 16(1)			—
	Article 16(2)			Article 164(1)
	Article 16(3)			Article 166
	Article 17(1)			Article 167
	Article 17(2), (3) and (4)			—

Directive 67/227/EEC	Directive 77/388/EEC	Amending Directives	Other acts	This Directive
	Article 17(5), first and second subparagraphs			Article 173(1), first and second subparagraphs
	Article 17(5), third subparagraph, points (a) to (e)			Article 173(2)(a) to (e)
	Article 17(6)			Article 176
	Article 17(7), first and second sentences			Article 177, first and second paragraphs
	Article 18(1)			—
	Article 18(2), first and second subparagraphs			Article 179, first and second paragraphs
	Article 18(3)			Article 180
	Article 18(4), first and second subparagraphs			Article 183, first and second paragraphs
	Article 19(1), first subparagraph, first indent			Article 174(1), first subparagraph, point (a)
	Article 19(1), first subparagraph, second indent, first sentence			Article 174(1), first subparagraph, point (b)
	Article 19(1), first subparagraph, second indent, second sentence			Article 174(1), second subparagraph
	Article 19(1), second subparagraph			Article 175(1)
	Article 19(2), first sentence			Article 174(2)(a)
	Article 19(2), second sentence			Article 174(2)(a) and (b)

Directive 67/227/EEC	Directive 77/388/EEC	Amending Directives	Other acts	This Directive
	Article 19(2), third sentence			Article 174(3)
	Article 19(3), first subparagraph, first and second sentences			Article 175(2), first subparagraph
	Article 19(3), first subparagraph, third sentence			Article 175(2), second subparagraph
	Article 19(3), second subparagraph			Article 175(3)
	Article 20(1), introductory sentence			Article 186
	Article 20(1)(a)			Article 184
	Article 20(1)(b), first part of the first sentence			Article 185(1)
	Article 20(1)(b), second part of the first sentence			Article 185(2), first subparagraph
	Article 20(1)(b), second sentence			Article 185(2), second subparagraph
	Article 20(2), first subparagraph, first sentence			Article 187(1), first subparagraph
	Article 20(2), first subparagraph, second and third sentences			Article 187(2), first and second subparagraphs
	Article 20(2), second and third subparagraphs			Article 187(1), second and third subparagraphs
	Article 20(3), first subparagraph, first sentence			Article 188(1), first subparagraph
	Article 20(3), first subparagraph, second sentence			Article 188(1), second and third subparagraphs

Directive 67/227/EEC	Directive 77/388/EEC	Amending Directives	Other acts	This Directive
	Article 20(3), first subparagraph, third sentence			Article 188(2)
	Article 20(3), second subparagraph			Article 188(2)
	Article 20(4), first subparagraph, first to fourth indents			Article 189(a) to (d)
	Article 20(4), second subparagraph			Article 190
	Article 20(5)			Article 191
	Article 20(6)			Article 192
	Article 21			—
	Article 22			—
	Article 22a			Article 249
	Article 23, first paragraph			Article 211, first paragraph Article 260
	Article 23, second paragraph			Article 211, second paragraph
	Article 24(1)			Article 281
	►C1 Article 24(2), introductory sentence ◄			Article 292
	Article 24(2)(a), first subparagraph			Article 284(1)
	Article 24(2)(a), second and third subparagraphs			Article 284(2), first and second subparagraphs
	Article 24(2)(b), first and second sentences			Article 285, first and second paragraphs

Directive 67/227/EEC	Directive 77/388/EEC	Amending Directives	Other acts	This Directive
	Article 24(2)(c)			Article 286
	Article 24(3), first subparagraph			Article 282
	Article 24(3), second subparagraph, first sentence			Article 283(2)
	Article 24(3), second subparagraph, second sentence			Article 283(1)(a)
	Article 24(4), first subparagraph			Article 288, first paragraph, points (1) to (4)
	Article 24(4), second subparagraph			Article 288, second paragraph
	Article 24(5)			Article 289
	Article 24(6)			Article 290
	Article 24(7)			Article 291
	Article 24(8)(a), (b) and (c)			Article 293, points (1), (2) and (3)
	Article 24(9)			Article 294
	►C1 Article 24a, first paragraph, first to tenth indents ◄			Article 287, points (7) to (16)
	Article 24a, second paragraph			—
	Article 25(1)			Article 296(1)

Directive 67/227/EEC	Directive 77/388/EEC	Amending Directives	Other acts	This Directive
	Article 25(2), first to eighth indents			Article 295(1), points (1) to (8)
	Article 25(3), first subparagraph, first sentence			Article 297, first paragraph, first sentence and second paragraph
	Article 25(3), first subparagraph, second sentence			Article 298, first paragraph
	Article 25(3), first subparagraph, third sentence			Article 299
	Article 25(3), first subparagraph, fourth and fifth sentences			Article 298, second paragraph
	Article 25(3), second subparagraph			Article 297, first paragraph, second sentence
	Article 25(4), first subparagraph			Article 272(1), first subparagraph, point (e)
	Article 25(5) and (6)			—
	Article 25(7)			Article 304
	Article 25(8)			Article 301(2)
	Article 25(9)			Article 296(2)
	Article 25(10)			Article 296(3)
	Article 25(11) and (12)			—
	Article 26(1) first and second sentences			Article 306(1), first and second subparagraphs
	Article 26(1) third sentence			Article 306(2)

Directive 67/227/EEC	Directive 77/388/EEC	Amending Directives	Other acts	This Directive
	Article 26(2), first and second sentences			Article 307, first and second paragraphs
	Article 26(2), third sentence			Article 308
	Article 26(3), first and second sentences			Article 309, first and second paragraphs
	Article 26(4)			Article 310
	Article 26a(A)(a), first subparagraph			Article 311(1), point (2)
	Article 26a(A)(a), second subparagraph			Article 311(2)
	Article 26a(A)(b) and (c)			Article 311(1), points (3) and (4)
	Article 26a(A)(d)			Article 311(1), point (1)
	Article 26a(A)(e) and (f)			Article 311(1), points (5) and (6)
	Article 26a(A)(g), introductory sentence			Article 311(1), point (7)
	Article 26a(A)(g), first and second indents			Article 311(3)
	Article 26a(B)(1)			Article 313(1)
	Article 26a(B)(2)			Article 314
	►C1 Article 26a(B)(2), first to fourth indents ◄			Article 314(a) to (d)

Directive 67/227/EEC	Directive 77/388/EEC	Amending Directives	Other acts	This Directive
	Article 26a(B)(3), first subparagraph, first and second sentences			Article 315, first and second paragraphs
	Article 26a(B)(3), second subparagraph			Article 312
	Article 26a(B)(3), second subparagraph, first and second indents			Article 312, points (1) and (2)
	Article 26a(B)(4), first subparagraph			Article 316(1)
	Article 26a(B)(4), first subparagraph, points (a), (b) and (c)			Article 316(1)(a), (b) and (c)
	Article 26a(B)(4), second subparagraph			Article 316(2)
	Article 26a(B)(4), third subparagraph, first and second sentences			Article 317, first and second paragraphs
	Article 26a(B)(5)			Article 321
	Article 26a(B)(6)			Article 323
	Article 26a(B)(7)			Article 322
	Article 26a(B)(7)(a), (b) and (c)			Article 322(a), (b) and (c)
	Article 26a(B)(8)			Article 324
	Article 26a(B)(9)			Article 325
	Article 26a(B)(10), first and second subparagraphs			Article 318(1), first and second subparagraphs

Directive 67/227/EEC	Directive 77/388/EEC	Amending Directives	Other acts	This Directive
	Article 26a(B)(10), third subparagraph, first and second indents			Article 318(2)(a) and (b)
	Article 26a(B)(10), fourth subparagraph			Article 318(3)
	Article 26a(B)(11), first subparagraph			Article 319
	Article 26a(B)(11), second subparagraph, point (a)			Article 320(1), first subparagraph
	Article 26a(B)(11), second subparagraph, points (b) and (c)			Article 320(1), second subparagraph
	Article 26a(B)(11), third subparagraph			Article 320(2)
	Article 26a(C)(1), introductory sentence			Article 333(1) Article 334
	Article 26a(C)(1), first to fourth indents			Article 334(a) to (d)
	Article 26a(C)(2), first and second indents			Article 336(a) and (b)
	Article 26a(C)(3)			Article 337
	Article 26a(C)(4), first subparagraph, first, second and third indents			Article 339, first paragraph, points (a), (b) and (c)
	Article 26a(C)(4), second subparagraph			Article 339, second paragraph
	Article 26a(C)(5), first and second subparagraphs			Article 340(1), first and second subparagraphs

Directive 67/227/EEC	Directive 77/388/EEC	Amending Directives	Other acts	This Directive
	Article 26a(C)(5), third subparagraph			Article 340(2)
	Article 26a(C)(6), first subparagraph, first and second indents			Article 338, first paragraph, points (a) and (b)
	Article 26a(C)(6), second subparagraph			Article 338, second paragraph
	Article 26a(C)(7)			Article 335
	Article 26a(D), introductory sentence			—
	Article 26a(D)(a)			Article 313(2) Article 333(2)
	Article 26a(D)(b)			Article 4(a) and (c)
	Article 26a(D)(c)			Article 35 Article 139(3), first subparagraph
	Article 26b(A), first subparagraph, point (i), first sentence			Article 344(1), point (1)
	Article 26b(A), first subparagraph, point (i), second sentence			Article 344(2)
	Article 26b(A), first subparagraph, point (ii), first to fourth indents			Article 344(1), point (2)
	Article 26b(A), second subparagraph			Article 344(3)
	Article 26b(A), third subparagraph			Article 345
	Article 26b(B), first subparagraph			Article 346
	Article 26b(B), second subparagraph			Article 347

Directive 67/227/EEC	Directive 77/388/EEC	Amending Directives	Other acts	This Directive
	Article 26b(C), first subparagraph			Article 348
	Article 26b(C), second subparagraph, first and second sentences			Article 349(1) and (2)
	Article 26b(C), third subparagraph			Article 350
	Article 26b(C), fourth subparagraph			Article 351
	Article 26b(D)(1)(a), (b) and (c)			Article 354(a), (b) and (c)
	Article 26b(D)(2)			Article 355
	Article 26b(E), first and second subparagraphs			Article 356(1), first and second subparagraphs
	Article 26b(E), third and fourth subparagraphs			Article 356(2) and (3)
	Article 26b(F), first sentence			Article 198(2) and (3)
	Article 26b(F), second sentence			Articles 208 and 255
	Article 26b(G)(1), first subparagraph			Article 352
	Article 26b(G)(1), second subparagraph			—
	Article 26b(G)(2)(a)			Article 353
	Article 26b(G)(2)(b), first and second sentences			Article 198(1) and (3)
	Article 26c(A)(a) to (e)			Article 358, points (1) to (5)
	Article 26c(B)(1)			Article 359

Directive 67/227/EEC	Directive 77/388/EEC	Amending Directives	Other acts	This Directive
	Article 26c(B)(2), first subparagraph			Article 360
	Article 26c(B)(2), second subparagraph, first part of the first sentence			Article 361(1)
	Article 26c(B)(2), second subparagraph, second part of the first sentence			Article 361(1)(a) to (e)
	Article 26c(B)(2), second subparagraph, second sentence			Article 361(2)
	Article 26c(B)(3), first and second subparagraphs			Article 362
	Article 26c(B)(4)(a) to (d)			Article 363(a) to (d)
	Article 26c(B)(5), first subparagraph			Article 364
	Article 26c(B)(5), second subparagraph			Article 365
	Article 26c(B)(6), first sentence			Article 366(1), first subparagraph
	Article 26c(B)(6), second and third sentences			Article 366(1), second subparagraph
	Article 26c(B)(6), fourth sentence			Article 366(2)
	Article 26c(B)(7), first sentence			Article 367, first paragraph
	Article 26c(B)(7), second and third sentences			Article 367, second paragraph

Directive 67/227/EEC	Directive 77/388/EEC	Amending Directives	Other acts	This Directive
	Article 6(2), first subparagraph, points (a) and (b)			Article 26(1)(a) and (b)
	Article 6(2), second subparagraph			Article 26(2)
	Article 6(3)			Article 27
	Article 6(4)			Article 28
	Article 6(5)			Article 29
	Article 7(1)(a) and (b)			Article 30, first and second paragraphs
	Article 7(2)			Article 60
	Article 7(3), first and second subparagraphs			Article 61, first and second paragraphs
	Article 8(1)(a), first sentence			Article 32, first paragraph
	Article 8(1)(a), second and third sentences			Article 36, first and second paragraphs
	Article 8(1)(b)			Article 31
	Article 8(1)(c), first subparagraph			Article 37(1)
	Article 8(1)(c), second subparagraph, first indent			Article 37(2), first subparagraph
	Article 8(1)(c), second subparagraph, second and third indents			Article 37(2), second and third subparagraphs
	Article 8(1)(c), third subparagraph			Article 37(2), fourth subparagraph

Directive 67/227/EEC	Directive 77/388/EEC	Amending Directives	Other acts	This Directive
	Article 8(1)(c), fourth subparagraph			Article 37(3), first subparagraph
	Article 8(1)(c), fifth subparagraph			—
	Article 8(1)(c), sixth subparagraph			Article 37(3), second subparagraph
	Article 8(1)(d), first and second subparagraphs			Article 38(1) and (2)
	Article 8(1)(e), first sentence			Article 39, first paragraph
	Article 8(1)(e), second and third sentences			Article 39, second paragraph
	Article 8(2)			Article 32, second paragraph
	Article 9(1)			Article 43
	Article 9(2) introductory sentence			—
	Article 9(2)(a)			Article 45
	Article 9(2)(b)			Article 46
	Article 9(2)(c), first and second indents			Article 52(a) and (b)
	Article 9(2)(c), third and fourth indents			Article 52(c)
	Article 9(2)(e), first to sixth indents			Article 56(1)(a) to (f)

Directive 67/227/EEC	Directive 77/388/EEC	Amending Directives	Other acts	This Directive
	Article 28(2)(a), third subparagraph, second and third sentences			Article 112, second paragraph
	Article 28(2)(b)			Article 113
	Article 28(2)(c), first and second sentences			Article 114(1), first and second subparagraphs
	Article 28(2)(c), third sentence			Article 114(2)
	Article 28(2)(d)			Article 115
	Article 28(2)(e), first and second subparagraphs			Article 118, first and second paragraphs
	Article 28(2)(f)			Article 120
	Article 28(2)(g)			—
	Article 28(2)(h), first and second subparagraphs			Article 121, first and second paragraphs
	Article 28(2)(i)			Article 122
	Article 28(2)(j)			Article 117(2)
	Article 28(2)(k)			Article 116
	Article 28(3)(a)			Article 370
	Article 28(3)(b)			Article 371
	Article 28(3)(c)			Article 391
	Article 28(3)(d)			Article 372

Directive 67/227/EEC	Directive 77/388/EEC	Amending Directives	Other acts	This Directive
	Article 28(3)(e)			Article 373
	Article 28(3)(f)			Article 392
	Article 28(3)(g)			Article 374
	Article 28(3a)			Article 376
	Article 28(4) and (5)			Article 393(1) and (2)
	Article 28(6), first subparagraph, first sentence			Article 106, first and second paragraphs
	Article 28(6), first subparagraph, second sentence			Article 106, third paragraph
	Article 28(6), second subparagraph, points (a), (b) and (c)			Article 107, first paragraph, points (a), (b) and (c)
	Article 28(6), second subparagraph, point (d)			Article 107, second paragraph
	Article 28(6), third subparagraph			Article 107, second paragraph
	Article 28(6), fourth subparagraph, points (a), (b) and (c)			Article 108(a), (b) and (c)
	Article 28(6), fifth and sixth subparagraphs			—
	Article 28a(1), introductory sentence			Article 2(1)
	Article 28a(1)(a), first subparagraph			Article 2(1)(b)(i)

Directive 67/227/EEC	Directive 77/388/EEC	Amending Directives	Other acts	This Directive
	Article 28a(1)(a), second subparagraph			Article 3(1)
	Article 28a(1)(a), third subparagraph			Article 3(3)
	Article 28a(1)(b)			Article 2(1)(b)(ii)
	Article 28a(1)(c)			Article 2(1)(b)(iii)
	Article 28a(1a)(a)			Article 3(1)(a)
	Article 28a(1a)(b), first subparagraph, first indent			Article 3(1)(b)
	Article 28a(1a)(b), first subparagraph, second and third indents			Article 3(2), first subparagraph, points (a) and (b)
	Article 28a(1a)(b), second subparagraph			Article 3(2), second subparagraph
	Article 28a(2), introductory sentence			—
	Article 28a(2)(a)			Article 2(2), point (a) (i), (ii), and (iii)
	Article 28a(2)(b), first subparagraph			Article 2(2), point (b)
	Article 28a(2)(b), first subparagraph, first and second indents			Article 2(2), point (b) (ii, iii) and (iii)
	Article 28a(2)(b), second subparagraph			Article 2(2), point (c)

Directive 67/227/EEC	Directive 77/388/EEC	Amending Directives	Other acts	This Directive
	Article 28a(3), first and second subparagraphs			Article 20, first and second paragraphs
	Article 28a(4), first subparagraph			Article 9(2)
	Article 28a(4), second subparagraph, first indent			Article 172(1), second subparagraph
	Article 28a(4), second subparagraph, second indent			Article 172(1), first subparagraph
	Article 28a(4), third subparagraph			Article 172(2)
	Article 28a(5)(b), first subparagraph			Article 17(1), first subparagraph
	Article 28a(5)(b), second subparagraph			Article 17(1), second subparagraph and (2), introductory sentence
	Article 28a(5)(b), second subparagraph, first indent			Article 17(2)(a) and (b)
	Article 28a(5)(b), second subparagraph, second indent			Article 17(2)(c)
	Article 28a(5)(b), second subparagraph, third indent			Article 17(2)(e)
	Article 28a(5)(b), second subparagraph, fifth, sixth and seventh indents			Article 17(2)(f), (g) and (h)
	Article 28a(5)(b), second subparagraph, eighth indent			Article 17(2)(d)
	Article 28a(5)(b), third subparagraph			Article 17(3)

Directive 67/227/EEC	Directive 77/388/EEC	Amending Directives	Other acts	This Directive
	Article 28a(6), first subparagraph			Article 21
	Article 28a(6), second subparagraph			Article 22
	Article 28a(7)			Article 23
	Article 28b(A)(1)			Article 40
	Article 28b(A)(2), first and second subparagraphs			Article 41, first and second paragraphs
	Article 28b(A)(2), third subparagraph, first and second indents			Article 42(a) and (b)
	Article 28b(B)(1), first subparagraph, first and second indents			Article 33(1)(a) and (b)
	Article 28b(B)(1), second subparagraph			Article 33(2)
	Article 28b(B)(2), first subparagraph			Article 34(1)(a)
	Article 28b(B)(2), first subparagraph, first and second indents			Article 34(1)(b) and (c)
	Article 28b(B)(2), second subparagraph, first and second sentences			Article 34(2), first and second subparagraphs
	Article 28b(B)(2), third subparagraph, first sentence			Article 34(3)
	Article 28b(B)(2), third subparagraph, second and third sentences			—
	Article 28b(B)(3), first and second subparagraphs			Article 34(4), first and second subparagraphs

Directive 67/227/EEC	Directive 77/388/EEC	Amending Directives	Other acts	This Directive
	Article 28b(C)(1), first indent, first subparagraph			Article 48, first paragraph
	Article 28b(C)(1), first indent, second subparagraph			Article 49
	Article 28b(C)(1), second and third indents			Article 48, second and third paragraphs
	Article 28b(C)(2) and (3)			Article 47, first and second paragraphs
	Article 28b(C)(4)			Article 51
	Article 28b(D)			Article 53
	Article 28b(E)(1), first and second subparagraphs			Article 50, first and second paragraphs
	Article 28b(E)(2), first and second subparagraphs			Article 54, first and second paragraphs
	Article 28b(E)(3), first and second subparagraphs			Article 44, first and second paragraphs
	Article 28b(F), first and second paragraphs			Article 55, first and second paragraphs
	Article 28c(A), introductory sentence			Article 131
	Article 28c(A)(a), first subparagraph			Article 138(1)
	Article 28c(A)(a), second subparagraph			Article 139(1), first and second subparagraphs
	Article 28c(A)(b)			Article 138(2)(a)

Directive 67/227/EEC	Directive 77/388/EEC	Amending Directives	Other acts	This Directive
	Article 28c(A)(c), first subparagraph			Article 138(2)(b)
	Article 28c(A)(c), second subparagraph			Article 139(2)
	Article 28c(A)(d)			Article 138(2)(c)
	Article 28c(B), introductory sentence			Articles 131
	Article 28c(B)(a), (b) and (c)			Article 140(a), (b) and (c)
	Article 28c(C)			Article 142
	Article 28c(D), first subparagraph			Article 143(d)
	Article 28c(D), second subparagraph			Article 131
	Article 28c(E), point (1), first indent, replacing Article 16(1)			
	— paragraph 1, first subparagraph			Article 155
	— paragraph 1, first subparagraph, point (A)			Article 157(1)(a)
	— paragraph 1, first subparagraph, point (B), first subparagraph, points (a), (b) and (c)			Article 156(1)(a), (b) and (c)
	— paragraph 1, first subparagraph, point (B), first subparagraph, point (d), first and second indents			Article 156(1)(d) and (e)
	— paragraph 1, first subparagraph, point (B), first subparagraph, point (e), first subparagraph			Article 157(1)(b)

Directive 67/227/EEC	Directive 77/388/EEC	Amending Directives	Other acts	This Directive
	— paragraph 1, first subparagraph, point (B), first subparagraph, point (e), second subparagraph, first indent			Article 154
	— paragraph 1, first subparagraph, point (B), first subparagraph, point (e), second subparagraph, second indent, first sentence			Article 154
	— paragraph 1, first subparagraph, point (B), first subparagraph, point (e), second subparagraph, second indent, second sentence			Article 157(2)
	— paragraph 1, first subparagraph, point (B), first subparagraph, point (e), third subparagraph, first indent			—
	— paragraph 1, first subparagraph, point (B), first subparagraph, point (e), third subparagraph, second, third and fourth indents			Article 158(1)(a), (b) and (c)
	— paragraph 1, first subparagraph, point (B), second subparagraph			Article 156(2)
	— paragraph 1, first subparagraph, point (C)			Article 159
	— paragraph 1, first subparagraph, point (D), first subparagraph, points (a) and (b)			Article 160(1)(a) and (b)
	— paragraph 1, first subparagraph, point (D), second subparagraph			Articles 160(2)
	— paragraph 1, first subparagraph, point (E), first and second indents			Article 161(a) and (b)
	— paragraph 1, second subparagraph			Article 202
	— paragraph 1, third subparagraph			Article 163

Directive 67/227/EEC	Directive 77/388/EEC	Amending Directives	Other acts	This Directive
	Article 28c(E), point (1), second indent, inserting paragraph 1a into Article 16			
	— paragraph 1a			Article 162
	Article 28c(E), point (2), first indent, amending Article 16(2)			
	— paragraph 2, first subparagraph			Article 164(1)
	Article 28c(E), point (2), second indent, inserting the second and third subparagraphs into Article 16(2)			
	— paragraph 2, second subparagraph			Article 164(2)
	— paragraph 2, third subparagraph			Article 165
	Article 28c(E), point (3), first to fifth indents			Article 141(a) to (e)
	Article 28d(1), first and second sentences			Article 68, first and second paragraphs
	Article 28d(2) and (3)			Article 69(1) and (2)
	Article 28d(4), first and second subparagraphs			Article 67(1) and (2)
	Article 28e(1), first subparagraph			Article 83
	Article 28e(1), second subparagraph, first and second sentences			Article 84(1) and (2)
	Article 28e(2)			Article 76

Directive 67/227/EEC	Directive 77/388/EEC	Amending Directives	Other acts	This Directive
	Article 28e(3)			Article 93, second paragraph, point (b)
	Article 28e(4)			Article 94(1)
	Article 28f, point (1), replacing Article 17(2), (3) and (4)			
	— paragraph 2(a)			Article 168(a)
	— paragraph 2(b)			Article 168(e)
	— paragraph 2(c)			Article 168(b) and (d)
	— paragraph 2(d)			Article 168(c)
	— paragraph 3(a), (b) and (c)			Article 169(a), (b) and (c) Article 170(a) and (b)
	— paragraph 4, first subparagraph, first indent			Article 171(1), first subparagraph
	— paragraph 4, first subparagraph, second indent			Article 171(2), first subparagraph
	— paragraph 4, second subparagraph, point (a)			Article 171(1), second subparagraph
	— paragraph 4, second subparagraph, point (b)			Article 171(2), second subparagraph
	— paragraph 4, second subparagraph, point (c)			Article 171(3)
	Article 28f, point (2), replacing Article 18(1)			
	— paragraph 1(a)			Article 178(a)
	— paragraph 1(b)			Article 178(e)

Directive 67/227/EEC	Directive 77/388/EEC	Amending Directives	Other acts	This Directive
	— paragraph 1(c)			Article 178(b) and (d)
	— paragraph 1(d)			Article 178(f)
	— paragraph 1(e)			Article 178(c)
	Article 28f, point (3) inserting paragraph 3a into Article 18			
	— paragraph 3a, first part of the sentence			Article 181
	— paragraph 3a, second part of the sentence			Article 182
	Article 28g replacing Article 21			
	— paragraph 1(a), first subparagraph			Article 193
	— paragraph 1(a), second subparagraph			Article 194(1) and (2)
	— paragraph 1(b)			Article 196
	— paragraph 1(c), first subparagraph, first, second and third indents			Article 197(1)(a), (b) and (c)
	— paragraph 1(c), second subparagraph			Article 197(2)
	— paragraph 1(d)			Article 203
	— paragraph 1(e)			Article 200
	— paragraph 1(f)			Article 195
	— paragraph 2			—
	— paragraph 2(a), first sentence			Article 204(1), first subparagraph

Directive 67/227/EEC	Directive 77/388/EEC	Amending Directives	Other acts	This Directive
	— paragraph 2(a), second sentence			Article 204(2)
	— paragraph 2(b)			Article 204(1), second subparagraph
	— paragraph 2(c), first subparagraph			Article 199(1)(a) to (g)
	— paragraph 2(c), second, third and fourth subparagraphs			Article 199(2), (3) and (4)
	— paragraph 3			Article 205
	— paragraph 4			Article 201
	Article 28h replacing Article 22			
	— paragraph 1(a), first and second sentences			Article 213(1), first and second subparagraphs
	— paragraph 1(b)			Article 213(2)
	— paragraph 1(c), first indent, first sentence			Article 214(1)(a)
	— paragraph 1(c), first indent, second sentence			Article 214(2)
	— paragraph 1(c), second and third indents			Article 214(1)(b) and (c)
	— paragraph 1(d), first and second sentences			Article 215, first and second paragraphs
	— paragraph 1(e)			Article 216
	— paragraph 2(a)			Article 242

Directive 67/227/EEC	Directive 77/388/EEC	Amending Directives	Other acts	This Directive
—	►C1 paragraph 2(b), first and second subparagraphs ◄			Article 243(1) and (2)
	— paragraph 3(a), first subparagraph, first sentence			Article 220, point (1)
	— paragraph 3(a), first subparagraph, second sentence			Article 220, points (2) and (3)
	— paragraph 3(a), second subparagraph			Article 220, points (4) and (5)
	— paragraph 3(a), third subparagraph, first and second sentences			Article 221(1), first and second subparagraphs
	— paragraph 3(a), fourth subparagraph			Article 221(2)
	— paragraph 3(a), fifth subparagraph, first sentence			Article 219
	— paragraph 3(a), fifth subparagraph, second sentence			Article 228
	— paragraph 3(a), sixth subparagraph			Article 222
	— paragraph 3(a), seventh subparagraph			Article 223
	— paragraph 3(a), eighth subparagraph, first and second sentences			Article 224(1) and (2)
	— paragraph 3(a), ninth subparagraph, first and second sentences			Article 224(3), first subparagraph
	— paragraph 3(a), ninth subparagraph, third sentence			Article 224(3), second subparagraph
	— paragraph 3(a), tenth subparagraph			Article 225

Directive 67/227/EEC	Directive 77/388/EEC	Amending Directives	Other acts	This Directive
	— paragraph 3(b), first subparagraph, first to twelfth indents			Article 226, points (1) to (12)
	— paragraph 3(b), first subparagraph, thirteenth indent			Article 226, points (13) and (14)
	— paragraph 3(b), first subparagraph, fourteenth indent			Article 226, point (15)
	— paragraph 3(b), second subparagraph			Article 227
	— paragraph 3(b), third subparagraph			Article 229
	— paragraph 3(b), fourth subparagraph			Article 230
	— paragraph 3(b), fifth subparagraph			Article 231
	— paragraph 3(c), first subparagraph			Article 232
	— paragraph 3(c), second subparagraph, introductory sentence			Article 233(1), first subparagraph
	— paragraph 3(c), second subparagraph, first indent, first sentence			Article 233(1), first subparagraph, point (a)
	— paragraph 3(c), second subparagraph, first indent, second sentence			Article 233(2)
	— paragraph 3(c), second subparagraph, second indent, first sentence			Article 233(1), first subparagraph, point (b)
	— paragraph 3(c), second subparagraph, second indent, second sentence			Article 233(3)
	— paragraph 3(c), third subparagraph, first sentence			Article 233(1), second subparagraph

Directive 67/227/EEC	Directive 77/388/EEC	Amending Directives	Other acts	This Directive
	— paragraph 3(c), third subparagraph, second sentence			Article 237
	— paragraph 3(c), fourth subparagraph, first and second sentences			Article 234
	— paragraph 3(c), fifth subparagraph			Article 235
	— paragraph 3(c), sixth subparagraph			Article 236
	— paragraph 3(d), first subparagraph			Article 244
	— paragraph 3(d), second subparagraph, first sentence			Article 245(1)
	— paragraph 3(d), second subparagraph, second and third sentences			Article 245(2), first and second subparagraphs
	— paragraph 3(d), third subparagraph, first and second sentences			Article 246, first and second paragraphs
	— paragraph 3(d), fourth, fifth and sixth subparagraphs			Article 247(1), (2) and (3)
	— paragraph 3(d), seventh subparagraph			Article 248
	— paragraph 3(e), first subparagraph			Articles 217 and 241
	— paragraph 3(e), second subparagraph			Article 218
	— paragraph 4(a), first and second sentences			Article 252(1)
	— paragraph 4(a), third and fourth sentences			Article 252(2), first and second subparagraphs
	— paragraph 4(a), fifth sentence			Article 250(2)

Directive 67/227/EEC	Directive 77/388/EEC	Amending Directives	Other acts	This Directive
	— paragraph 4(b)			Article 250(1)
	— paragraph 4(c), first indent, first and second subparagraphs			Article 251(a) and (b)
	— paragraph 4(c), second indent, first subparagraph			Article 251(c)
	— paragraph 4(c), second indent, second subparagraph			Article 251(d) and (e)
	— paragraph 5			Article 206
	— paragraph 6(a), first and second sentences			Article 261(1)
	— paragraph 6(a), third sentence			Article 261(2)
	— paragraph 6(b), first subparagraph			Article 262
	— paragraph 6(b), second subparagraph, first sentence			Article 263(1), first subparagraph
	— paragraph 6(b), second subparagraph, second sentence			Article 263(2)
	— paragraph 6(b), third subparagraph, first and second indents			Article 264(1)(a) and (b)
	— paragraph 6(b), third subparagraph, third indent, first sentence			Article 264(1)(d)
	— paragraph 6(b), third subparagraph, third indent, second sentence			Article 264(2), first subparagraph
	— paragraph 6(b), fourth subparagraph, first indent			Article 264(1)(c) and (e)

Directive 67/227/EEC	Directive 77/388/EEC	Amending Directives	Other acts	This Directive
	— paragraph 6(b), fourth subparagraph, second indent, first sentence			Article 264(1)(f)
	— paragraph 6(b), fourth subparagraph, second indent, second sentence			Article 264(2), second subparagraph
	— paragraph 6(b), fifth subparagraph, first and second indents			Article 265(1)(a) and (b)
	— paragraph 6(b), fifth subparagraph, third indent, first sentence			Article 265(1)(c)
	— paragraph 6(b), fifth subparagraph, third indent, second sentence			Article 265(2)
	— paragraph 6(c), first indent			Article 263(1), second subparagraph
	— paragraph 6(c), second indent			Article 266
	— paragraph 6(d)			Article 254
	— paragraph 6(e), first subparagraph			Article 268
	— paragraph 6(e), second subparagraph			Article 259
	— paragraph 7, first part of the sentence			Article 207, first paragraph Article 256 Article 267
	— paragraph 7, second part of the sentence			Article 207, second paragraph
	— paragraph 8, first and second subparagraphs			Article 273, first and second paragraphs
	— paragraph 9(a), first subparagraph, first indent			Article 272(1), first subparagraph, point (c)
	— paragraph 9(a), first subparagraph, second indent			Article 272(1), first subparagraph, points (a) and (d)
	— paragraph 9(a), first subparagraph, third indent			Article 272(1), first subparagraph, point (b)
	— paragraph 9(a), second subparagraph			Article 272(1), second subparagraph
	— paragraph 9(b)			Article 272(3)
	— paragraph 9(c)			Article 212
	— paragraph 9(d), first subparagraph, first and second indents			Article 238(1)(a) and (b)
	— paragraph 9(d), second subparagraph, first to fourth indents			Article 238(2)(a) to (d)
	— paragraph 9(d), third subparagraph			Article 238(3)
	— paragraph 9(e), first subparagraph			Article 239
	— paragraph 9(e), second subparagraph, first and second indents			Article 240, points (1) and (2)
	— paragraph 10			Articles 209 and 257
	— paragraph 11			Articles 210 and 258
	— paragraph 12, introductory sentence			Article 269
	— paragraph 12(a), first, second and third indents			Article 270(a), (b) and (c)
	— paragraph 12(b), first, second and third indents			Article 271(a), (b) and (c)

Directive 67/227/EEC	Directive 77/388/EEC	Amending Directives	Other acts	This Directive
	Article 28i inserting a third subparagraph into Article 24(3)			
	— paragraph 3, third subparagraph			Article 283(1)(b) and (c)
	Article 28j, point (1) inserting a second subparagraph into Article 25(4)			
	— paragraph 4, second subparagraph			Article 272(2)
	Article 28j, point (2) replacing Article 25(5) and (6)			
	— paragraph 5, first subparagraph, points (a), (b) and (c)			Article 300, points (1), (2) and (3)
	— paragraph 5, second subparagraph			Article 302
	— paragraph 6(a), first subparagraph, first sentence			Article 301(1)
	— paragraph 6(a), first subparagraph, second sentence			Article 303(1)
	— paragraph 6(a), second subparagraph, first, second and third indents			Article 303(2)(a), (b) and (c)
	— paragraph 6(a), third subparagraph			Article 303(3)
	— paragraph 6(b)			Article 301(1)
	Article 28j, point (3) inserting a second subparagraph into Article 25(9)			
	— paragraph 9, second subparagraph			Article 305

Directive 67/227/EEC	Directive 77/388/EEC	Amending Directives	Other acts	This Directive
	Article 28k, point (1), first subparagraph			—
	Article 28k, point (1), second subparagraph, point (a)			Article 158(3)
	Article 28k, point (1), second subparagraph, points (b) and (c)			—
	Article 28k, points (2), (3) and (4)			—
	Article 28k, point (5)			Article 158(2)
	Article 28l, first paragraph			—
	Article 28l, second and third paragraphs			Article 402(1) and (2)
	Article 28l, fourth paragraph			—
	Article 28m			Article 399, first paragraph
	Article 28n			—
	Article 28o(1), introductory sentence			Article 326, first paragraph
	Article 28o(1)(a), first sentence			Article 327(1) and (3)
	Article 28o(1)(a), second sentence			Article 327(2)
	Article 28o(1)(b)			Article 328
	Article 28o(1)(c), first, second and third indents			Article 329(a), (b) and (c)

Directive 67/227/EEC	Directive 77/388/EEC	Amending Directives	Other acts	This Directive
	Article 28o(1)(d), first and second subparagraphs			Article 330, first and second paragraphs
	Article 28o(1)(e)			Article 332
	Article 28o(1)(f)			Article 331
	Article 28o(1)(g)			Article 4(b)
	Article 28o(1)(h)			Article 35 Article 139(3), second subparagraph
	Article 28o(2)			Article 326, second paragraph
	Article 28o(3)			Article 341
	Article 28o(4)			—
	Article 28p(1), first, second and third indents			Article 405, points (1), (2) and (3)
	Article 28p(2)			Article 406
	Article 28p(3), first subparagraph, first and second indents			Article 407(a) and (b)
	Article 28p(3), second subparagraph			—
	Article 28p(4)(a) to (d)			Article 408(1)(a) to (d)
	Article 28p(5), first and second indents			Article 408(2)(a) and (b)

Directive 67/227/EEC	Directive 77/388/EEC	Amending Directives	Other acts	This Directive
	Article 28p(6)			Article 409
	Article 28p(7), first subparagraph, points (a), (b) and (c)			Article 410(1)(a), (b) and (c)
	Article 28p(7), second subparagraph, first indent			—
	►C1 Article 28p(7), second subparagraph, second and third indents ◄			►C1 Article 410(2)(a) and (b) ◄
	Article 29(1) to (4)			Article 398(1) to (4)
	Article 29a			Article 397
	Article 30(1)			Article 396(1)
	Article 30(2), first and second sentences			Article 396(2), first subparagraph
	Article 30(2), third sentence			Article 396(2), second subparagraph
	Article 30(3) and (4)			Article 396(3) and (4)
	Article 31(1)			—
	Article 31(2)			Article 400
	Article 33(1)			Article 401
	Article 33(2)			Article 2(3)
	Article 33a(1), introductory sentence			Article 274
	Article 33a(1)(a)			Article 275

Directive 67/227/EEC	Directive 77/388/EEC	Amending Directives	Other acts	This Directive
	Article 33a(1)(b)			Article 276
	Article 33a(1)(c)			Article 277
	Article 33a(2), introductory sentence			Article 278
	Article 33a(2)(a)			Article 279
	Article 33a(2)(b)			Article 280
	Article 34			Article 404
	Article 35			Article 403
	Articles 36 and 37			—
	Article 38			Article 414
	Annex A(I)(1) and (2)			Annex VII, point (1)(a) and (b)
	Annex A(I)(3)			Annex VII, points (1)(c) and (d)
	Annex A(II)(1) to (6)			Annex VII, points (2)(a) to (f)
	Annex A(III) and (IV)			Annex VII, points (3) and (4)
	Annex A(IV)(1) to (4)			Annex VII, points (4)(a) to (d)
	Annex A(V)			Article 295(2)
	Annex B, introductory sentence			Article 295(1), point (5)
	Annex B, first to ninth indents			Annex VIII, points (1) to (9)
	Annex C			—

Directive 67/227/EEC	Directive 77/388/EEC	Amending Directives	Other acts	This Directive
	Annex D(1) to (13)			Annex I, points (1) to (13)
	Annex E(2)			Annex X, Part A, point (1)
	Annex E(7)			Annex X, Part A, point (2)
	Annex E(11)			Annex X, Part A, point (3)
	Annex E(15)			Annex X, Part A, point (4)
	Annex F(1)			Annex X, Part B, point (1)
	Annex F(2)			Annex X, Part B, points (2)(a) to (j)
	Annex F(5) to (8)			Annex X, Part B, points (3) to (6)
	Annex F(10)			Annex X, Part B, point (7)
	Annex F(12)			Annex X, Part B, point (8)
	Annex F(16)			Annex X, Part B, point (9)
	Annex F(17), first and second subparagraphs			Annex X, Part B, point (10)
	Annex F(23)			Annex X, Part B, point (11)
	Annex F(25)			Annex X, Part B, point (12)
	Annex F(27)			Annex X, Part B, point (13)
	Annex G(1) and (2)			Article 391
	Annex H, first paragraph			Article 98(3)
	Annex H, second paragraph, introductory sentence			—
	Annex H, second paragraph, points (1) to (6)			Annex III, points (1) to (6)

Directive 67/227/EEC	Directive 77/388/EEC	Amending Directives	Other acts	This Directive
	Annex H, second paragraph, point (7), first and second subparagraphs			Annex III, points (7) and (8)
	Annex H, second paragraph, points (8) to (17)			Annex III, points (9) to (18)
	Annex I, introductory sentence			—
	Annex I(a), first to seventh indents			Annex IX, Part A, points (1) to (7)
	Annex I(b), first and second indents			Annex IX, Part B, points (1) and (2)
	Annex I(c)			Annex IX, Part C
	Annex J, introductory sentence			Annex V, introductory sentence
	Annex J			Annex V, points (1) to (25)
	Annex K(1), first, second and third indents			Annex IV, points (1)(a), (b) and (c)
	Annex K(2) to (5)			Annex IV, points (2) to (5)
	Annex L, first paragraph, points (1) to (5)			Annex II, points (1) to (5)
	Annex L, second paragraph			Article 56(2)
	Annex M, points (a) to (f)			Annex VI, points (1) to (8)
		Article 1, point (1), second subparagraph, of Directive 89/465/EEC		Article 133, second paragraph
		Article 2 of Directive 94/5/EC		Article 342
		Article 3, first and second sentences, of Directive 94/5/EC		Article 343, first and second paragraphs

Directive 67/227/EEC	Directive 77/388/EEC	Amending Directives	Other acts	This Directive
		Article 4 of Directive 2002/38/EC		Article 56(3) Article 57(2) Article 357
		Article 5 of Directive 2002/38/EC		—
			Annex VIII(II), point (2)(a) of the Act of Accession of Greece	Article 287, point (1)
			Annex VIII(II), point (2)(b) of the Act of Accession of Greece	Article 375
			Annex XXXII(IV), point (3)(a), first indent and second indent, first sentence, of the Act of Accession of Spain and Portugal	Article 287, points (2) and (3)
			Annex XXXII(IV), point (3)(b), first subparagraph, of the Act of Accession of Spain and Portugal	Article 377
			Annex XV(IX), point (2)(b), first subparagraph, of the Act of Accession of Austria, Finland and Sweden	Article 104
			Annex XV(IX), point (2)(c), first subparagraph, of the Act of Accession of Austria, Finland and Sweden	Article 287, point (4)

Directive 67/227/EEC	Directive 77/388/EEC	Amending Directives	Other acts	This Directive
			Annex XV(IX), point (2)(f), first subparagraph, of the Act of Accession of Austria, Finland and Sweden	Article 117(1)
			Annex XV(IX), point (2)(g), first subparagraph, of the Act of Accession of Austria, Finland and Sweden	Article 119
			Annex XV(IX), point (2)(h), first subparagraph, first and second indents, of the Act of Accession of Austria, Finland and Sweden	Article 378(1)
			Annex XV(IX), point (2)(i), first subparagraph, first indent, of the Act of Accession of Austria, Finland and Sweden	—
			Annex XV(IX), point (2)(i), first subparagraph, second and third indents, of the Act of Accession of Austria, Finland and Sweden	Article 378(2)(a) and (b)
			Annex XV(IX), point (2)(j) of the Act of Accession of Austria, Finland and Sweden	Article 287, point (5)
			Annex XV(IX), point (2)(l), first subparagraph, of the Act of Accession of Austria, Finland and Sweden	Article 111(a)

Directive 67/227/EEC	Directive 77/388/EEC	Amending Directives	Other acts	This Directive
			Annex XV(IX), point (2)(m), first subparagraph, of the Act of Accession of Austria, Finland and Sweden	Article 379(1)
			Annex XV(IX), point (2)(n), first subparagraph, first and second indents, of the Act of Accession of Austria, Finland and Sweden	Article 379(2)
			Annex XV(IX), point (2)(x), first indent, of the Act of Accession of Austria, Finland and Sweden	Article 253
			Annex XV(IX), point (2)(x), second indent, of the Act of Accession of Austria, Finland and Sweden	Article 287, point (6)
			Annex XV(IX), point (2)(z), first subparagraph, of the Act of Accession of Austria, Finland and Sweden	Article 111(b)
			Annex XV(IX), point (2)(aa), first subparagraph, first and second indents, of the Act of Accession of Austria, Finland and Sweden	Article 380
			Protocol No 2 of the Act of Accession of Austria, Finland and Sweden concerning the Åland Islands	Article 6(1)(d)

Directive 67/227/EEC	Directive 77/388/EEC	Amending Directives	Other acts	This Directive
			Annex V(5), point (1)(a) of the 2003 Act of Accession of the Czech Republic, Estonia, Cyprus, Latvia, Lithuania, Hungary, Malta, Poland, Slovenia and Slovakia	Article 123
			Annex V(5), point (1)(b) of the 2003 Act of Accession	Article 381
			Annex VI(7), point (1)(a) of the 2003 Act of Accession	Article 124
			Annex VI(7), point (1)(b) of the 2003 Act of Accession	Article 382
			Annex VII(7), point (1), first and second subparagraph, of the 2003 Act of Accession	Article 125(1) and (2)
			Annex VII(7), point (1), third subparagraph, of the 2003 Act of Accession	—
			Annex VII(7), point (1), fourth subparagraph, of the 2003 Act of Accession	Article 383(a)
			Annex VII(7), point (1), fifth subparagraph, of the 2003 Act of Accession	—

Directive 67/227/EEC	Directive 77/388/EEC	Amending Directives	Other acts	This Directive
			Annex VII(7), point (1), sixth subparagraph, of the 2003 Act of Accession	Article 383(b)
			Annex VIII(7), point (1)(a) of the 2003 Act of Accession	—
			Annex VIII(7), point (1)(b), second subparagraph, of the 2003 Act of Accession	Article 384(a)
			►C1 Annex VIII(7), point (1)(b), third subparagraph, of the 2003 Act of Accession ◄	Article 384(b)
			Annex IX(8), point (1) of the 2003 Act of Accession	Article 385
			Annex X(7), point (1)(a)(i) and (ii) of the 2003 Act of Accession	Article 126(a) and (b)
			Annex X(7), point (1)(c) of the 2003 Act of Accession	Article 386
			Annex XI(7), point (1) of the 2003 Act of Accession	Article 127
			Annex XI(7), point (2)(a) of the 2003 Act of Accession	Article 387(c)
			Annex XI(7), point (2)(b) of the 2003 Act of Accession	Article 387(a)

Directive 67/227/EEC	Directive 77/388/EEC	Amending Directives	Other acts	This Directive
			Annex XI(7), point (2)(c) of the 2003 Act of Accession	Article 387(b)
			Annex XII(9), point (1)(a) of the 2003 Act of Accession	Article 128(1) and (2)
			Annex XII(9), point (1)(b) of the 2003 Act of Accession	Article 128(3), (4) and (5)
			Annex XII(9), point (2) of the 2003 Act of Accession	Article 388
			Annex XIII(9), point (1)(a) of the 2003 Act of Accession	Article 129(1) and (2)
			Annex XIII(9), point (1)(b) of the 2003 Act of Accession	Article 389
			Annex XIV(7), first subparagraph, of the 2003 Act of Accession	Article 130(a) and (b)
			Annex XIV(7), second subparagraph, of the 2003 Act of Accession	—
			Annex XIV(7), third subparagraph, of the 2003 Act of Accession	Article 390

António Calisto Pato / Marlon Marques

VAT e-Consultant app

VISIT US

AT

WWW.EASYGOTAX.COM

And test our VAT e-Consultant

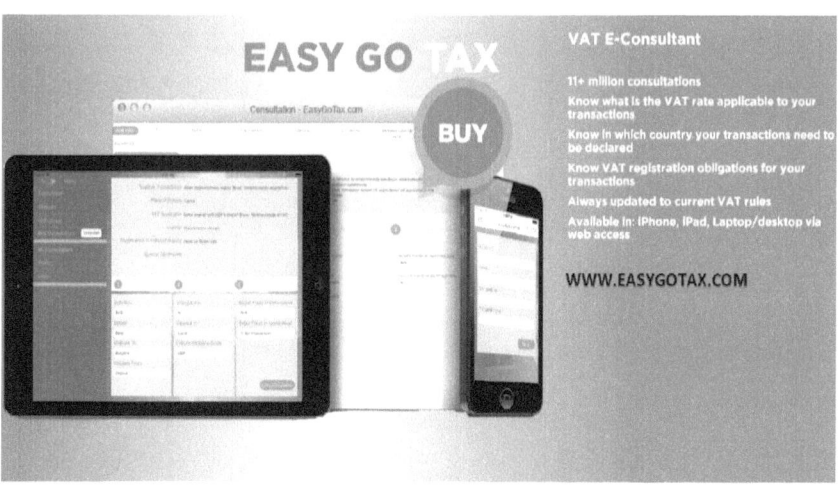

www.ingramcontent.com/pod-product-compliance
Lightning Source LLC
Chambersburg PA
CBHW020853180526
45163CB00007B/2488